Ceauşescu's Romania

Recent Titles in
Bibliographies and Indexes in World History

World Racism and Related Inhumanities: A Country-by-Country Bibliography
Meyer Weinberg, compiler

A Selected Bibliography of Modern Historiography
Attila Pók, editor

The Rise and Fall of the Soviet Union: A Selected Bibliography of Sources in English
Abraham J. Edelheit and Hershel Edelheit, editors

History of Canadian Childhood and Youth: A Bibliography
Neil Sutherland, Jean Barman, and Linda Hale, compilers

Contemporary Canadian Childhood and Youth: A Bibliography
Neil Sutherland, Jean Barman, and Linda Hale, compilers

Spanish and Portuguese Jewry: A Classified Bibliography
Robert Singerman, compiler

Crime in Victorian Britain: An Annotated Bibliography from Nineteenth-Century
British Magazines
E.M. Palmegiano, compiler

Joseph Chamberlain: A Bibliography
Scott Newton and Dilwyn Porter, compilers

Agriculture in Britain and America, 1660-1820: An Annotated Bibliography of the
Eighteenth-Century Literature
Samuel J. Rogal, compiler

Annales Historiography and Theory: A Selective and Annotated Bibliography
Jean-Pierre V. M. Hérubel, compiler

The Polish-German Borderlands: An Annotated Bibliography
Barbara Dotts Paul, compiler

Ceauşescu's Romania

An Annotated Bibliography

Compiled by
Opritsa D. Popa & Marguerite E. Horn

*Bibliographies and Indexes
in World History, Number 36*

Greenwood Press
Westport, Connecticut • London

Library of Congress Cataloging-in-Publication Data

Ceauşescu's Romania : an annotated bibliography / compiled by Opritsa
    D. Popa and Marguerite E. Horn.
        p.   cm.—(Bibliographies and indexes in world history, ISSN
    0742–6852 ; no. 36)
    Includes bibliographical references and index.
    ISBN 0–313–28939–5 (alk. paper)
    1. Romania—Bibliography. 2. Romania—History—1944–1989—
Bibliography. I. Popa, Opritsa D. II. Horn, Marguerite E.
III. Series.
Z2921.C43 1994
[DR205]
016.9498—dc20   94–13055

British Library Cataloguing in Publication Data is available.

Library of Congress Catalog Card Number: 94–13055
ISBN: 0–313–28939–5
ISSN: 0742–6852

First published in 1994

Greenwood Press, 88 Post Road West, Westport, CT 06881
An imprint of Greenwood Publishing Group, Inc.

Printed in the United States of America

∞™

The paper used in this book complies with the
Permanent Paper Standard issued by the National
Information Standards Organization (Z39.48–1984).

10 9 8 7 6 5 4 3 2 1

To my parents
In the eye of the nightmare,
they taught me to dream

～Opritsa Popa

Contents

Introduction

Ceauşescu's Romania: An Annotated Bibliography is a selected and classified guide that brings together over one thousand citations, spanning close to three decades of Western research.

The bibliography offers to its readers a one-stop information source on Romania's recent communist history. It is designed for students, teachers, and researchers in Romanian and East European studies. Students will find the bibliography easy to use with its topically arranged chapters to a large variety of subjects, from reproductive legislation and human rights abuses, to the cult of personality and international espionage. Teachers will find the bibliography useful in planning lessons or developing reading lists. Researchers will discover numerous sources of information for inter-disciplinary research.

The bibliography lists writings published outside Romania, mostly in Western Europe and the United States, for the period from March 1965, when Ceauşescu rose to power, to his execution in December 1989. While the focus of the bibliography remains on English language materials, items published in French and German literature are also included.

The bibliography focuses exclusively on topics in the social sciences dealing with aspects of life during Ceauşescu's dictatorship. Citations are primarily to scholarly works. A number of informative journalistic analyses and personal accounts offering unique insights into Ceauşescu's Romania have also been included. The bibliography brings together books, journal articles, reports, occasional papers, chapters in books, U.S. doctoral dissertations, and government documents, whose focus is Romania.

In compiling the bibliography, citations were identified by searching computerized databases and mainstream printed indexes in the social sciences, by consulting existing bibliographies, (e.g. Viorel Roman's *The Romanian Economic Politics: A Developmental Strategy,* Paul Michelson's *Nationalism in the Balkans, Südosteuropa-Bibliographie*, and Fischer-Galaţi's early work *Rumania: A Bibliographic Guide*), and by reviewing bibliographies of cited works. While the bibliography strives for completeness within stated parameters, pragmatic reasons, such as space restrictions and physical availability of sources for inspection, affected the inclusion of some pertinent citations. Items that could not be obtained for verification through interlibrary loan services, were largely omitted. Not represented are unpublished papers, student papers, (other then U.S. Ph.D. dissertations), U.S. documents with restricted circulation, and foreign documents. Although searches revealed thousands of informational writings on Romania, space concerns mandated that most popular articles, newspaper commentaries, and most statistical series not be included. Space constraints also did not permit extensive inclusion of studies on Eastern Europe, which presented data on Romania among other countries within the region. Cited, but not analyzed issue by issue, were sources that record developments in Romania on an ongoing basis, such as the expert analyses provided by Radio Free Europe, the hundreds of commentaries in

Wissenschaftlicher Dienst Südosteuropa (continued by *Südosteuropa*), or in *Soviet-East European Survey*, encyclopedia articles, annual handbooks, (e.g. *Die Wirtschaftliche Entwicklung in Osteuropa zur Jahreswende*), etc. Also omitted were older materials, when superseded by or subsumed within more recent ones.

Citations are grouped by subject under major fields of knowledge. When a citation covers more than one subject, it is placed under the subject of major emphasis and indexed under its sub-topics. Where appropriate, see also references direct readers from one subject category to another. Within each category, citations are arranged alphabetically by author. Entries are numbered consecutively, and each citation is preceded by its entry number. Author and subject indexes, referring to citation number, provide additional levels of recall and precision.

Each citation offers sufficient information to identify a given bibliographic unit. In addition to standard bibliographic elements, numbered series statements have been noted. Unnumbered series titles were not recorded. Government documents include Superintendent of Documents numbers, and theses include University Microfilm International (UMI) order numbers, when available. For foreign language materials, titles appear in the original language, with English translations provided by the authors in brackets. When appropriate, earlier or subsequent versions are noted. Citation formats follow as closely as possible the conventions prescribed by *The Chicago Manual of Style*.

Annotations are brief and kept on the informative, descriptive level. They are intended to allow the reader enough insight to reach an informed decision about the usefulness of the source. Where individual titles are fully descriptive of contents, no annotation is appended. Occasionally, a full or partial rendition of the table of contents is used to reflect diverse aspects treated or chapters by various authors. Chapters on Romania included in monographs dealing with Eastern Europe as a region are analyzed. Where monographs consist exclusively of contributions on Romania, only the monograph is cited, with information on the chapters presented in the form of a contents note. All authors listed in the contents note are included in the author index.

No bibliography is complete and the authors are aware of the existing large body of literature on the field. It is our sincere hope that other bibliographies will soon complement the one at hand. The authors request the indulgence of the readers for any omission that might have occurred and will thankfully acknowledge any comments concerning such omissions. In spite of its limitations, it is hoped that this bibliography will partially close an existing informational gap on Romania, and will be useful to all those interested in Eastern European studies.

The authors wish to acknowledge the financial assistance provided by the Librarians Association of the University of California-Davis (LAUC-D) and the financial and professional development support of the Academic Federation of the University of California, Davis. Our heartfelt thanks go to our Library Administration, who allowed extensive use of interlibrary loan services during difficult financial times and insured an atmosphere conducive to research.

Many individuals have helped to make this work possible. It is a pleasure to acknowledge the help received from Sandra Lamprecht, in the incipient phases of this project, and from Melanie Hughbanks, whose skill and perseverance, allowed us to locate most of the sources used in the bibliography. A special vote of thanks goes to Ted Hostetler, Head, Access Services and to the staff of the interlibrary loan department at University of California, Davis Library. Raleigh Elliott, Christine Alan, Muriel Suleiman, and Ann Maloney devoted endless hours locating and requesting obscure articles and books from libraries across the state or across the continent. Finally, we want to express our appreciation to Mykl Herdklotz, graphic artist, for applying his talent and professional knowledge to the careful preparation of the manuscript in camera-ready format. The timely completion of the bibliography is due to their support, professionalism, patience, and tenacity.

Ceauşescu's Romania

1. Overview Works & Bibliographies

1. Bachman, Ronald D., ed. *Romania: A Country Study*. 2nd ed. Washington, D.C.: Federal Research Division, Library of Congress, 1991.
   Describes and analyzes the country's history, society, economy, government, politics, and national security to 1989.

2. Blanc, André. *La Roumanie: Le Fait National dans une Économie Socialiste [Romania: Nationalism in a Socialist Economy]*. Bordas Études, 139. Paris: Bordas, 1973.
   Following an overview of people and geography, discusses the country's economic development, domestic policies, urban growth, manufacturing and service industry, foreign policy and tourism.

3. Brogan, Patrick. *Eastern Europe, 1939-1989: The Fifty Years War*. London: Bloomsbury, 1990.
   The chapter on Romania (pp. 209-239) summarizes the country's history, describes the Ceauşescu dictatorship and the revolution that toppled it.

4. Buonincontro, Pasquale. *La Presenza della Romania in Italia nel Secolo XX: Contributo Bibliografico, 1900-1980 [The Presence of Romania in Twentieth Century Italy: A Bibliographic Guide, 1900-1980]*. Napoli: De Simone, 1988.
   Following an essay on 20th century Italian research on Romania is a chronological list of 2553 un-annotated citations in the humanities and social sciences, published in Italian periodicals.

5. Fischer-Galaţi, Stephen. "National Minorities in Romania, 1919-1980." In *Eastern European National Minorities, 1919-1980: A Handbook*, edited by Stephan M. Horak, Richard Blanke, [et al.], 190-215. Littleton, CO: Libraries Unlimited, 1985.
   The chapter on Romania (pp. 190-215) opens with a historical overview on the treatment of minorities, followed by an annotated bibliographic guide of monographs and articles on Germans, Hungarians, Jews, and other minority populations.

6. Fischer-Galaţi, Stephen. *Twentieth Century Rumania*. New York: Columbia University Press, 1970.
   Studies the attempts to identify Communist Romania with its historic past. "Legacy Restated" (pp. 183-210) deals with Ceauşescu's ascent to power and his policy of independence, culminating with the threat of military resistance against a Soviet invasion in August 1968.

7. Fischer-Galaţi, Stephen. *Twentieth Century Rumania*. 2nd ed. New York: Columbia University Press, 1991.
   Reassesses the Ceauşescu era and follows the historical legacy of Greater Romania to the end of the communist regime.

8. Georgescu, Vlad, ed. *Romania: 40 Years (1944-1984)*. The Washington Papers, XIII, 115. New York: Praeger, 1985.
    Essays on economics, agriculture, foreign policy, and nationalities policy, published on the occasion of Romania's 40th anniversary under communism.

9. Georgescu, Vlad. *The Romanians: A History*. Columbus: Ohio State University Press, 1991.
    Translation of *Istoria Românilor*. Los Angeles: ARA, 1984.
    History of Romania from its earliest times to 1991.

10. Grothusen, Klaus-Detlev, ed. *Rumänien [Romania]*. Südosteuropa-Handbuch, 2. Göttingen: Vandenhoeck & Ruprecht, 1977.
    Consists of four major parts: politics, economy, society and social structure, and culture and science, followed by an appendix. Partial Contents: D. Ghermani "Die Rumänische Kommunistische Partei;" S. Fischer-Galaţi "Foreign Policy;" W. Kowarik "Landesverteidigung;" I. M. Matley "The Geographical Basis of Romania;" W. Gumpel "Das Wirtschaftssystem;" R. Schönfeld "Industrie und Gewerbliche Wirtschaft;" G. E. Schmutzler "Land- und Forstwirtschaft;" H. Gross, G. E. Schmutzler, R. Schönfeld "Aussenwirtschaft;" F. Ronneberger "Sozialstruktur;" M. R. Jackson, S. K. Happel "Population Structure;" E. C. Suttner "Kirche und Staat;" W. Mitter "Schulsystem und Volksbildung;" A. U. Gabanyi "Literatur;" A. Coulin "Massenmedia." The appendix consists of a listing of government officials, a 1944-1977 chronology of major events, a selection of international treaties, biographies of political personalities, and an extensive bibliography.

11. Kellogg, Frederick. *A History of Romanian Historical Writing*. Bakersfield, CA: Charles Schlacks, Jr., 1990.
    A bibliographic essay analyzing Romanian and non-Romanian historical writings to 1989, including works on the Ceauşescu era.

12. Marcou, Lilly. "La République Socialiste de Roumanie: L'Évolution de la Recherche Historique et Idéologique [Socialist Republic of Romania: Evolution of Historical and Ideological Research]." *Revue Française de Science Politique* 23, no. 3 (1973): 595-616.
    Bibliographic essay on history and political science research conducted in Romania and in the West.

13. Matley, Ian M. *Romania: A Profile*. New York: Praeger, 1970.
    An introduction to the historical formation and development of Romania to the present. Describes Ceauşescu's "Romania first" policy, and the popular support generated by his anti-Soviet attitude.

14. Michelson, Paul E. "Romania." In *Nationalism in the Balkans: An Annotated Bibliography*, edited by Gail Stokes, 31-67. Canadian Review of Studies in Nationalism, 3. Garland Reference Library of Social Sciences, vol.160. New York: Garland, 1984.
    A bibliographic essay discussing the dominant themes of unity, continuity, and nationalism in Romanian scholarship of the Ceauşescu era introduces an annotated review of literature published in Romania and abroad.

15. Nelson, Daniel N., ed. *Romania in the 1980's*. Boulder: Westview, 1981.
    East European scholars assess Romania's outlook in the 1980's. Organized in three parts: Part 1. The setting of Romanian Communism. Chapters: S. Fischer-Galaţi, "Romania's Development as a Communist State." P. A. Shapiro, "Romania's Past as Challenge for the Future: A Developmental Approach to Interwar Politics." Part 2. Leaders and Citizens in Romanian Communism. Chapters: J. W. Cole, "Family, Farm, and Factory: Rural Workers in Contemporary Romania." M. E. Fischer, "Idol or Leader? The Origins and Future of the Ceauşescu Cult." T. Gilberg, "Political Socialization in Romania: Prospects and Performance." D. N. Nelson, "Workers in a Workers' State." Part 3. Foreign and Economic Policies. Chapters: W. M. Bacon, Jr., "Romanian Military Policy in the 1980's." R. H. Linden, "Romanian Foreign

Policy in the 1980's." M. R. Jackson, "Perspectives on Romania's Economic Development." D. N. Nelson, "Conclusion: Development, Communism, and Balkan Traditions."

16. Radio Free Europe. *Background Reports. Country Series. Romania.* N.p.: RFE-RL, 1956-1989.
    Other forms of title: Rumanian [or Romanian] Background Report; Radio Free Europe Research; RAD Background Report.
    A most important source of information on ongoing issues and events relating to Romania.

17. Radio Free Europe. *Radio Free Europe Research.* New York [etc.]: RFE/RL, 1976-1989.
    Basic source of information on current events in Romania. Since 1989 it is continued by *Report on Eastern Europe,* formed by the union of the Situation Report sections on all Eastern European countries, including *RFE/East Europe. Rumania.*

18. Roman, Viorel S. *The Romanian Economic Politics: A Development Strategy: Theses-Bibiography-Maps.* Offenbach: Falk, 1988.
    Un-annotated bibliography including works published between 1965-1987 and dealing with Romania's economic and development policy.

19. Salzmann, Zdenek. "A Bibliography of Sources Concerning the Czechs and Slovaks in Romania." *East European Quarterly* 13, no. 4 (1979): 465-488.
    A bibliography of ethnohistorical sources concerning Czechs and Slovaks who have settled in Romania.

20. Siegert, Heinz. *Rumänien Heute [Romania Today].* Vienna: Econ, 1966.
    Profiles the history, development, population, economy, social and political organization of the country and describes Bucharest as a city in transition.

21. *Soviet/East European Survey: Selected Research and Analysis from Radio Free Europe/Radio Liberty.* Boulder: Westview, 1983.
    Series of annual reports analyzing important events and trends in all Eastern European countries, including Romania.

22. *Südosteuropa.* München: Abteilung Gegenwartsforschung des Südost-Instituts,1982-.
    Continues *Wissenschaftlicher Dienst Südosteuropa.* This monthly periodical includes many excellent commentaries on current social, economic, and policital events relating to Ceauşescu's Romania. Indexed selectively by *Foreign Language Index.*

23. *Südosteuropa-Bibliographie.* München: Oldenbourg, 1956-.
    International bibliography on the history of the region. Volume 5, part 1 (1982) covers works on Romania published between 1966-1970; Volume 6, part 1, "Rumänien" (1991) covers works published between 1971-1981.

24. Wagner, Ernst. *Quellen zur Geschichte der Siebenbürger Sachsen, 1191-1975 [Sources on the History of the Transylvanian Saxons, 1191-1975].* Schriften zur Landeskunde Siebenbürgens, 1. Köln: Böhlau, 1976.
    Sources are listed chronologically. For the period 1965-1975, the list includes excerpts from the Romanian constitution, Party documents, Ceauşescu's speeches, and various laws and legal documents concerning minorities.

25. *Wissenschaftlicher Dienst Südosteuropa.* München: Südost-Institut München, 1952-1981.
    Monthly periodical featuring hundreds of excellent commentaries on current social, economic, and political events relating to Ceauşescu's Romania. Indexed selectively in *Foreign Language Index.* Continued since 1982 by *Südosteuropa* (q.v.).

2. Agriculture: Economics, History & Policy

26. Acker, Udo W. "Das Ländliche Genossenschaftswesen in Rumänien von seinen Anfängen bis Heute: Eine Wirtschaftsgeschichtliche Studie mit einer Einführung in die Agrarverhältnisse des Landes [The Agricultural Cooperatives in Romania from the Beginning to the Present: A Study in Economic History with an Introduction to the Agricultural Situation of the Country]." *Acta Scientiarum Socialium* 5 (1972): 66-152.

    Studies three periods in the development of agriculture: before World War I, the inter-war period, and the time from the communist takeover to 1970. Concludes that the agricultural policy imposed by the Party has resulted in total failure.

27. Argyras, Andreas E. "Peasant Production, State Articulation and Competing Rationalities: The Collective Economy of Rural Romania." Ph.D. diss., University of California, Davis, 1988. Ann Arbor: UMI, 1988. AAD8821680.

    Study of tensions and contradictions among state, "collective," and peasant household production in the Banat Region.

28. Beck, Sam. "'Privat' - Bauern in Rumänien: Die Sozialistische Umgestaltung in den 1970er Jahren [Private Farmers in Romania: The Socialist Reorganization in the 1970s]." *Osteuropa* 37, no. 11 (1987): 851-861.

    A non-collectivized agricultural labor force does not imply the existence of private "capitalist" farmers, opposing the socialist system. The so-called private farmers are an accepted, integral part of the socialist economy, providing vital products for domestic and foreign markets.

29. Ciorănescu, George. "How Efficient is Rumanian Agriculture?" *East Europe* 16, no. 9 (1967): 9-13.

    Romania's efficient agricultural economy is a myth.

30. Clayton, Elizabeth M. "Economic Reforms in Bulgaria and Romania: Prospects for the 1980s." In *Economic Reforms in Eastern Europe and Prospects for the 1980's*, by the Information Directorate, North Atlantic Treaty Organization, 141-148. New York: Pergamon Press, 1980.

    Colloquium 16-18 April 1980, Brussels.

    Focuses on the agricultural sector and shows that reforms so far have been administrative in nature and that incentives for economic reforms are nonexistent.

31. Cummings, Robert. *Romania: Economic Crisis and Agricultural Management*. Washington, D.C.: U.S. Economic Research Service, March 1986. A93.44:AGES860127.

    Surveys economic achievements of the 1970's and 1980's and casts a pessimistic picture of the country's future in the agricultural sector based on its continued centralized management, economic difficulties, and disappointing performance.

32. Dando, William A. "Wheat in Romania." *Annals of the Association of American Geographers* 64, no. 2 (1974): 241-257.
    Describes the historical importance of the crop and explains the institutional and environmental factors influencing modern wheat production.

33. Deutsch, Robert. *The Food Revolution in the Soviet Union and Eastern Europe*. Boulder: Westview, 1986.
    "The Petrified Economies" (pp.103-106) reviews Romania's consistently unsuccessful agricultural policies.

34. Gartner, E. "Ökonomische Aspekte Rumänischer Agrarpolitik: Ein Ergänzender Kommentar [Economic Aspects of Romania's Agricultural Policies: An Additional Comment]." In *Current Trends in the Soviet and East European Food Economy*, edited by Karl-Eugen Wädekin, 262-272. Berlin: Duncker & Humbolt, 1982.
    A follow-up on T. Gilberg's contribution "Romanian Agricultural Policy," in the same work.
    Summarizes general characteristics of Romanian agriculture and its role in the overall economy, and discusses size and structure of farms, investment allocations, workforce, distribution of producer and consumer prices, and 1981-1985 plan targets.

35. Gilberg, Trond. "The Costly Experiment: Collectivization of Romanian Agriculture." In *The Political Economy of Collectivized Agriculture: Comparative Study of Communist and Non-Communist Systems*, edited by Ronald A. Francisco, Betty A. Laird, and Roy D. Laird, 23-62. Pergamon Policy Studies, 14. New York: Pergamon, 1979.
    After a historical overview of pre-communist Romania, discusses the rural transformation under the collectivization program and concludes that it represented a "considerable handicap in terms of production and in terms of the establishment of regime legitimacy in the population"(p.59).

36. Gilberg, Trond. "Romanian Agricultural Policy in the Quest of 'the Multilateral Developed Society'." In *Agricultural Policies in the USSR and Eastern Europe*, edited by Ronald A. Francisco, Betty A. Laird, and Roy D. Laird, 137-164. Boulder: Westview, 1980.
    Ceauşescu's vision of the "multilaterally developed society" confers upon agriculture a new and important economic role. Nonetheless, recent results and future prospects are mixed, as the government is unwilling to come to grips with the problems plaguing socialist agriculture.

37. Gilberg, Trond. "Romanian Agricultural Policy: Persisting Problems." In *Current Trends in the Soviet and East European Food Economy*, edited by Karl-Eugen Wädekin, 239-261. Berlin: Duncker & Humbolt, 1982.
    Focuses on agricultural policy since collectivization and examines land distribution, plans and performance in the 1970's, and the need for agricultural reforms.

38. Lambert, Miles J. "Romania Moves to Revamp its Lagging Agriculture." *Foreign Agriculture* 13, no. 34 (1975): 12-16.
    Examines incentives implemented by the government to stimulate agricultural efficiency.

39. Lambert, Miles J. "U.S.-Romanian Farm Trade Up." *Foreign Agriculture* 13, no. 33 (1975): 2-4.
    Investigates agricultural production and U.S.-Romanian trade relations.

40. Lazarcik, Gregor, and George Pall. *Rumania: Agricultural Production, Output, Expenses, Gross and Net Product, and Productivity, 1938, 1948, and 1950-1971*. Occasional Papers of the Research Project on National Income in East Central Europe, OP-38. New York: Economic Studies, Riverside Research Institute, 1973.
    Develops measures for agricultural production that are similar to those used in Western countries and compares results with official Romanian statistics.

41. Organisation for Economic Co-operation and Development (OECD). "Romania." In *Prospects for Agricultural Production and Trade in Eastern Europe: Bulgaria, Czecholsovakia, Romania*, v. 2, 67-128. Paris: OECD, 1982.
    Looks at trends in food consumption, production plans, agricultural production, inputs, and trade.

42. Schinke, Eberhard. *Der Anteil der Privaten Landwirtschaft an der Agrarproduktion in den RGW-Ländern [The Contribution of Private Agriculture in the Agricultural Production of COMECON Countries].* Giessener Abhandlungen zur Agrar- und Wirtschaftsforschung des Europäische Ostens, 127. Berlin: Duncker & Humbolt, 1983.
    The chapter on Romania (pp.53-56) reveals that, encouraged by the state, the country's private small farms produce more than all other similar entities in Eastern Europe and that this production is on the increase.

43. Sporea, C. "Gegenwartsfragen der Rumänischen Landwirtschaft [Current Issues in Romanian Agriculture]." *Acta Scientiarum Socialium* 3 (1971): 136-171.
    Assesses 25 years of agricultural development, 1945-1970.

44. Sporea, C., and K.-E. Wädekin. "Arbeitskräfte in der Landwirtschaft Rumäniens [Labor Force in Romanian Agriculture]." *Osteuropa* 27, no. 3 (1977): 226-234.
    Statistical overview and report on the organization of agricultural manpower.

45. Sporea, C., and K.-E. Wädekin. "Arbeitseinkommen und Lohnsystem in der Rumänischen Landwirtschaft [Labor Income and Wage System in Romanian Agriculture]." *Osteuropa* 27, no. 4 (1977): 331-339.
    Discussion of median income, wages and benefits for agricultural laborers.

46. Turnock, David. "Geographical Aspects of Romanian Agriculture." *Geography* 55, pt.2, no. 247 (1970): 169-186.
    Presents, with a historical overview, issues relating to farming enterprises, livestock rearing, pomiculture, viticulture, fish-farming, and supply of raw materials to industry. Agriculture continues to play a vital role in Romania's economic growth.

47. Wooley, Douglas Charles, Jr. "The Role of the Agricultural Sector in the Development of the Romanian Economy Since 1950." Ph.D. diss., University of Connecticut, 1976. Ann Arbor: UMI, 1976. AAD: 7614287.
    Analyzes the administrative development, input/output and short and long run efficiency of the Romanian socialist agriculture.

3. Anthropology & Folklore

48. Andreesco, Ioana, and Mihaela Bacou. *Mourir à l'Ombre des Carpathes [To Die in the Shadow of the Carpathiens]*. Paris: Payot, 1986.
    Describes funeral rites and ceremonies in the Transylvanian Alps.

49. Andreesco-Miereanu, Ioana. "Espace et Temps de la Magie dans un Village Roumain Actuel [Space and Time in the Magic of a Contemporary Romanian Village]." *Cahiers Internationaux de Sociologie* 73 (July-December 1982): 251-266.
    Popular perceptions of magical powers and symbols have changed and adapted to the socialist transformation of the Romanian village. Changes occurred in the type of magical manipulations, in the selection of new magical objects, but most of all in the importance given to the magical language. The imaginary has adopted new structures but still represents a bond and communication link in the village community.

50. Banc, C., and Alan Dundes. *First Prize: Fifteen Years! An Annotated Collection of Romanian Political Jokes*. London: Associated University Presses, 1986.
    Political jokes mirror reality and are used as weapons against oppression. The name of the first author appears to be a pseudonym, which translates as "what a joke."

51. Barth, Frederick H. "Marriage Traditions and Customs among Transylvanian Saxons." *East European Quarterly* 12, no. 1 (1978): 93-110.
    Describes courtship and wedding rituals in contemporary Jidvei (Seiden) and Soria (Schönau).

52. Beck, Sam. "The Emergence of the Peasant-Worker in a Transylvanian Mountain Community." *Dialectical Anthropology* 1, no. 4 (1976): 365-375.
    A study of Poiana Mărului, including ecology and history, ethnic composition, settlement patterns, subsistence, labor force, and social stratification. Shows that Poiana can no longer survive strictly as an agro-pastoral community. The state's investment policies in rural development have allowed the population to retain some of its traditional pursuits while adapting to an industrial socialist economy.

53. Beck, Sam. "Indigenous Anthropologists in Socialist Romania." *Dialectical Anthropology* 10, no. 3-4 (1986): 265-274.
    After the communist takeover, sociology was discredited and members of the old sociological school imprisoned. The discipline revived twenty years later, in December 1965, when mentioned in a speech by Nicolae Ceaușescu. There remains a taboo on ethnic research, as Marxism denies any existing frictions between ethnic populations. Ethnic research is conducted only in areas of ancient practices, folklore, material culture, or historical instances that led to harmonious inter-ethnic relations. Research outside these areas remains unpublished or, if published, places the authors at considerable risk.

54. Beck, Sam. "Transylvania: The Political Economy of a Frontier." Ph.D. diss., University of Massachusetts, 1979. Ann Arbor: UMI, 1979. AAD80-04897.
    Study of the Transylvanian mountain community of Poiana Mărului, its history, settlement patterns, population, upland expansion, economic development, family relations, and the fundamental changes brought about by the socialist transformation of the country.

55. Bernabé, Jean. *Le Symbolisme de la Mort: Croyances et Rites Roumains [Symbolism of Death: Romanian Beliefs and Rites]*. Gent: Communication & Cognition, 1980.
    Chronicles death and funeral customs in the village of Dobriţa, Oltenia.

56. Bouras, Alain. *Quand l'Arbre Deviens Bois: Techniques et Croyances des Paysans Roumains [When the Tree Becomes Wood: Techniques and Beliefs of Romanian Peasants]*. Études et Documents Balkaniques et Méditerranéens, 11. Paris: [Laboratoire d'Anthropologie Sociale], 1986.
    Examines uses of wood throughout Romania and explores its relation to existing myths, beliefs, customs, history, professions, and folkart.

57. Brunvand, Jan Harold. "'Don't Shoot, Comrades': A Survey of the Submerged Folklore of Eastern Europe." *North Carolina Folklore Journal* 21, no. 4 (1973): 181-188.
    Presents major themes of jokelore and sample jokes reflecting life and political dissent in communist Romania.

58. Brunvand, Jan Harold. "Gingerbread in Romania." *Natural History* 84, no. 6 (June 1975): 66-71.
    The forced pace of industrialization, brings hardships and limits choices. Romanians express their creative spirit in colorful house decorations.

59. Brunvand, Jan Harold. "The Merry Cemetery of Transylvania." *North Carolina Folklore Journal* 21, no. 3 (September 1973): 83-88.
    Describes the Săpînţa cemetery whose ornate tombstones were created by one single accomplished craftsman.

60. Brunvand, Jan Harold. "The Study of Romanian Folklore." *Journal of the Folklore Institute* 9 (1972): 133-161.
    Introduces Western scholars to the organization of folklore research in Romania and describes some of the most representative Romanian works in the field.

61. Brunvand, Jan Harold. "Traditional House Decoration in Romania: Survey and Bibliography." *East European Quarterly* 14, no. 3 (1980): 255-301.
    A survey of Romania's traditional house decorations, an art that remains a popular mode of expression, despite being neither government sponsored nor saleable to tourists.

62. Cochran, Robert. "'What Courage': Romanian 'Our Leader' Jokes." *Journal of American Folklore* 102, no. 405 (1989): 259-274.
    Studies jokes about Ceauşescu and their psychological function.

63. Cole, John W. "In a Pig's Eye: Daily Life and Political Economy in Southeastern Europe." In *Economy, Society, and Culture in Contemporary Romania*, edited by John W. Cole, 159-174. Research Report, 24. Amherst: University of Massachusetts, Department of Anthropology, 1984.
    Expresses reservations about Western research on Southeastern Europe and stresses the importance of field work for a clear understanding of a country's internal dynamics.

64. Cole, John W. "Notes on Anthropology in Romania." In *Economy, Society, and Culture in Contemporary Romania*, edited by John W. Cole, xiii-xx. Research Report, 24. Amherst: University of Massachusetts, Department of Anthropology, 1984.
    Compares American anthropology to social sciences in Romania.

65. Coussens, Regina. "Folk Culture as a Symbol in Contemporary Romania." In *Economy, Society, and Culture in Contemporary Romania*, edited by John W. Cole, 129-138. Research Report, 24. Amherst: University of Massachusetts, Department of Anthropology, 1984.
    Reports on folk traditions in the village of Bucium and political use to legitimize changes.

66. Dundes, Alan. "Laughter Behind the Iron Curtain: A Sample of Rumanian Political Jokes." *The Ukrainian Quarterly* 27, no. 1 (1971): 50-59.
    Lacking such instruments as questionnaires or controlled interviews, political jokes collected in 1969 in Bucharest are viewed as uncensored and trustworthy expressions of popular attitude towards political realities.

67. Edes, Daniel King. "Romanian Children's Knowledge of Social Categories: A Social Anthropological Approach to Person Perception." Ph.D. diss., University of Rochester, 1986. Ann Arbor: UMI, 1986. AAD8708226.
    Studies children's awareness of kinship, occupation, and life-cycle stages.

68. Erler, J., H. D. Schmidt, and F. W. Rösing. "Partnerwahl - Eine Untersuchung an Verschiedenen Ethnischen Gruppen der Rumänischen Bevölkerung [Mate Choice - an Investigation of Different Ethnic Groups of the Romanian Population]." *Homo: Zeitschrift für die Vergleichende Forschung am Menschen* 34, no. 2 (1983): 93-99.
    Presents mate correlations for four Romanian population samples: German, Czech, Gypsy, and Romanian.

69. Evascu, Thomas Lynn. "Segagea: Economic and Social Change in a Transylvanian Mountain Village of Romania." Ph.D. diss., Ohio State University, 1980. Ann Arbor: UMI, 1980. AAD8022270.
    Reviews the economic, social and cultural changes in a noncollectivized mountain community. Analyzes the sociological and ethnographic role of the peasant worker, problems of rural urban migration, kinship and family structure.

70. Freedman, Diane C. "Dance as Communicative Code in Romanian Courtship and Marriage Rituals." Ph.D. diss., Temple University, 1984. Ann Arbor: UMI, 1984. AAD8410194.
    Studies contemporary Transylvanian village dances and argues that movements express complex social concepts related to gender relations.

71. Freedman, Diane C. "Gender Identity and Dance Style in Rural Transylvania." *East European Quarterly* 23, no. 4 (1990): 419-430.
    Describes courtship, dance and family relations in a non-collectivized village of the Ţara Oaşului. Modernization and participation in cultural activities sponsored by the Party are changing the role and nature of folk dance.

72. Hauck, Shirley A. "Ethnicity and Kirchweih Ritual: Symbolism for German-Romanians of Banat." In *Papers for the V. Congress of Southeast European Studies, Belgrade, September 1984*, edited by Kot K. Shangriladze and Erica W. Townsend, 217-226. Columbus, OH: Slavica, 1984.
    Uses the annual Kirchweih ritual to demonstrate ethnic strength and cohesion of Germans in Banat.

73. Husum, Jean Serge. "L'Enterrement à Masques dans la Region de Vrancea [Masqued Burials in the Vrancea Region]." *Journal of the American-Romanian Academy of Arts and Sciences* 11 (1988): 210-230.
    Describes ancient masqued burial rituals, still performed secretly in the village of Nereju (Vrancea).

74. Kideckel, David A. "Economic Images and Social Change in the Romanian Socialist Transformation." *Dialectical Anthropology* 12, no. 4 (1987): 399-411.
    Traces the uses of ideology in social change by examining local (Făgăraş/south

central Transylvania region) folklore versus state propaganda in presenting industrial events and processes.

75. Kideckel, David A., and Steven L. Sampson. "Field Work in Romania: Political, Practical, and Ethical Aspects." In *Economy, Society, and Culture in Contemporary Romania*, edited by John W. Cole, 85-102. Research Report, 24. Amherst: University of Massachusetts, Department of Anthropology, 1984.
    Describes how research is conducted in a socialist country and what contributes to the successful completion of a research plan.

76. Kligman, Gail. *Căluş: Symbolic Transformation in Romanian Ritual*. Chicago: University of Chicago Press, 1981.
    Studies the Căluş ritual as an art form, as well as a fertility and healing ritual, and discusses its place in a socialist society.

77. Kligman, Gail. "Poetry and Politics in a Transylvanian Village." *Anthropological Quarterly* 56, no. 2 (1983): 83-89.
    Describes how oral poetry in the form of shouted couplets, laments and songs reflect social changes and political attitudes in a Maramureş community.

78. Kligman, Gail. "The Rites of Women: Oral Poetry, Ideology, and the Socialization of Peasant Women in Contemporary Romania." *Journal of American Folklore* 97, no. 384 (1984): 167-88.
    A revised version was published in Sharon L. Wolchick, et al. *Women, State and Party in Eastern Europe*. Durham: Duke University Press, 1985.
    While socialism claims to have achieved equality between sexes, reality shows that women's subordinate role has been not only maintained but exacerbated. Wedding rituals of a Maramureş village reflect these social and cultural relationships.

79. Kligman, Gail. *The Wedding of the Dead: Ritual, Poetics, and Popular Culture in Transylvania*. Studies on the History of Society and Culture, [4]. Berkeley: University of California Press, 1988.
    Explores how life-cycle rituals, illustrated by Maramureş wedding and funeral rituals, are created, enacted, understood, and made meaningful in a socialist state.

80. Marrant, Joel Patrick. "The Idea of Folk Tradition in Romania." Ph.D. diss., University of Oregon, 1977. Ann Arbor: UMI, 1977. AAD78-02541.
    Field research conducted in the village of Poienile Izei (Maramureş) to study changing attitudes towards folk traditions in light of current nationalistic tendencies.

81. Matley, Ian M. "Traditional Pastoral Life in Romania." *The Professional Geographer* 22, no. 6 (1970): 311-316.
    Transhumance, the movement of livestock to winter pastures, is disappearing. The role of the "stâna" (the shepherd's hut and livestock pen), however, retains its traditional economic and social function.

82. Musset, Danielle. *Le Mariage à Moiseni, Roumanie [Marriage in Moiseni, Romania]*. Études et Documents Balkaniques, 3. Paris: Laboratoire d'Anthropologie Sociale, 1981.
    Detailed study of wedding and marriage rites and customs and their place in the socioeconomic life of a non-collectivized northern Transylvanian village.

83. Patterson, G. James. "National Styles in the Development and Profession of Anthropology: The Case of Romania." *East European Quarterly* 14, no. 2 (1980): 207-218.
    Highlights trends in Romanian anthropological research. Lists major institutions conducting research and offering training in anthropology, comments on types of publications and scientific meetings in the field, and discusses the role played by the government in furthering research.

84. Randall, Steven G. "The Family Estate in an Upland Carpathian Village." *Dialectical Anthropology* 1, no. 3 (1976): 277-285.
    A report on the impact of socialist economic transformations on the noncollectivized village of Paltin, in the Carpathian foothills.

85. Randall, Steven G. "The Household Estate under Socialism: The Theory and Practice of Socialist Transformation and the Political Economy of Upland Peasant Workers in Romania." Ph.D. diss., University of Massachusetts, 1983. Ann Arbor: UMI, 1983. AAD8401098.
    A theoretical discussion of "socialist transformation" with an analysis of household economic strategies in the uncollectivized mountain commune of Fundata.

86. Salzmann, Zdenek. "Peasant Life Histories as a Source of Data for the Study of Socio-cultural Change." In *Economy, Society, and Culture in Contemporary Romania*, edited by John W. Cole, 119-128. Research Report, 24. Amherst: University of Massachusetts, Department of Anthropology, 1984.
    Studies the impact of socialist changes on six isolated Czech-speaking villages in the Banat.

87. Sampson, Steven L. "Bureaucracy and Corruption as Anthropological Problems: A Case Study from Romania." *Folk: Dansk Etnografisk Tidsskrift* 25 (1983): 63-96.
    A theoretical discussion is followed by an illustration of the link between corruption and bureaucracy in Romania's planning process and in the behavior of rural elite bureaucrats.

88. Sampson, Steven L. "National Integration Through Socialist Planning: An Anthropological Study of a Romanian New Town." Ph.D. diss., University of Massachusetts, 1980. Ann Arbor: UMI, 1980. AAD81-01392.
    A revision of this work was published under the same title as East European Monographs, 148. New York: Columbia University Press, 1984.
    To achieve rapid industrialization, Romania plans to convert 300 villages into urban areas, thus eliminating differences between city and rural life styles. Braşov County and the village of Feldioara illustrate this integration process. Discusses implications for development planning theory.

89. Sampson, Steven L. *The Planners and the Peasants: An Anthropological Study of Urban Development in Romania*. Monographs in East-West Studies, 4. Esbjerg, Denmark: University Center of South Jutland, Institute of East-West Studies, 1982.
    Abridged version of the author's 1980 Ph.D. thesis.

90. Sampson, Steven L. "Rich Families and Poor Collectives: An Anthropological Approach to Romania's 'Second Economy'." *Bidrag Till Oststatsforskningen: Contributions to Soviet and East European Research* 11, no. 1 (1983): 44-77.
    Argues that the "second economy" is not governed by bureaucratic structures but by social relations, and demonstrates its functioning in the private sector of Romania's agriculture.

91. Schneider, Karl Günther. "Fernweidewirtschaft in den Südost-Karpaten (Rumänien) [Migrant Pasturing in the South-Eastern Carpathians (Romania)]." *Geographische Rundschau* 25, no. 7 (1973): 282-289.
    Collectivization and improved means of transportation have reduced the role of shepherds in leading flocks to distant mountain pastures. Rules on distance traveled, use of grazing grounds, wages, and prices govern today's transhumance activities.

92. Senn, Harry A. "Some Werewolf Legends and the Căluşari Ritual in Romania." *East European Quarterly* 11, no. 1 (1977): 1-14.
    Mythological traditions and rituals to counteract potentially maleficent powers are still alive and practiced in Romanian villages.

93. Senn, Harry A. "Were-Beings and Strigoi Legends in Village Life: Romanian Folk Beliefs." *East European Quarterly* 14, no. 3 (1980): 303-314.
     Beliefs and rituals of villagers in Transylvania, Moldova, and Ilfov.

94. Senn, Harry A. *Were-Wolf and Vampire in Romania*. East European Monographs, 99. New York: Columbia University Press, 1982.
     Analyzes stories and beliefs about the origin and significance of super-human beings as they endure in Romanian popular mythology.

95. Summers, David. "Living Legends in Romania." *Folklore* 83 (1972): 321-328.
     Reports on legends collected in the mountainous region of Maramureş.

96. Verdery, Katherine. "The 'Etatization' of Time in Ceauşescu's Romania." In *The Politics of Time*, edited by Henry J. Rutz, 37-61. American Ethnological Society Monograph Series, 4. Washington, D.C.: American Anthropological Association, 1992.
     Using the example of 1980's Romania, demonstrates how regime politics can create struggles over time, as people were subjected to and resisted new temporal organizations.

97. Verdery, Katherine. *Transylvanian Villagers: Three Centuries of Political, Economic, and Ethnic Change*. Berkeley, CA: University of California Press, 1983.
     Presents the political, economic, and social changes in the Transylvanian community of Binţinţi (Aurel Vlaicu). Of special interest is Part I, which focuses on the Ceauşescu era.

4. Armed Forces & Defense Policy

98. Alexiev, Alex. "Party-Military Relations in Eastern Europe: The Case of Romania." In *Soldiers, Peasants, and Bureaucrats: Civil-Military Relations in Communist and Modernizing Societies*, edited by Roman Kolkowicz and Andrzej Korbonski, 199-227. London: Allen & Unwin, 1982.
  Published originally as ACIS Working Paper, 15, by the Center for International and Strategic Affairs, University of California, Los Angeles, January 1979.
  Analyzes the evolution of party-military relations in Romania in light of growing nationalism and includes an overview of civil-miltary relations in Eastern Europe.

99. Alexiev, Alex. *Romania and the Warsaw Pact: The Defense Policy of a Reluctant Ally*. Rand Paper, P-6270. Santa Monica, CA: Rand Corporation, 1979.
  See also the author's article in *Journal of Strategic Studies* 4, no. 1 (1981): 5-18, and his chapter in Adelman, Johnathan R. *Communist Armies in Politics*. Boulder: Westview, 1982.
  Discusses Romania's threat perception and its concept of "people's war."

100. Alexiev, Alex. "Romania and the Warsaw Pact: The Defense Policy of a Reluctant Ally." *Journal of Strategic Studies* 4, no. 1 (1981): 5-18.
  See also the author's monograph of the same title, published in 1979, and his chapter in Adelman, Johnathan R. *Communist Armies in Politics*. Boulder: Westview, 1982.
  Overview of military-political and strategic implications resulting from Romania's defiant defense posture within the Warsaw Pact. Discusses Romania's concept of defense, "the people's war," its threat perception, its weapon production, and its relations with Warsaw Pact and non-Warsaw Pact countries.

101. Alexiev, Alex. "The Romanian Army." In *Communist Armies in Politics*, edited by Jonathan R. Adelman, 149-166. Boulder: Westview, 1982.
  Based in part on the author's *Romania and the Warsaw Pact: The Defense Policy of a Reluctant Ally*. Rand Paper, P-6270. Santa Monica, CA: The Rand Corporation, 1979. See also the author's article in *Journal of Strategic Studies* 4, no. 1 (1981): 5-18.
  Documents changes occurring in the Romanian military throughout its communist history, with special emphasis on Ceauşescu's defense doctrine.

102. Bacon, Walter M., Jr. "Civil-Military Relations in Romania: Value Transformations in the Military." *Studies in Comparative Communism* 11, no. 3 (1978): 237-249.
  Study of civil-military relations and their conformance to and deviations from the Herspring-Volgyes model.

103. Bacon, Walter M., Jr. "The Military and the Party in Romania." In *Civil-Military Relations in Communist Systems*, edited by Dale R. Herspring and Ivan Volgyes,

165-180. Boulder: Westview, 1978.
Reviews party-military relations since the 1960's.

104. Bacon, Walter M., Jr. "Romania." In *Soviet Allies: The Warsaw Pact and the Issue of Reliability*, edited by Daniel N. Nelson, 250-263. Boulder: Westview, 1984.
Describes Romania's divergent military policy and assesses its mobilizing potential. Concludes that Romania's degree of participation in an armed conflict outside its frontiers is likely to be lower than that of its Warsaw Pact allies.

105. Barany, Zoltan D. "East European Armed Forces in Transitions and Beyond." *East European Quarterly* 26, no. 1 (1992): 1-30.
Examines the role of the armed forces in the collapse of the Ceauşescu government and concludes that "in domestic emergencies [armed forces] usually shied away from turning against the enemies of the regime" (p. 23).

106. Breyer, Siegfried. "Neubauten für Rumäniens Marine [New Ships for the Romanian Navy]." *Marine Rundschau* 80 (July 1983): 311-313.
Ceauşescu is building two new classes of warships.

107. Breyer, Siegfried. "Rumänische Kriegschiffbau im Aufwind [Romanian Warship Building on the Increase]." *Marine-Rundschau* 82 (November-December 1985): 356-358.
Describes Ceauşescu's new fleet.

108. Burke, David P. "Defense and Mass Mobilization in Romania." *Armed Forces and Society* 7, no. 1 (1980): 31-49.
Contends that Romania has successfully maximized its freedom by maneuvering prudently along the fine edge of Soviet tolerance and by creating a defense policy of mass mobilization to deter invasion by its allies, which is unique within the Warsaw Pact.

109. Burke, David P. "The Defense Policy of Romania." In *The Defense Policies of Nations: A Comparative Study*, edited by Douglas J. Murray and Paul R. Viotti, 323-341. Baltimore: Johns Hopkins University Press, 1982.
Adapted from "Defense and Mass Mobilization in Romania" published in *Armed Forces and Society* 7, no. 1 (1980).

110. Cason, Thomas O. "The Warsaw Pact Today: The East European Military Forces." In *The Warsaw Pact: Political Purpose & Military Means*, edited by Robert W. Clawson and Lawrence S. Kaplan, 158-160. Wilmington, DE: Scholarly Resources, 1982.
Papers originally presented at a conference held at Kent, Ohio, April 22-23, 1981.
The sub-chapter on Romania (pp.158-160) looks at military units and equipment and underscores the reluctance of Romania to participate in Warsaw Pact activities.

111. Chaplin, Ari. "The 'Popular War' Doctrine in Romanian Defense Policy." *East European Quarterly* 17, no. 3 (1983): 267-282.
Analyzes the justification for and legal adaptation of the popular war doctrine, and its practical implementation. Discusses the political and psychological education of the population and issues of armed and non-violent resistance.

112. Chaplin, Ari. "Security of Weak States: The 'Popular War' Doctrine in Romanian Defense Policy." Ph.D. diss., New School for Social Research, 1977. Ann Arbor: UMI, 1977. AAD77-28206.
Analyzes Romania's adaptation of popular/guerilla warfare as a defense option. Compares it with the defense doctrines of Finland, Sweden, Austria, and Yugoslavia.

113. Crowther, William. "'Ceauşescuism' and Civil-Military Relations in Romania." *Armed Forces and Society* 15, no. 2 (1989): 207-225.

Ceauşescu exercises maximum control over the army. Through budget cuts and decreased autonomy, the army has seen its power eroded and transferred to the security forces.

114. Eyal, Jonathan. "Ceauşescu's Armed Forces." *Armed Forces* 6, no. 3 (1987): 114-117.
Offers a historical overview of the organization, equipment, and training and describes the 1966-1972 "golden years" of the Romanian armed forces and its subsequent decline and neglect. Ill-equiped and demoralized, the military has little to contribute to the strength of the Warsaw Pact.

115. Ghermani, Dionisie. "Die Rumänische Volksarmee [The Romanian Popular Army]." In *Zur Geschichte der Europäischen Volksarmeen*, edited by Peter Gosztony, 189-226. Bonn: Hohwacht, [1976].
Describes how changes in foreign policy have an impact on the organization, characteristics, and historical interpretation of the role of defense.

116. Ghermani, Dionisie. "Sozialistische Republik Rumänien [Socialist Republic Romania]." In *Reservesysteme des Warschauer Paktes: Ein Weissbuch*, edited by Rudolf Woller, 51-62. München: Bernard & Graefe, 1978.
Army reserves are the centerpiece of Ceauşescu's ideology of people's war. Describes pre-military and military training, responsibilities and ranks, and aspects of mobilization and deployment.

117. Gilberg, Trond. "Eastern European Military Assistance to the Third World." In *Communist Nations' Military Assistance*, edited by John F. Copper and Daniel S. Papp, 86-87. Boulder: Westview, 1983.
Asia and Africa have been the object of Romanian military assistance, while Latin America has received economic and political support.

118. Holmes, Richard, and David Isby. "Romania." In *World Armies*, edited by John Keegan, 491-493. 2nd ed. Hants, England: Macmillan, 1983.
Describes Romania's military strength, budget, organization, recruitment and training, constitutional status, and role as a member of the Warsaw Pact. Lists military ranks, dress and distinctions.

119. Jacobini, H. B. "International Law, Defense and Aspects of Rumanian Military Doctrine." *International Journal of Rumanian Studies* 5, no. 1 (1987): 85-103.
Romanian military doctrine is grounded in historical tradition as well as contemporary international law. It is well conceived, well structured, and well articulated.

120. Jessup, John. "Romania Celebrates the Centennial of its Independence." *Military Affairs* 42, no. 3 (1978): 147-149.
Report on the Bucharest Commemorative Conference on the War of Independence, May 1977, attended by military representatives from 18 nations, including the United States. Discusses issues, papers and commentaries presented at the conference.

121. Jones, Christopher D. "Romania." In *Warsaw Pact: The Question of Cohesion. Phase II - Volume 2: Poland, German Democratic Republic, and Romania*, by Teresa Rakowska-Harmstone, Christopher D. Jones, and Ivan Sylvain, 348-411. ORAE Extra-Mural Paper, 33. Ottawa, Canada: Department of Defense, November 1984.
Reviews Romania's treaty obligations, its position on European Security, its military doctrine, and its participation in joint alliance activities. Discusses weapon production and acquisition. Concludes that in the event of war, Romanian armed forces may continue to remain non-aligned.

122. Jones, Christopher D. *Soviet Influence in Eastern Europe: Political Autonomy and the Warsaw Pact*. New York: Praeger, 1981.
Demonstrates how Romania, Yugoslavia, and Albania have retained a certain degree of independence from the Soviet Union. Presents Romania's doctrine of war of the entire people, its national plan for territorial defense, and its military educational system.

123. King, Robert R. "Die Paramilitärischen Organisationen in Rumänien [The Paramilitary Organizations in Romania]." In *Paramilitärische Organisationen im Sowjetblock*, edited by Peter Gosztony, 215-236. Bonn: Hohwacht, 1977.
Various paramilitary units were created after World War II. After the invasion of Czechoslovakia, however, Romania's new military doctrine of people's war mandated the introduction of military education and the creation of patriotic guards. These, together with the militia, security forces, and border and paramilitary units, are under strict Party control.

124. Marey, Georges. "L'Armée de la République Socialiste de Roumanie [The Army of the Socialist Republic of Romania]." *Est & Ouest* 624 (31 January 1979): 15-21.
Reviews Romania's military forces, weapons, suppliers, and military expenditures, in the aftermath of the invasion of Czechoslovakia.

125. Mason, David S. "Romanian Autonomy and Arms Control Policies." *Arms Control* 3, no. 1 (May 1982): 13-36.
Reviews Romania's position and concludes that in an era of re-militarization, small states can play a role in maintaining peace.

126. Mushkat, Marion. *Kann Ein Kleiner Staat Sich Selbst Verteidigen? Die Rumänische Version [Can a Small State Defend Itself? The Romanian Version].* Berichte, 6. Köln: Bundesinstitut für Ostwissenschaftliche und Internationale Studien, 1979.
Analyzes the origins of the Romanian defense doctrine and its impact on the present and future unity of the Warsaw Pact and on Euro-communism.

127. Nelson, Daniel N. "Ceaușescu and the Romanian Army." *International Defense Review* 22, no. 6 (1989): 737-741.
Since the 1970's the army's role as defender of national sovereignty was diluted by the emergence of patriotic guards. Military expenditures remain low and armed forces are increasingly used in economic and repressive activities. No military coup is predicted, but the military will have a say in Ceaușescu's succession and future political decisions.

128. O'Ballance, Edgar. "The Three Southern Members of the Warsaw Pact." In *The Warsaw Pact: Political Purpose & Military Means*, edited by Robert W. Clawson and Lawrence S. Kaplan, 49-63. Wilmington, DE: Scholarly Resources, 1982.
Papers originally presented at a conference held at Kent, OH, April 22-23, 1981.
Examines Ceaușescu's defense policy in the aftermath of the Soviet invasion of Czechoslovakia.

129. *Report of the Delegation to Romania, Hungary, Federal Republic of Germany, and France, of the Committee on Armed Services, House of Representatives ... .* Washington: U.S. G.P.O., 1982. Committee Print. Y4.Ar5/2:D37/5.
Updates the Committee's information on conditions and stability factors in Romania via discussions with high ranking Romanian officials including President Ceaușescu. Summarizes economic, foreign and defense conditions as well as prospects for the future.

130. Van Tol, Robert, and Jonathan Eyal. "New Romanian Navy: A Weapon Without Target." *RUSI Journal* 132, no. 1 (1987): 37-46.
A history of the Romanian navy is followed by a discussion of Ceaușescu's wasteful naval rearmament program.

131. Volgyes, Ivan. *The Political Reliability of the Warsaw Pact Armies: The Southern Tier.* Durham, NC: Duke University Press, 1982.
Profiles Romania's independent policy stance in light of potential implications for NATO. Discusses the size, composition, and equipment of its armed forces, its military doctrine, and party-military relations (pp.41-59).

5. Ceauşescu & the Cult of Personality

132. Almond, Mark. *The Rise and Fall of Nicolae and Elena Ceauşescu*. London: Chapmans, 1992.
     Narrates the Ceauşescus' rise to power, their abusive policies and self-aggrandizing image, and the revolution that brought them down.

133. Behr, Edward. *Kiss the Hand You Cannot Bite: The Rise and Fall of the Ceauşescus*. New York: Villard Books, 1991.
     Explores the social and political conditions that permitted Ceauşescu's ascent to power, depicts his abusive rule and the revolutionary forces that brought about his demise, and comments on the shadow his legacy casts on Romania's future.

134. Braun, Aurel. *Ceauşescu: The Problems of Power*. Behind the Headlines, vol. 37, no. 6. Toronto: Canadian Institute of International Affairs, 1979.
     Examines potential short, medium, and long-term impact of Ceauşescu's leadership and speculates on the future of a post-Ceauşescu Romania.

135. Brown, J. F. *Eastern Europe and Communist Rule*. Durham: Duke University Press, 1988.
     Chapter eight (pp.263-293) on Romania presents the debilitating effects of power on Ceauşescu's personality and the political and moral disintegration of his regime at the close of the 1980's.

136. Brown, J. F. *The New Eastern Europe: The Khrushchev Era and After*. Praeger Publications in Russian History and World Communism, 169. New York: Praeger, 1966.
     A brief discussion of relevant events and policy trends during the transition from Gheorghiu-Dej to Ceauşescu (pp.202-211) is followed by a biographical sketch of Ceauşescu and Maurer (pp.282-289).

137. Castex, Michel. *Un Mensonge Gros Comme le Siècle: Roumanie, Histoire d'une Manipulation [A Lie as Big as the Century: Romania, the History of a Manipulation]*. Paris: Albin Michel, 1990.
     Contends that the Romanian revolution was a coup d'état organized by the KGB and not a spontaneous uprising.

138. Catchlove, Donald. *Romania's Ceauşescu*. London: Abacus, 1972.
     Flattering biographical profile of Ceauşescu.

139. De Flers, René. "Socialism in One Family." *Survey (London)* 28, no. 4 (1984): 165-174.
     Describes the dynastic nature of Ceauşescu's government.

140. Dima, Nicholas. "Nicolae Ceauşescu of Communist Romania: A Portrait of Power." *Journal of Social, Political and Economic Studies* 13, no. 4 (December 1988): 429-454.
     A biographical portrait of Ceauşescu's ascent to power, his methods of consolida-

tion and preservation of political control, and his relationship to the West and to the Soviet Union. Predicts the imminent end of the Ceauşescu era and warns against the longlasting disastrous effects of his policies.

141. Durandin, Catherine. *Nicolae Ceauşescu: Verités et Mensonges d'un Roi Communiste [Nicolae Ceauşescu: Truths and Lies of a Communist King]*. Paris: Albin Michel, 1990.
     Portrait of Ceauşescu, his regime and his demise.

142. Fischer, Mary Ellen. *Nicolae Ceauşescu: A Study in Political Leadership*. Boulder: Lynne Rienner, 1989.
     Examines Ceauşescu's ascension to power, his personality and character, and the effects of his policies on Romania's present and future.

143. Fischer, Mary Ellen. *Nicolae Ceauşescu and the Romanian Political Leadership: Nationalism and Personalization of Power*. Saratoga Springs, NY: Skidmore College, 1983.
     Explores Ceauşescu's background, political activities and policies, his ascent to the rank of "supreme ruler" (1969-1979), and the 1979 economic crisis and its management. Discusses potential political scenarios for the post-Ceauşescu era.

144. Fischer, Mary Ellen. "Nicolae Ceauşescu: His Political Life and Style." *Balkanistica* 5 (1979): 84-99.
     Examines Ceauşescu's biography and attempts "to place his current political priorities and leadership style in the context of his early life and past political experience" (p. 86).

145. Fischer, Mary Ellen. "Women in Romanian Politics: Elena Ceauşescu, Pronatalism, and the Promotion of Women." In *Women, State, and Party in Eastern Europe*, edited by Sharon L. Wolchik and Alfred G. Meyer, 121-137. Durham: Duke University Press, 1985.
     Charts the development of the official "Elena cult," despised by the people, who consider her responsible for the 1966 pronatalist measures. Contends that since 1979, Ceauşescu has pushed for greater representation of women in positions of political power.

146. Fischer-Galaţi, Stephen. "Nicolae Ceauşescu: Rumania's Leader." *Communist Affairs* 5, no. 2 (1967): 23-26.
     Profiles Ceauşescu, his early prison years, his rise as heir-apparent to Gheorghiu-Dej, and his ascension to power.

147. Frankland, Mark. *The Patriots' Revolution: How East Europe Won its Freedom*. London: Sinclair-Stevenson, 1990.
     "Romania's Bitter Revolution" (pp.296-333) outlines Ceauşescu's life and policies, and the revolution that ended his dictatorship. Concludes that post-Ceauşescu Romania is ill prepared to face the future.

148. Gabanyi, Anneli Ute. "Personenkult und Kulturperson: Rumänien Feierte Ceauşescus Geburtstag [Personality Cult and Cult Figure: Romania Celebrates Ceauşescu's Birthday]." *Osteuropa* 28, no. 8 (1978): 714-718.
     The cult of personality is used to rally the country around Ceauşescu.

149. Galloway, George, and Bob Wylie. *Downfall: The Ceauşescus and the Romanian Revolution*. London: Futura, 1991.
     Chronicles the Ceauşescu era, the revolution, and the Ceauşescus' trial and execution.

150. Georgescu, Vlad. "Politics, History and Nationalism: The Origins of Romania's Socialist Personality Cult." In *The Cult of Power: Dictators in the Twentieth Century*, edited by Joseph Held, 129-142. East European Monographs, 140. New York:

Columbia University Press, 1983.
Using Ceaușescu as one example, asserts that regimes of socialist societies are potential breeding grounds for personality cults built around un-charismatic dictators.

151. Hamelet, Michel P. *Nicolae Ceaușescu: Présentation, Choix de Textes, Aperçu Historique, Documents Photographiques [Nicolae Ceaușescu: Presentation, Selected Literature, Historical Overview, Photographic Documents].* Destinus Politiques, 9. Paris: Seghers, 1971.
Sympathetic biography of Ceaușescu.

152. Kozinski, Alex. "Death, Lies & Videotapes: The Ceaușescu Show Trial and the Future of Romania." *ABA Journal* 77, no. 1 (1991): 70-73.
Concludes that due process of law was not followed. The legal farce does not bode well for the future of the country.

153. Masson, Danièle. "La Roumanie et l'Époque Ceaușescu: Édification d'un Cult [Romania and the Ceaușescu Era: The Building of a Cult]." *International Journal of Rumanian Studies* 5, no. 1 (1987): 53-59.
Analyzes the themes of Ceaușescu's personality cult.

154. Maxwell, Robert, ed. *Nicolae Ceaușescu: Builder of Modern Romania and International Statesman.* Oxford: Pergamon, 1983.
Biographical account praising his dedication to his people and his international efforts for peace and a new world economic order.

155. Nelson, Daniel N. "Ceaușescu-Kult und Lokale Politikbereiche in Rumänien [Ceaușescu-Cult and Local Politics in Romania]." *Osteuropa* 39, no. 4 (1989): 371-384.
Romania has become a chaotic autocracy. The disintegration of the centralized political system, weakens sub-national political organizations which form the very base of the regime.

156. Nelson, Daniel N. "Le Fiasco Politique de la Roumanie [Romania's Political Fiasco]." *Revue d'Études Comparatives Est-Ouest* 20, no. 3 (1989): 5-16.
For over fifteen years Romania's Nicolae Ceaușescu was the toast of the West. However, in the 1980s, he lost credibility. Analyzes his demise as an important player in the international political arena and as a leader of his own people. Concludes that Romania's hope for a better future could begin only after the disappearance of Ceaușescu and his family.

157. Olschewski, Malte. *Der Conducator Nicolae Ceaușescu: Phänomen der Macht [The Leader Nicolae Ceaușescu: Materialization of Power].* Vienna: Ueberreuter, 1990.
Portrait of Ceaușescu from his humble origins to his execution and secret burial. Based on personal observations, and testimonials of dissidents and of opponents of the neo-communist regime.

158. Pacepa, Ion Mihai. *Red Horizons: Chronicles of a Communist Spy Chief.* Washington, D.C.: Regnery Gateway, 1987.
Draws a picture of the political ruthlessness and moral decay of Nicolae Ceaușescu and his family. Describes the "Horizon" operation, a masterful plan of deception conceived by Ceaușescu to gain Western political and financial support.

159. Pakula, Hanna. "Elena Ceaușescu: The Shaping of an Ogress." *Vanity Fair* 53, no. 8 (1990): 120-125+.
A biographical sketch, laced with anecdotes and personal testimonies, tracing Elena's humble origins and describing her marriage to Nicolae, her rapacity for the trappings of power, and her sordid end.

160. Rupnik, Jacques. *The Other Europe.* London: Weidenfeld and Nicolson, 1988.
The chapter "Romania's Dynastic Communism" (pp.150-158) depicts scenes of

adulation orchestrated for the benefit of Ceauşescu and his family while the population suffers under repressive domestic policies and witnesses the irrevocable damage inflicted in the name of urban renewal.

161. Selbourne, David. *Death of the Dark Hero: Eastern Europe, 1987-90.* London: Jonathan Cape, 1990.
Personal account of experiences in Eastern Europe and in Romania during the last years under Ceauşescu and the revolutionary wave that swept over Eastern Europe in 1989.

162. Siegert, Heinz. *Ceauşescu: Management für ein Modernes Rumänien [Ceauşescu: Management for a Modern Romania].* München: Bertelsmann, 1973.
Favorable portrait of Ceauşescu's life.

163. Sweeney, John. *The Life and Evil Times of Nicolae Ceauşescu.* London: Hutchinson, 1991.
Based on testimony of people close to Ceauşescu and on the author's personal experiences in Romania during the revolution, this journalistic account profiles life under the cruel and grotesque regime of the dictator.

164. Tismăneanu, Vladimir. "The Agony of a Marxist Monarchy." *The World & I,* 3, no. 3-4 (1988): 108-114.
While the economy is crumbling, Ceauşescu's personality cult is more strident than ever. Discusses possible scenarios for succession.

165. Tismăneanu, Vladimir. "The Ambiguity of Romanian National Communism." *Telos* 60 (Summer 1984): 65-79.
Explains the Stalinist traditions of Romanian communist leaders, with emphasis on Ceauşescu's bureaucratic despotism and personality cult.

166. Tismăneanu, Vladimir. "Byzantine Rites, Stalinist Follies: The Twilight of Dynastic Socialism in Romania." *Orbis* 30, no. 1 (1986): 65-90.
Analyzes the dynamics of the Ceauşescus' personality cult and likens it to a quasi-mystical tradition of Byzantine heritage in which Nicolae, Elena and Nicu act as "the trinity." At the same time, a rigid internal Stalinist system is upheld by ruthless suppression of all opposition and dissent. This unique combination of dynastic socialism stemming from Gheorghiu-Dej's rule has led to alienation and political and economic crises for Romania's people, resulting in a psychology of national despair.

167. Tismăneanu, Vladimir. "Ceauşescu at Seventy." *East European Reporter* 3, no. 2 (1988): 60-61.
Traces briefly Ceauşescu's life and his use of xenophobic nationalism to gain popular support. While his birthday is celebrated with pageantry, economic crises and dissent are gripping the country.

168. Tismăneanu, Vladimir. "Ceauşescu's Socialism." *Problems of Communism* 34, no. 1 (1985): 50-66.
Analyzes the roots of Ceauşescu's "dynastic socialism" from a biographical and institutional point of view.

6. Communications & Media

169. Gabanyi, Anneli Ute. "...im Einklang mit den Allgemeinen Bestrebungen des Volkes: Die Zensur in Rumänien - Nicht Abgeschafft, Sondern Verstärkt [...In Accordance with the General Aspirations of the People: Censorship in Romania - Toughened Rather than Abolished]." *Osteuropa* 29, no. 4 (1979): 334-340.
An open protest against continuing censorship characterized the May 1978 Cluj Colloquium on Drama. While censorship was officially abolished in 1977, Ceaușescu's new "system of self-control" has resulted in even more stringent suppression of free speech.

170. Gabanyi, Anneli Ute. "Rumania's New Press Law." *Index on Censorship* 3, no. 3 (1974): 65-71.
Reviews the provisions of the first post-World War II law of the press adopted by the Great National Assembly in 1974.

171. Gilberg, Trond. "Romania: In Quest of Development." In *Political Socialization in Eastern Europe*, edited by Ivan Volgyes, 147-199. New York: Praeger, 1975.
Studies the "political socialization" process in Romania by examining how citizens are informed about the political system, and how they evaluate its performance.

172. Gross, Peter. "Exercises in Cynicism and Propaganda: Law, Legality, and Foreign Correspondence in Romania." *Political Communication and Persuasion* 6, no. 3 (1989): 179-190.
In most East European countries, the advent of *glasnost* meant improved freedom of movement and access to sources for the press. Not so in Romania, where deportation, visa denials, and harassment of accredited Western journalists continues, proof of Ceaușescu's stubborn resistance to change.

173. Gross, Peter. "The Romanian Press and Its Party-State Relatonship: A Study of the 1974/1977 Press Laws." Ph.D. diss., University of Iowa, 1984. Ann Arbor: UMI, 1984. AAD8507942.
The new press law of 1974/77, legitimizes the Soviet tradition of stringent party control over all mass media.

174. Gross, Peter. "The USA as Seen Through the Eyes of the Romanian Press: A Study of Images Created by the Romanian Communist Party's 'Scînteia'." *East European Quarterly* 24, no. 3 (1990): 373-392.
Outlines the negative portrayal of the U.S. as reflected in the pages of the premier Communist Party newspaper, *Scinteia*, during the first six months of 1988.

175. Harrington, Joseph F., and Bruce J. Courtney. "Romania's Changing Image: Bucharest and the American Press: 1952-1975." In *The United States and Romania: American-Romanian Relations in the Twentieth Century*, edited by Paul D. Quinlan, 105-

123. American-Romanian Academy of Arts and Sciences, 6. Woodland Hills, CA: ARA, 1988.
    From 1964-1968 Ceaușescu has been depicted as "an energetic and youthful leader". From 1969 to 1975 Romania's mixed press image reflected Washington ambivalent attitude towards communism.

176. Jorgensen, Rebekah Lee. "The Screening of America: The Use and Influences of American Films and Television Programs by Adolescents in a Romanian Community." Ph.D. diss., Ohio State University, 1980. Ann Arbor: UMI, 1980. AAD8100174.
    American films, television programs and music, although selected by official decision makers to support socialist ideology, are very popular with Romanian adolescents and are not a threat to their cultural heritage.

177. Lendvai, Paul. *The Bureaucracy of Truth: How Communist Governments Manage the News.* Boulder: Westview, 1981.
    Illustrates with Romanian examples how information is handled in repressive societies. Shows the importance of western broadcasts and government attempts to intimidate listeners.

178. Leonhardt, Peter. *Das Rumänische Presserecht Nach dem Gesetz vom 28.3.1974 [The Romanian Press Rights after the Law of 3/28/1974].* Sonderdruck aus *Jahrbuch für Ostrecht*, 1974, 15 (1/2). Tübingen: Erdmann Verlag für Internationalen Kulturaustausch, 1980.
    The 1974 Press Law consolidates Party control over information and eliminates any possible liberalization tendencies. Describes the social function of the press, its organization, and activities, the journalistic rights and consequences for infractions.

179. Lovinescu, Monica. "La Littérature en Roumanie [Literature in Romania]." *L'Alternative (Paris)* 13 (November-December 1981): 59-63.
    Illusions of freedom of expression after the Prague Spring are dashed by Ceaușescu's 1971 cultural mini-revolution. While some artists resort to sycophancy and duplicity to survive, others resist openly and suffer the consequences. The 1981 writers' meeting turns into an open rebellion against the regime.

180. Manea, Ion. "The Romanian Press: Does It Exist in Today's Romania?" *Journal of the Romanian American Academy for Arts and Sciences* 6-9 (1985-1986): 142-147, 149-155.
    A two part article on Ceaușescu's tight control over information. Discusses the dismanteling of the foreign press corps and the grooming of a generation of subservient press cadres.

181. Masson, Danièle. "Discours et Pratiques de l'État vis-à-vis de la Paysannerie à Travers la Presse Officielle en Roumanie [The State's Attitudes and Actions vis-à-vis the Peasants as Reflected in the Official Romanian Press]." *Revue d'Études Comparatives Est-Ouest* 16, no. 1 (1985): 107-120.
    With the installation of the communist regime, Romania's economy underwent drastic changes. The agricultural sector lost its dominant role to heavy industry. The Soviet model of collectivization met with the resistance of Romanian peasantry. The State conducted an intensive ideological campaign to change the mentality of the small farm worker into that of a "modern citizen of a socialist society multilaterally developed." The State also struggled to preserve those characteristics of the peasantry, that affirmed its legitimacy and continuity. Concludes that this campaign did not succeed.

182. Oschlies, Wolf. "'Die Behörden mit Deutschen Sorgen bombardieren...': 30 Jahre Rumäniendeutsche Tageszeitung 'Neuer Weg' ['Bombard the Authorities with German Issues...': Thirty Years of the Romanian-German Daily Newspaper 'Neuer Weg']." *Deutschland Archiv* 12, no. 5 (May 1979): 518-521.
    The paper has served the German minority well. Romania now has additional German papers, an unprecedented news media phenomenon in Eastern Europe.

183. Sampson, Steven L. "The Communications Revolution: Rumours in Socialist Romania." *Survey (London)* 28, no. 4 (1984): 142-164.
Studies origin, typology, diffusion and social function of rumors as informal communication channels.

184. Schoengrund, Charles Alan. "Visual Tradition and Indoctrination: A Study of Cultural Manipulation in Portugal and Romania." Ph.D. diss., University of Wisconsin - Madison, 1982. Ann Arbor: UMI, 1982. AAD8216266.
Studies propaganda manipulation of visual artifacts by policy makers in order to indoctrinate and control masses.

7. Demography & Pronatalist Policies

185. Berelson, B. "Romania's 1966 Anti-Abortion Decree: The Demographic Experience of the First Decade." *Population Studies* 33, no. 2 (1979): 209-222.
   In 1966 the government made abortion legal only under limited conditions, discouraged the use of contraceptive methods, instituted divorce restrictions, and introduced pronatalistic incentives. Over the next decade the reproductive rate increased 33% and is compared to the U.S. "baby boom" with an expected echo effect in the 1990s. In Romania, however, the demographic increase is the result of unwanted pregnancies. From the standpoint of the government, the policy achieved its purpose.

186. Calot, Gérard. "Oú en est la Natalité en Roumanie? [The Status of Natality in Romania]." *Économie et Statistique* 36 (1972): 55-58.
   Studies the effects of the anti-abortion law (1966) to the end of 1970.

187. Cole, John W., and Judith A. Nydon. "Class, Gender and Fertility: Contradictions of Social Life in Contemporary Romania." *East European Quarterly* 23, no. 4 (1990): 469-476.
   Explores reasons for and failures of Romania's pronatalist policies.

188. "Les Conséquences de l'Interdiction de l'Avortement en Roumanie [Consequences of Prohibition of Abortions in Romania]." *Population* 27, no. 4-5 (1972): 882-884.
   The change in abortion laws (1966) led to an increase in natality. Recently, births have declined. The number of wanted pregancies is very low among educated women. It is doubtful that these tendencies could be overcome by legislation.

189. David, Henry P. *Family Planning and Abortion in the Socialist Countries of Central and Eastern Europe.* New York: Population Council, 1970.
   Partial contents of the chapter "Romania" (pp. 127-160): Historical Trends, Illegal Abortions, Family Allowances and Tax Policy, Contraceptives, Family Planning Centers, Medical and Postgraduate Training, Sex Education, Public Education.

190. David, Henry P., and Robert J. McIntyre. *Reproductive Behavior: Central and Eastern European Experience.* New York: Springer, 1981.
   Chapter nine, part 2, "Romania" (pp. 176-197), begins with a history of demographic trends and population policies and focuses on Ceauşescu's pronatalist measures, fertility planning, and questions of sex and society.

191. David, Henry P., and Nicholas H. Wright. "Abortion Legislation: The Romanian Experience." *Studies in Family Planning* 2, no. 10 (October 1971): 205-210.
   Reprinted in *The Population Problem*, edited by Stanley Johnson, 120-128. New York: Wiley, 1973.

Explores Romanian demographics before and after the restrictive abortion law of 1966 and its long-term effect on patterns of fertility behavior.

192. Doh, Rainer, and Wienfried Senker. *Bevölkerungsentwicklung, Wirtschaftsordnung und Industrialisierungsprozess in Südosteuropa: Dargestellt am Beispiel der Länder Rumänien und Türkei [Demographic Development, Economic System, and Industrialization in South-East Europe: The Case of Romania and Turkey]*. Wirtschaft und Gesellschaft in Südosteuropa, 4. Neuried: Hieronymus, 1985.
    Detailed demographic analysis emphasizing data since World War II and dealing with geographic distribution, age and sex breakdown, mortality, fertility, natality and abortions, life expectancy, marital status, divorce, number of children, education and occupations, and income.

193. Galaction, Virgil. "Das Neue Abtreibungsverbot und die Krise in der Bevölkerungsentwicklung Rumäniens [The New Ban on Abortions and the Crisis in Romania's Demographic Development]." *Jahrbuch für Ostrecht* 7, no. 2 (1966): 221-235.
    Romania could address the population crisis by addressing its economic, social, and religious causes. The new abortion law focuses on the symptoms and not the causes.

194. Hord, Charlotte, Henry P. David, France Donnay, and M. Wolf. "Reproductive Health in Romania: Reversing the Ceauşescu Legacy." *Studies in Family Planning* 22, no. 4 (1991): 231-240.
    Pronatalist policies and illegal abortions resulted in the highest maternal mortality in Europe. Post-communist Romania has legalized abortion and is improving education and services related to reproductive health.

195. Ionescu, Dan. "Abortions in Romania." *Survey (London)* 29, no. 4 (1987): 113-114.
    Abortions, legal and illegal, are still being performed in high numbers despite harsh anti-abortion legislation.

196. Kligman, Gail. "The Politics of Reproduction in Ceauşescu's Romania: A Case Study in Political Culture." *East European Politics and Societies* 6, no. 3 (1992): 364-418.
    Explores "the relationship between official rhetoric, policy, and everyday practice" and unveils the tragic results of political demography.

197. Kligman, Gail. "Women and Reproductive Legislation in Romania: Implications for the Transition." In *Dilemmas of Transition in the Soviet Union and Eastern Europe*, edited by George W. Breslauer, 141-166. Berkeley: University of California at Berkeley, International and Area Studies, 1991.
    Explains the political and economic consequences of Ceauşescu's pronatalist policies for post-communist measures on family planning and of the role of women in economy and society.

198. Kostanick, Huey Louis. "Characteristics and Trends in Southeastern Europe: Romania, Yugoslavia, Bulgaria, Albania, Greece, and Turkey." In *Population and Migration Trends in Eastern Europe*, edited by Huey Louis Kostanick, 11-22. Boulder: Westview, 1977.
    Summarizes Romania's demographic structure between 1953 and 1973.

199. Legge, Jerome S., Jr. *Abortion Policy: An Evaluation of the Consequences for Maternal and Infant Health*. Albany: State University of New York Press, 1985.
    Chapter four "Romania: A Tightening of Liberal Policy" (pp.56-71), shows that the shift in abortion policy in 1966 had severe negative health consequences for women and infants.

200. McIntyre, Robert J. "Demographic Policy and Sexual Equality: Value Conflicts and Policy Appraisal in Hungary and Romania." In *Women, State, and Party in Eastern*

Europe, edited by Sharon L. Wolchik and Alfred G. Meyer, 270-285. Durham: Duke University Press, 1985.

Presents Hungary's positive incentives to increase natality in contrast to Romania's draconic pronatalist measures and probes into the motives, goals, and social values of decision-makers in the two societies.

201. McIntyre, Robert J. "Pronatalist Programmes in Eastern Europe." *Soviet Studies* 27, no. 3 (1975): 366-380.

Falling fertility levels in Romania have been reversed since 1966 by legislation restricting legal abortion. In contrast, other East-European countries have introduced positive incentives to parenthood, which appear to be partially successful.

202. Nydon, Judith A. "Public Policy and Private Fertility Behavior: The Case of Pronatalist Policy in Socialist Romania." Ph.D. diss., University of Massachusetts, 1984. Ann Arbor: UMI, 1984. AAD8500110.

Analysis of contradictions between strong pronatalist governmental policies and personal aspirations. Reasons for the failure of coercive and non-coercive measures are discussed.

203. Peyfuss, Max Demeter. "Ethnopolitische Fragen des Rumänentums [Romanian Ethnopolitical Issues]." *Österreichische Osthefte* 20, no. 1, 3 (1978): 141-146, 428-434.

A two part article comparing the presentation of data on minorities in the 1977 Romanian population census and the treatment of data on Romanian minority populations in the Soviet Union, Yugoslavia, and Bulgaria.

204. Satmarescu, G. D. "The Changing Demographic Structure of the Population of Transylvania." *East European Quarterly* 8, no. 4 (1975): 425-439.

Studies population growth and distribution, fertility and mortality rates, age and sex structures, as well as ethnic composition. Comments on differences between the "Regat" and Transylvania.

205. Suga, Alexander. "Die Volkszählung in Rumänien [Population Census in Romania]." *Osteuropa* 17, no. 2/3 (1967): 167-171.

Compares population data in 1930, 1956, and 1966, with special emphasis on natality/mortality data and on demographics of minority groups.

206. Tabah, Leon. "The Significance of the Bucharest Conference on Population." *International Social Science Journal* 27, no. 2 (1975): 375-384.

Assessment of the World Population Conference, Bucharest, August 1974, and its main themes: growth potential and the need for anticipating future demographic trends, the relationship between population and development, human rights and the role of the family, birth control and education concerning parenthood.

207. Teitelbaum, Michael S. "Fertility Effects of the Abolition of Legal Abortion in Romania." *Population Studies* 26, no. 3 (1972): 405-417.

By withdrawing the means of birth control from Romanian women, the government achieved in 1967 "the largest one year fertility increase ever experienced by a large human population," (p. 414) which resulted in an important economic, educational, psychological, and medical impact. However, 1969-1970 data suggest an accelerating downtrend in fertility as women find ways other than abortions for birth control. Thus, various medical, educational and other facilities, forced to expand to accommodate the baby-boom, will need to contract sharply only a few years after expansion.

208. Wright, Nicholas H. "Restricting Legal Abortion: Some Maternal and Child Health Effects in Romania." *American Journal of Obstetrics and Gynecology* 121, no. 2 (1975): 246-256.

Discusses the 1966 decree restricting legal abortion and the resulting fertility changes, maternal, fetal and infant mortality rates. Offers explanations on causes of death.

8. Economic & Business Conditions

209. Alton, Thad P. *Indexes of Rumanian Industrial Production, 1938, 1948, and 1950-1967.* Occasional Papers of the Research Project on National Income in East Central Europe, 10. New York: Riverside Research Institute, 1972.
    Presents independently calculated data, using methods compatible to Western measurements of economic capacity.

210. Backe-Dietrich, Berta. "Übersicht über die Wirtschaftliche Entwicklung Rumäniens seit 1960 [Overview of Romanian Economic Development since 1960]." *Osteuropa Wirtschaft* 15, no. 2 (1970): 127-135.
    Highlights successes in economic, social, and educational development and discusses the slowdown in industrial and agricultural output since 1969.

211. Banister, C. E. "Transport in Romania: A British Perspective." *Transport Reviews* 1, no. 3 (1981): 251-270.
    Describes organization and function of road, rail, water, and air passenger and goods transport and compares it to the British system.

212. Barbaza, Yvette. "Trois Types d'Intervention du Tourisme dans l'Organisation de l'Espace Littoral [Three Ways in Which the Tourist Industry Can Influence the Development of Coastal Regions]." *Annales de Géographie* 79, no. 434 (1970): 446-469.
    Describes the impact of the developing tourist industries on three areas: Costa-Brava, the Romanian-Bulgarian Black Sea Coast, and Longedoc-Rousillon.

213. Brada, Josef C., Marvin R. Jackson, and Arthur E. King. "The Optimal Rate of Industrialization in Developed and Developing Centrally-Planned Economies: A General Equilibrium Approach." *World Development* 9, no. 9-10 (1981): 991-1004.
    Examines the investment policies of Czechoslovakia and Romania in a series of simulations utilizing econometric models. Examines the effects of three policy options. Indicates that a change in investment strategy would have generated faster economic growth. Shows that Romania would have benefited from a shift of investments to services.

214. Brezinski, Horst, and Paul Petersen. "The Second Economy in Romania." In *The Second Economy in Marxist States*, edited by Maria Los, 69-84. London: Macmillan, 1990.
    As the socialist economy is failing to satisfy the needs of the population, legal and illegal second economy activities have become a necessity. Explains the causes of the existence and rise of the second economy and the dilemma it represents for socialist systems.

215. Catoiu, Iacob I. "Modelling the Demand for Consumer Durables in Romania." Ph.D. diss., Indiana University, Graduate School of Business, 1975. Ann Arbor: UMI, 1975. AAD76-04712.
Creates a demand model for radio sets, televisions, refrigerators, sewing and washing machines by using market data collected over a 20 year period (1955-1974).

216. Cismarescu, Michael. "Romania's Industrial Development." *East Europe* 19, no. 1 (1970): 2-8.
Reviews progress and shortcomings and concludes that further economic expansion at the expense of the standard of living will generate enormous difficulties.

217. Crane, Keith. *Romanian Economic Mess After Ceauşescu: What can We Expect?* Rand Paper Series, P-7296. Santa Monica, CA: Rand Corporation, 1986.
An overview of the economic situation of the mid 1980's is followed by economic policy scenarios for a post-Ceauşescu Romania.

218. Demekas, Dimitri G., and Mohsin S. Khan. *The Romanian Economic Reform Program.* IMF Occasional Paper, 89. Washington, D.C.: International Monetary Fund, 1991.
Discusses Romania's economy during the 1970's and 1980's and maps its transition to a market-based system after the revolution.

219. Dion, Michel. "L'Autogestion en Roumanie [Self-Management in Romania]." *International Journal of Rumanian Studies* 5, no. 1 (1987): 71-82.
Presents the legal and political framework and functions of industrial self-management.

220. *East European Economies: Slow Growth in the 1980's: Selected Papers Submitted to the Joint Economic Committee, Congress of the United States.* Washington: U.S. G.P.O., 1985. 3 vols. Committee Print. Y4.Ec7:Eu7/10/v.1-3.
Volume One, "Economic Performance and Policy," provides an overview of economic performance in Eastern Europe, analyzing economic adjustments to external factors; measurements of GNP and growth; industry and employment; consumption and population; energy; agriculture; defense; political factors and policy implications. Volume Two, "Foreign Trade and International Finance," compiles studies assessing the economies of Eastern Europe by analyzing trade patterns and perspectives; international finance and debt; and intra-CMEA relations. Volume Three, "Country Studies on Eastern Europe and Yugoslavia," analyzes individual countries. "Romania's Debt Crisis: Its Causes and Consequences," by M. R. Jackson (pages 489-542), reviews economic performance since 1975, and discusses the impact of the debt crisis.

221. Fink, Gerhard, and Gabriele Tuitz. *Rumänien: Wirtschafts- und Systempolitik [Romania: Economic and System Policy].* Berichte, 51. Köln: Bundesinstitut für Ostwissenschaftliche und Internationale Studien, 1984.
Based on legal and party documents as well as on published articles, analyzes the results and outlook of economic policies and reforms to the 1980's.

222. Fink, Gerhard, and Gabriele Tuitz. "Wirtschafts- und Reformpolitische Massnahmen in Rumäniens Industrie [Economic and Political Reform Decisions in Romania's Industry]." *Europäische Rundschau* 12, no. 3 (1984): 111-125.
While reforms in economic decision-making have been implemented since the 1970's, Romania's economy remains highly centralized and rigidly under Party control.

223. Ghermani, Dionisie. "Rumänien [Romania]." In *Internationales Gewerkschaftshandbuch*, edited by Siegfried Mielke, 931-935. Opladen: Leske und Budrich, 1983.
Historical overview of the organization, role, and activities of unions since World War II.

224. Gianaris, Nicholas V. *The Economies of the Balkan Countries: Albania, Bulgaria, Greece, Romania, Turkey, and Yugoslavia.* New York: Praeger, 1982.

Greece, Romania, Turkey, and Yugoslavia. New York: Praeger, 1982.
Historical overview of the establishment and development of Balkan states followed by a discussion of their modern economic organization, resources and productivity, development, foreign trade, and economic cooperation.

225. Goodman, Seymour E. "From Under the Rubble: Computing and the Resuscitation of Romania." *Communications of the ACM* 34, no. 9 (1991): 19-22.
Overview of the computing industry, computer related instruction, and research under Elena Ceauşescu, as well as present efforts to cope with crushing economic realities.

226. Granick, David. *Enterprise Guidance in Eastern Europe: A Comparison of Four Socialist Economies.* Princeton, NJ: Princeton University Press, 1975.
Based on his article "The Orthodox Model of the Socialist Enterprise in the Light of Romanian Experience," *Soviet Studies* 26, no. 2, (1974).
Compares characteristics of managerial systems in Romania, the German Democratic Republic, Hungary and Yugoslavia. Looks at the Romanian industrial setting, its organization, planning, allocation of manpower and materials, wages, and decision-making at the "centrale" and enterprise level, and compares it to the orthodox model of Soviet-type economies.

227. Granick, David. "The Orthodox Model of the Socialist Enterprise in the Light of Romanian Experience." *Soviet Studies* 26, no. 2 (1974): 205-223.
Argues that the Soviet orthodox model of production units' operation, which is based upon managers' achieving major plan targets at the expense of lesser objectives by attempting to maximize their bonuses, cannot be successfully applied to the Romanian industry. Bonuses for Romanian managers are too small and too subjectively distributed to constitute a motivator for managerial behavior. Due to the centralization of management in the ministries and above, very little economic decision-making is achieved at the "centrale" level.

228. Granick, David. "La Planification Centrale de l'Industrie en Roumanie [Central Planning of Industry in Romania]." *Revue de l'Est* 4, no. 2 (1973): 5-58.
Analyzes industrial management by studying prices, five-year plans and their annual target figures, manpower planning, wages, decision-making in production, investment, and trade.

229. Guha, Amalendu B. "Rumania as a Development Model." *Journal of Peace Research* 11, no. 4 (1974): 297-323.
Comparative study of representative developing countries in Asia and Latin America in 1968 with 1938 Romania, the peak year of capitalist economic progress, including a socioeconomic analysis of 1968 Romania. Analyzes the characteristics of a thirty year development span in Romania to ascertain whether socioeconomic measures introduced after World War II in Romania apply to other countries from 1968 to the present.

230. Gumpel, Werner. "Ursachen der Krise der Rumänischen Wirtschaft [Causes of the Romanian Economic Crisis]." *Südosteuropa Mitteilungen* 30, no. 1 (1990): 22-28.
Years of economic mismanagement have bankrupted the economy. Discusses the disastrous consequences of Ceauşescu's economic policies and megalomaniacal plans.

231. Halpin, Daniel W., Mihai Nemţeanu, and Ronald W. Woodhead. "Structure of Construction Industry in Romania." *Journal of the Construction Division-ASCE* 100, no. CO2 (1974): 141-152.
Describes the industry and discusses its organization, project development and cost determination, cash flow, labor costs and pay scales, production and management incentives, resource control, and labor force requirements.

232. Halpin, Daniel W., and Nicolai Tutos. "Construction Information-Systems in Romania." *Journal of the Construction Division-ASCE* 102, no. CO2 (1976): 335-355.
Describes the Romanian Management System, an information system for schedul-

233. Hoffman, George W. "The Problems of the Underdeveloped Regions in Southeast Europe: A Comparative Analysis of Romania, Yugoslavia, and Greece." *Annals of the Association of American Geographers* 57, no. 4 (1967): 637-648.
     Compares the three countries' approach to economic development, industrialization, and diversification. Analyzes Romania's limited success in locating industries in underdeveloped regions.

234. Hoffman, George W. *Regional Development Strategy in Southeast Europe: A Comparative Analysis of Albania, Bulgaria, Greece, Romania and Yugoslavia.* New York: Praeger, 1972.
     Describes important pre- and post-World War II transformations affecting the Balkan region and reviews key elements of development strategies, and regional development concepts, policies, and applications in individual countries.

235. Howell, Thomas. "Steel and the State in Romania." *Comparative Economic Studies* 29, no. 2 (1987): 71-100.
     Since the 1950's, Romania's centrally-planned economy has embarked on a massive steel industry expansion program. During the economic crisis of the 1970's, Romania "dumped" steel abroad at below production costs. This represents a desperate struggle to overcome economic difficulties rather than a sign of international competitiveness.

236. Hunt, Scott Edward. "A Time Series Production Function Analysis of Postwar Romanian Industry: Its Branches and Regions." Ph.D. diss., Ohio State University, 1992. Ann Arbor: UMI, 1992. AAD9307783.
     Analyzes causes of the rise (1951-1972) and fall (1972-1985) of growth rates in industrial production and shows which industrial branches were the prime contributors to the decline.

237. Jackson, Marvin R. "Industrialization, Trade, and Mobilization in Romania's Drive for Economic Independence." In *East European Economies Post-Helsinki: A Compendium of Papers*, 886-940. U.S. Congress. Joint Economic Committee. Washington, D. C.: U.S. G.P.O., 25 August 1977. Committee Print. Y4.Ec7:Eu7/8.
     Partial Contents: "The Remobilization Process: 1971-1980," "Sources and Uses of Resources for Industrialization," "Investment Supplies and the International Economy," "Investment Allocations and the Growth of Industry," "The Sources and Uses of Industrial and Agricultural Products," "Sources and Uses of Labor Resources."

238. Jackson, Marvin R. "Inflation und Depression: Der Preis des Rumänischen Nationalismus [Inflation and Depression: The Price of Romania's Nationalism]." *Europäische Rundschau* 14, no. 4 (1986): 45-58.
     Discusses the economic crisis and points out the unreliability of Romanian statistics. Warns that with no political change in sight, the country's future looks bleak.

239. Jackson, Marvin R. *National Accounts and the Estimation of Gross Domestic Product and Its Growth Rates for Romania.* World Bank Staff Working Paper, 774. Washington, D.C.: The World Bank, 1985.
     Discusses Net Material Product Accounts, estimates of Gross Domestic Product (GDP) in domestic currency, and addresses problems in the estimation of GDP growth rates.

240. Jackson, Marvin R. "Romania's Economy at the End of the 1970's: Turning the Corner on Intensive Developments." In *East European Economic Assessment. Part 1 - Country Studies, 1980*, 231-297. U.S. Congress. Joint Economic Committee. Washington, D.C.: U.S. G.P.O., 27 February 1981. Committee Print. Y4.Ec7:Eu7/9/pt.1.
     Examines Romania's rapid economic growth from 1970 to 1978, and its slowdown thereafter, by discussing annual and five year economic plans, labor resources, consumption, income, investment, capital resources, foreign trade, and industrial and agricultural performance.

241. Jackson, Marvin R. "Statistical and Political Economy in Romania: What Comes Next - Relief or More Exploitation?" In *Pressures for Reform in the East European Economies: Study Papers Submitted to the Joint Economic Committee, Congress of the United States*, v.2, pp. 307-327. Washington: U.S. G.P.O, 1989. Committee Print. Y4.Ec7:Eu7/13/v.2.
Discusses Romania's allocation policy which is centered on repayment of the foreign debt and on giving rewards to Ceauşescu's household and chosen elite. Proposes economic scenarios for the future.

242. Jackson, Marvin R., and James D. Woodson, Jr., eds. *New Horizons in East-West Economic and Business Relations*. East European Monographs, 156. New York: Columbia University Press, 1984.
Papers presented at the third Romanian American conference on trade and economic cooperation, Bucharest 1978. Partial contents: J. C. Brada, M. R. Jackson, A. E. King "The Romanian Balance of Payment Crisis: An Econometric Study of its Causes and Cures;" E. Neuberger, A. Ben-Ner "Romania's Reactions to International Commodity Inflation;" P. Marer "U.S. Market Disruption Procedures Involving Romanian and Other CPC Products, With Policy Recommendations;" G. P. Lauter "East-West Trade: Organizational Structures and Problems of United States Multinational Corporations;" S. G. Walters "Management Issues in U.S.-Romanian Trade and Cooperation;" R. C. Amacher "International Markets versus the New International Order: Challenges to Independence of Nation States;" H. S. Tapia "The Experience of Latin America in Marketing Exports to the U.S.: Some Lessons for Romania."

243. Jampel, Wilhem. "La Singularité de la Politique Économique Roumaine [The Peculiarity of the Romanian Economic Policy]." *Le Courrier des Pays de L'Est* 228 (April 1979): 29-41.
The country expressed its independence by distancing itself economically, politically, and ideologically from the communist bloc. However, its ambitious economic accomplishments are realized with sacrifices in the standard of living.

244. Joyner, Christopher C. "The Energy Situation in Eastern Europe: Problems and Prospects." *East European Quarterly* 10, no. 4 (1976): 496-516.
Reviews energy capability and requirements of Eastern European countries and assesses prospects for local economic growth and Soviet-CMEA cooperation.

245. Kaser, Michael. "An Estimate of the National Accounts of Rumania Following Both Eastern and Western Definitions." *Soviet Studies* 18, no. 1 (1966): 86-90.
Attempts to piece together existing partial economic information, since Romania fails to publish official estimates on national income or product in absolute figures.

246. Kaser, Michael. "Romania." In *The New Economic Systems of Eastern Europe*, edited by Hans-Hermann Höhmann, Michael Kaser, and Karl C. Thalheim, 171-197. Berkeley: University of California Press, 1975.
Presents a chronology of economic reforms since the mid-sixties and examines the legal and constitutional framework affecting plan indicators, foreign trade, prices, wages, banking, and the agricultural sector.

247. Kaser, Michael. "Rumania." In *The Prediction of Communist Economic Performance*, edited by P. J. D. Wiles, 271-286. London: Cambridge University Press, 1971.
An earlier version appeared as "L'Albanie et la Roumanie." *Analyse et Prévision* 4, no. 5 (1967): 759-776..
Speaks to the difficulties in assessing future macroeconomic activities due to the format in which statistics are published. Reviews economic performance between 1960-1966 and looks at projections to 1970.

248. Kaser, Michael, and Iancu Spigler. "Economic Reform in Romania in the 1970s." In *The East European Economies in the 1970's*, edited by Alec Nove, Hans-Hermann Höhmann, and Gertraud Seidenstecher, 253-279. London: Butterworths, 1982.
**Previously published as Papers in East European Economics, no.63. Oxford: St.

Anthony's College, 1980**.
Reviews published literature on Romania's economic system. Discusses the period between reforms (1972-1978) and the new economic mechanism and its implementation in 1978-1980.

249. Kaser, Michael, and Janusz G. Zielinski. *Planning in East Europe: Industrial Management by the State.* London: Bodley Head, 1970.
Analyzes Romania within the context of other Eastern European communist states. Topics include forms of public management, levels of authority, planning and planning objectives, prices, foreign trade, finance, and management objectives and styles.

250. Knight, Peter T. *Economic Reform in Socialist Countries: The Experiences of China, Hungary, Romania, and Yugoslavia.* World Bank Staff Working Papers, 579. Management and Development Series, 6. Washington, D.C.: The World Bank, 1983.
With limited opportunities for cooperation between enterprises, centrally set prices, and central planning, economic reforms are unlikely to bring radical changes. Nonetheless, reforms may lead to future increased decentralization.

251. Labrousse, René. "Roumanie: Problèmes Actuels [Romania: Current Problems]." *Cahiers du Communisme* 59, no. 3 (1983): 94-100.
Chronicles domestic and foreign policy measures taken due to the economic crisis of the 1980's.

252. Lavallée, Leon. *Croissance d'une Économie Socialiste: La Roumanie [Growth of a Socialist Economy: Romania].* [Roanne]: Horvath, [1979].
Describes the economic and social factors contributing to Romania's economic growth, and attributes all successes to the superiority of the socialist system.

253. Lhomel, Edith. "L'Année Économique Roumaine 1980: Une Économie 'Essoufflée' [Economic Year 1980 in Romania: An Economy Running out of Steam]." *Le Courrier des Pays de l'Est* 250 (April 1981): 62-68.
Reviews data on major economic sectors and notes that the economy has registered its lowest growth rates since the beginning of the five-year plan.

254. Lhomel, Edith. "L'Économie de la Roumanie en 1982: Un Redressement Fragile [Romanian Economy in 1982: A Fragile Recovery]." *Le Courrier des Pays de l'Est* 272 (April 1983): 50-55.
Surveys the industrial sectors, agriculture, and foreign trade. Concludes that significant industrial growth is imperative.

255. Lhomel, Edith. "L'Économie Roumaine en 1981: Un Bilan Douloureux [Romania's Economy in 1981: Painful Results]." *Le Courrier des Pays de l'Est* 264 (July 1982): 56-71.
The economic and financial situation continues to deteriorate. Both agriculture and industry appear paralyzed, the living standard is at an all time low. This is the price of the foreign debt repayment program.

256. Lhomel, Edith. "L'Économie Roumaine en 1984: des Résultats Équivoques [Romanian Economy in 1984: Mixed Results]." *Le Courrier des Pays de l'Est* 294 (April 1985): 61-66.
According to official data, the most recent economic figures exceed expectations of the five-year plan, but in 1985 Romania faces serious financial difficulties.

257. Lhomel, Edith. "L'Économie Roumaine en 1988: Toujours à Contre-Courant [Romanian Economy in 1988: Still an Uphill Battle]." *Le Courrier des Pays de l'Est* 341 (June 1989): 64-72.
In April 1989 Ceauşescu announced that the international debt had been fully repaid. On the domestic front, no change in policy is evident.

258. Lhomel, Edith. "La Politique Énergétique de la Roumanie pour les Années 80 [Romanian Energy Policy for the 1980's]." *Le Courrier des Pays de l'Est* 251 (May 1981): 57-64.

The energy crisis has forced Romania to explore alternative sources of energy. Reviews production and consumption figures of traditional and alternative energy sources.

259. Lhomel, Edith. "Les Problèmes de l'Environment en Roumanie [Problems of the Environment in Romania]." *Le Courrier des Pays de l'Est* 281 (February 1984): 39-46.
    Environmental damage caused by industrial pollution is irreversible. Discusses general air, water, and ground pollution and damage to the Danube Delta.

260. Lhomel, Edith. "Les Résultats du Plan 1983 en Roumanie [1983 Plan Results in Romania]." *Le Courrier du Pays de l'Est* 286 (July-August 1984): 67-73.
    Reviews such data as the balance of payments, agricultural production figures, industrial output and the energy situation, as well as the return to a more intensive trade activity within COMECON.

261. Lhomel, Edith. "Roumanie [Romania]." *Le Courrier des Pays de l'Est* 309-311 (August-October 1986): 109-130.
    Industrial development is at a virtual standstill. The country has become economically dependent on the East and the West. A severe austerity program is in place.

262. Lhomel, Edith. "Roumanie: L'Année Économique [Romania: The Economic Year in Review]." *Notes et Études Documentaires* 4673-4674 (22 June 1982): 212-230.
    Romania is in the grip of an economic and financial crisis. Discusses the main economic indicators, the agricultural and industrial sectors, and the deterioration of the living standard.

263. Lhomel, Edith. "Roumanie, l'Année Économique: Un Pays à la Dérive [Romania, Annual Economic Review: A Country Off Course]." *Notes & Études Documentaires* 4867-4868 (1988): 200-210.
    Ceaușescu is determined to repay the international debt at the expense of the standard of living. Official statistics become unreliable.

264. Lhomel, Edith. "Roumanie: La Pénurie s'Installe... [Romania: Deprivation Becomes Norm]." *Le Courrier des Pays de l'Est* 258 (January 1982): 39-45.
    Food rationing and sanctions for food hoarding are only the latest punishments imposed on the population. Ceaușescu appears obsessed with repaying the international debt and sustaining the pace of industrial development.

265. Lhomel, Edith. "Roumanie: Une Économie Verrouillée [Romania: A Closed Economy]." *Problèmes Economiques* 1975 (22 May 1986): 16-21.
    Reprinted from *Le Courrier des Pays de l'Est*, no. 301 (December 1985).
    Romania's decision to repay its international debt by 1990 is a pretext to continue domestic austerity and militarize the energy sector.

266. Lhomel, Edith. "Stratégie de Repli ou Suicide Économique? [Retrenchment or Economic Suicide?]." *Esprit* 147 (February 1989): 19-23.
    The decision to repay the international debt by 1990 has bankrupt the economy and has led to a rapprochement to COMECON.

267. Lhomel, Edith. "Le Tourisme en Roumanie [Tourism in Romania]." *Le Courrier des Pays de l'Est* 268 (December 1982): 48-57.
    Recent economic difficulties have tarnished Romania's image as a tourists' heaven.

268. Lhomel, Edith, and Madeleine Balussou. "L'Économie Roumaine a l'Heure de la Rigueur [Romanian Economy in Times of Adversity]." *Le Courrier des Pays de l'Est* 275 (July-August 1983): 3-35.
    Surveys the impact of the 1978 economic reforms in a country gripped by economic crisis.

269. Lhomel, Edith, and Anita Tiraspolsky. "En Roumanie, un Plan pour une Croissance Douce [In Romania, a Plan for Slow Growth]." *Le Courrier des Pays de l'Est*, no. 253 (July-August 1981): 59-67.
The five-year plan 1981-1985 reflects a distinctive slow-down in economic growth targets.

270. Linden, Ronald H. "Romania: The Search for Economic Sovereignty." In *Pressures for Reform in the East European Economies: Study Papers Submitted to the Joint Economic Committee, Congress of the United States*, v.2, pp. 291-306. Washington: U.S. G.P.O, 1989. Committee Print. Y4.Ec7:Eu7/13/v.2.
Charts Romania's poor economic performance, Ceauşescu's dominance of the political system, his policy of rotation of cadres, and concludes that there is little hope for reform.

271. Linden, Ronald H. "Socialist Patrimonialism and the Global Economy: The Case of Romania." In *Power, Purpose, and Collective Choice: Economic Strategy in Socialist States*, edited by Ellen Comisso and Laura D'Andrea Tyson, 171-204. Ithaca: Cornell University Press, 1986.
Also published in *International Organizations* 40, no.2 (1986): 347-380.
Examines Romania under Ceauşescu in light of Max Weber's definition of patrimonial state. Explores the country's response to recent economic disruptions and discusses whether the regime itself is affected by economic shocks.

272. Marczewski, Jean. *Crisis in Socialist Planning: Eastern Europe and the USSR*. New York: Praeger, 1974.
The discussion on Romania (see pp. 72-75) centers on the "reforms" in industrial management introduced in 1967.

273. Marer, Paul. *Dollar GNP's of the U.S.S.R. and Eastern Europe*. Baltimore: Johns Hopkins University Press, 1985.
Presents price systems and policies in centrally planned economies and specific information on Romania's price reforms, types of prices, structure, changes in price levels, and the relationship between foreign and domestic prices.

274. Mihalyi, Peter. "Common Patterns and Particularities in East European Investment Cycles." *Soviet Studies* 40, no. 3 (1988): 444-459.
Cross-country analysis of annual growth rate at constant prices for six East European countries, including Romania.

275. Montias, John Michael. "Romanian Economy: A Survey of Current Problems." In *The Path of Reform in Central and Eastern Europe*, by the Commission of the European Communities, Directorate-General for Economic and Financial Affairs, 177-198. European Economy - Special Edition, 2. Lanham, MD: Office for Official Publications of the European Communities, 1991.
Analyzes the economic situation during the last years of the Ceauşescu dictatorship and discusses the post-revolutionary transition to market economy and price liberalization.

276. Montias, John M. "Socialist Industrialization and Trade in Machinery Products: An Analysis Based on the Experience of Bulgaria, Poland, and Rumania." In *International Trade and Central Planning: An Analysis of Economic Interactions*, edited by Alan A. Brown and Egon Neuberger, 130-165. Berkeley: University of California Press, 1968.
Examines the role of equipment imports in a growing domestic industry that emphasizes machine building.

277. Naor, Jacob, and S. Tamer Cavusgil. "Recent Changes in Enterprise Management and Marketing Practices in Romania." *European Journal of Marketing* 20, no. 10 (1986): 43-54.
Discusses the economic reform of 1978, known as "the new economic mechanism,"

and its implications for marketing. The reform focuses on enterprise management and allows greater autonomy for individual enterprises in operational and financial decision making.

278. Narayanswamy, Ramnath. "Romania - Socialist Corporatism and Command Economy." *Economic and Political Weekly* 22, no. 15 (1987): 633-634.
Discusses innovations in economic reforms. Reforms were introduced because of an unfavorable economic situation and had nothing to do with a conscious desire for decentralization. Concludes that while economically they have resulted in more than cosmetic changes, their limited nature is characteristic for most reforms carried out in Eastern Europe.

279. Orescu, Şerban. *Zentrale und Dezentrale Elemente im Leitungssystem der Rumänischen Industrie [Features of Centralization and Dispersion of Control in Romanian Industry].* Berichte, 20. Köln: Bundesinstitut für Ostwissenschaftliche und Internationale Studien, 1979.
Studies the cyclical nature of centralization and decentralization in Romania's economy.

280. Pissulla, Petra. "Drückende Sorgen der Rumänischen Wirtschaft durch Planungsfehler in der Vergangenheit [Past Planning Mistakes are Plaguing the Romanian Economy]." *Osteuropa-Info* 53, no. 3 (1983): 41-49.
Faced with increasing domestic and foreign pressure, Romania is looking for ways to stabilize its failing economy.

281. Pissulla, Petra. "Rumänien [Romania]." In *Die Wirtschaft Osteuropas und der VR China 1980-1990*, edited by Hans-Hermann Höhmann and Gertraud Seidenstecher, 366-423. Hamburg: Weltarchiv, 1988.
Describes economic developments from the late 1970's to 1985 and the impact of economic and political changes on the 1981-1985 five year plan. Analyzes the outlook for the new plan in light of Ceauşescu's reluctance to introduce change.

282. Pissulla, Petra. "Wirtschaftslage, Aussenhandelbeziehungen und Zahlungsbilanzprobleme Rumäniens [Romania's Economy, Foreign Trade, and Problems of Balance of Payments]." In *Südosteuropa in Weltpolitik und Weltwirtschaft der Achtziger Jahre*, edited by Roland Schönfeld, 251-258. Untersuchungen zur Gegenwart Südosteuropas, 21. München: Oldenbourg, 1983.
The country faces serious problems especially in agriculture, energy, and foreign economic relations.

283. Poncet, Jean. *Le Sous-Développement Vaincu? La Lutte pour le Développement en Italie Méridionale, en Tunisie et en Roumanie [Conquered Underdevelopment? The Struggle for Development in Italy, Tunisia, and Romania].* Paris: Editions Sociales, 1970.
Reviews (pp. 187-272) the country's history and the achievements of its planned economy and concludes that underdevelopment will be fully eliminated when the entire world converts to socialist production.

284. Rahmer, B. A. "Romania: Oil at the Crossroads." *Petroleum Economist* 46, no. 9 (1979): 360-362.
Crude oil production is declining, making independence from the Soviet Union more difficult. Prospects for developing alternative energy sources are unclear.

285. Rek, Bron. "Romania's Rejuvenated Aircraft Industry: An On-the-Spot Report." *Interavia* 38, no. 8 (1983): 859-862.
Reviews the spectacular progress achieved by the Romanian aircraft industry in the 1970's and early 1980's. Describes production facilities and programs.

286. Rey, Violette. *La Roumanie: Essai d'Analyse Régionale [Romania: Contribution to a Regional Analysis].* Paris: Société d'Édition d'Enseignement Superieur, 1975.

Assessment of national and regional socioeconomic changes since the end of World War II.

287. Rohleder, Claus-Dieter. "Romania: The Laggard." In *Reforms in the Soviet and Eastern European Economies*, edited by L. A. D. Dellin and Hermann Gross, 115-122. Lexington, MA: Lexington Books, 1972.
While Ceauşescu is reluctant to introduce elements of market mechanism, his conservative economic reforms nonetheless call for "debureaucratization" and urge against excessive centralism.

288. Rohleder, Claus-Dieter. "Die Rumänische Wirtschaftsentwicklung: Beginn einer neuen Phase [Romania's Economic Development: Beginning of a New Phase]." In *Wirtschaftsreformen in Osteuropa*, edited by Karl Christian Thalheim and Hans-Hermann Höhmann, 230-258. Köln: Wissenschaft und Politik, 1968.
In 1967, Romania joined other East European coutries in introducing economic reforms. These, however, follow the Soviet model of rationalization rather than the Hungarian example of decentralization.

289. *Romania: Human Resources and the Transition to a Market Economy*. Washington: World Bank, 1992.
Offers a historical review of policies and programs concerning labor markets, social security and social assistance, education, training and scientific research, health, population and family planning. Provides recommendations for government action.

290. Ronnås, Per. "The Economic Legacy of Ceauşescu." In *Economic Change in the Balkan States: Albania, Bulgaria, Romania and Yugoslavia*, edited by Örjan Sjöberg and Michael L. Wyzan, 47-68. London: Pinter, 1991.
Examines economic and development policies from the "successful" 1960's and early 1970's, to the stagnation and economic crisis of the 1980's. The legacy of Ceauşescu is described as an "unmitigated disaster on all fronts"(p. 61).

291. Ronnås, Per. "The Role of the 'Second Economy' as a Source of Supplementary Income to Rural Communities in Romania: A Case Study." *Bidrag Till Oststatsforskningen: Contributions to Soviet and East European Research* 11, no. 1 (1983): 34-43.
To compensate for poor agricultural conditions, the villagers of Certezi used their entrepreneurial spirit to close profitable subcontracting deals with the government, trade within and across borders in distilled plum brandy and livestock, and thus turn their village into a prosperous community.

292. Samli, A. Coskun. "A Comparative Analysis of Marketing in Romania and Yugoslavia." *The Southern Journal of Business* 5, no. 3 (1970): 105-113.
Discusses product, prices, promotion, and business logistics in the two countries.

293. Samli, A. Coskun. "Comparative Marketing Systems in Eastern Europe: An Illustration of Marketing Evolution." In *Comparative Marketing Systems*, edited by Erdener Kaynak and Ronald Savitt, 217-232. New York: Praeger, 1984.
Explores the role of marketing in Eastern Europe (with references to Romania), and studies its characteristics, evolution, research, and application.

294. Schönfeld, Roland. "Rumäniens Wirtschaftslage und Beziehungen zum RGW [Romanian Economic Conditions and Relations to COMECON]." In *Südosteuropa in der Ära Gorbatschow: Auswirkungen der Sowjetischen Reformpolitik auf die Südosteuropäischen Länder*, edited by Walter Althammer, 83-101. Südosteuropa Aktuell, 2. München: Südosteuropa-Gesellschaft, 1987.
Criticizes prevailing economic conditions. Considers Romania's resistance to COMECON integration as a political maneuver rather than as an economic decision. Romania's autonomous policy appears to have failed.

295. Schönfeld, Roland. "Sozialistische Industrialisierungspolitik in Rumänien [The Socialist Industrial Policy in Romania]." *Südosteuropa-Mitteilungen* 17, no. 2 (1977): 32-47.

Depicts industrial development since the communist takeover. Contends that the struggle for economic and political independence, which has imposed enormous sacrifices on the population, has ushered in the era of industrialization.

296. Selucky, Radoslav. *Economic Reforms in Eastern Europe: Political Background and Economic Significance*, New York: Praeger, 1972.
Notes the absence of economic reforms to date and affirms that changes will not occur as long as Romania maintains its quest for independence in foreign policy (pp.151-155).

297. Smith, Alan H. "Is there a Romanian Economic Crisis? The Problems of Energy and Indebtedness." In *Crisis in the East European Economy: The Spread of the Polish Disease*, edited by Jan F. Drewnowski, 103-130. New York: St. Martin's Press, 1982.
Charts the historical background of the economic crisis and suggests possible outcomes.

298. Smith, Alan H. *The Planned Economies of Eastern Europe*. London: Croom Helm, 1983.
Cross-time and cross-country comparison of economic conditions in Eastern European states.

299. Smith, Alan H. "Romanian Economic Reforms." In *Economic Reforms in Eastern Europe and Prospects for the 1980's*, edited by the North Atlantic Treaty Organization, Economic Directorate, Information Directorate, 35-57. New York: Pergamon Press, 1980.
Colloquium 16-18 April 1980, Brussels.
Discussion of economic measures announced in March 1978 and implemented in 1979 that attempt to reduce production costs and stimulate enterprise responsiveness to world market pressures.

300. Smith, Alan H. "The Romanian Economy: Policy and Prospects for the 1990's." In *The Central and East European Economies in the 1990's: Prospects and Constraints*, edited by Reiner Weichhardt, 117-128. Brussels: NATO, 1990.
Colloquium, 4-6 April 1990, Brussels.
Romania's prospects for socio-political stability and economic recovery are overshadowed by Ceauşescu's legacy.

301. Smith, Alan H. "The Romanian Enterprise." In *Industrial Reform in Socialist Countries: From Restructuring to Revolution*, edited by Ian Jeffries, 201-218, 282-283. Albershot: Elgar, 1992.
Discusses differences between Romania and other countries of Eastern Europe, industrial policy and administration under communism, generally, and under Ceauşescu, in particular, and the industrial reform since the revolution.

302. Smith, Alan H. "The Romanian Industrial Enterprise." In *The Industrial Enterprise in Eastern Europe*, edited by Ian Jeffries, 63-83. New York: Praeger, 1981.
Papers presented at a symposium sponsored by the University of Wales, 6-9 September, 1980.
Discusses the 1967 Directives on the Perfecting of Management and Planning and the 1978 New Economic Mechanism, including their impact on future industrial development.

303. Spigler, Iancu. *Economic Reform in Rumanian Industry*. London: Oxford University Press, 1973.
Focuses on 1967 to 1972, and analyzes the origins of economic reform, and changes in macro- and microeconomic planning, management, and banking and finance.

304. Staubus, Sarah, and George J. Staubus. "The Use of Accounting Information in the Management of Socialist Enterprises in Poland and Romania." ICRA Occasional

Paper, 16. Bailrigg, Lancaster: University of Lancaster, International Center for Research in Accounting (ICRA), 1977.
Looks at the organization and programs of the Romanian Academy of Economic Studies. Discusses main economic aspects and accounting practices.

305. Tiraspolsky, Anita. "L'Évolution Économique de la Roumanie en 1978 [Romanian Economic Development in 1978]." *Le Courrier des Pays de l'Est* 230 (June 1979): 49-51.
While Romanian economic growth rates remain high compared with other COMECON countries, in 1978 several plan objectives were not met.

306. Tiraspolsky, Anita. "Les Résultats Économiques de la Roumanie en 1979 [Romanian Economic Achievements in 1979]." *Le Courrier des Pays de l'Est* 239 (April 1980): 46-53.
Economic growth failed to meet planned expectations. This is partly due to inertia in the workforce.

307. Tsantis, Andreas C., and Roy Pepper. *Romania: The Industrialization of an Agrarian Economy under Socialist Planning.* Washington, D.C.: World Bank., 1979.
Report of a mission sent to Romania by the World Bank. This is the first World Bank descriptive and analytic study of individual economic sectors in Romania (1950-1977), with forecast to 1990.

308. Tuitz, Gabriele. "Romania." *Eastern European Economics* 19, no. 4 (1981): 41-46.
Report on Romania's economic stagnation in the late 1970's.

309. Turnock, David. *An Economic Geography of Romania.* London: Bell & Sons, 1974.
Studies the history, physical resources, industrial, agricultural and infrastructural development, international trade and relations.

310. Turnock, David. "Forest Exploitation and its Impact on Transport and Settlement in the Romanian Carpathians." *Journal of Transport History* 12, no. 1 (1991): 37-60.
Historical account of the timber industry and its impact on transportation, tourism, water management, employment, and services.

311. Turnock, David. "Industrial Railways in Eastern Europe: The Case of Forest Railways in Romania." In *Essays for Professor R.E.H. Mellor*, edited by William Ritchie, Jeffrey C. Stone, and Alexander S. Mather, 79-87. Aberdeen: University of Abderdeen, Department of Geography, 1986.
The rise in oil prices has led to a revival of forest railway transportation in Romania. Describes several systems operating in the 1980's.

312. Turnock, David. "The Pattern of Industrialization in Romania." *Annals of the Association of American Geographers* 60, no. 3 (1970): 540-559.
Describes pre-World War II industrial development, and changes in infrastructure, industrialization policy, and regional distribution in socialist Romania. Rapid industrial growth has been realized through strong central planning and at the expense of internal consumption.

313. Turnock, David. "Romania." In *Tourism and Economic Development in Eastern Europe and the Soviet Union*, edited by Derek R. Hall, 203-219. London: Belhaven, 1991.
Analyzes existing resources and domestic and international tourism from 1965 to the present and concludes that the communist legacy and the post-revolutionary turmoil makes the immediate future of tourism very uncertain.

314. Turnock, David. *The Romanian Economy in the Twentieth Century.* London: Croom Helm, 1986.
Overview of economic development from a historical perspective to the post-World War II socialist economic program, describing collectivization of agriculture, nationalization of industry, transportation, foreign trade, and settlements patterns.

315. Turnock, David. "Rumania and the Geography of Tourism." *Geoforum* 8, no. 1 (1977): 51-56.
Examines the development of tourism as a centrally planned economic activity.

316. Turnock, David. "Tourism in Romania: Rural Planning in the Carpathians." *Annals of Tourism Research* 17, no. 1 (1990): 79-102.
Examines opportunities for tourism with special emphasis on the Iron Gates and the Semenic, Retezat, and Lotru mountains.

317. Turnock, David. "Transport for Romania's Carpathian Forests: Improved Accessibility Through Technological Change." *GeoJournal* 22, no. 4 (1990): 409-428.
Investigates traditional transport of timber via rivers and forest railroads. In the post-nationalization period, increasing value of raw materials has led to a comprehensive program of road building, development of factories, and selective retention of existing railways and funiculars. Improved access to remote areas has strengthened tourism.

318. Tyson, Laura D'Andrea. "Economic Adjustment in Romania." In *Economic Adjustment in Eastern Europe*, 73-101. Rand Publication, R-3146-AF. Santa Monica, CA: Rand, September 1984.
Examines how Romania has adjusted to the economic shocks of the mid and late 1970's.

319. Vogel, Heinrich. "Rumänien [Romania]." In *Die Wirtschaft Ungarns, Bulgariens und Rumäniens*, by Werner Gumpel and Heinrich Vogel, 113-160. Gegenwartsfragen der Ostwirtschaft, 5. München: Olzog, 1968.
Addresses aspects of economic development, structure, growth, and productivity. Looks at the standard of living, reforms, and commerce and speculates on the outlook for expansion in foreign trade.

320. Welzk, Stefan. "Bedingungen Autozentrierter Entwicklung: Paradigma Rumänien [Conditions of Centralized Development: The Romanian Paradigm]." In *Auf dem Weg zu einer Neuen Weltwirtschaftsordnung? Bedingungen und Grenzen für eine Eigenständige Entwicklung*, edited by Hans-Dieter Evers, Dieter Senghaas, and Hüberta Wienholtz, 117-137. Baden-Baden: Nomos, 1983.
While central planning is a strategy to modernize agricultural societies, it should not be confused with a post-capitalist system. Such a misrepresentation is at the root of the Romanian economic crisis.

321. Welzk, Stefan. *Entwicklungskonzept Zentrale Planwirtschaft - Paradigma Rumänien [Central Planning as Development Concept - The Romanian Paradigm].* Sozialwissenschaftliche Studien zu Internationalen Problemen, 77. Saarbrücken: Breitenbach, 1982.
Detailed analysis of Romania's economic history since World War II.

322. Wessely, Kurt. "Le Budget d'État de la Roumanie [Romanian State Budget]." *Revue d'Études Comparatives Est-Ouest* 9, no. 1 (1978): 135-163.
The scarcity of official data makes research and analysis of the state budget close to impossible. Attempts to describe the function and organization of the financial system.

323. Wessely, Kurt. "Rumänien [Romania]." In *Die Wirtschaft Osteuropas zu Beginn der 70er Jahre*, edited by Hans-Hermann Höhmann, 205-239. Stuttgart: Kohlhammer, 1972.
Presents an overview of the economy, results of the 1966-1970 plan, and goals of the new five year plan, 1971-1975.

324. Wild, Gerard. "Le Développement Économique de la Roumanie [Romanian Economic Development]." *Notes et Études Documentaires* 3943-3944 (20 November 1972): 1-62.

Studies Romania's economic development stages from 1944 to 1970. Highlights industrial growth, successes and failures in agriculture, and overtures in foreign trade. Speculates on the country's future.

325. *Die Wirtschaftliche Entwicklung in den sozialistischen Ländern Osteuropas.* Hamburg: Weltarchiv, 1978/79-.
Continues *Die Wirtschaftliche Entwicklung in Osteuropa.* Each annual volume features a chapter on the economic situation in Romania.

326. *Die Wirtschaftliche Entwicklung in Osteuropa.* Hamburg: HWWA-Institut für Wirtschaftsforschung, 1974-1977/78.
Continued by *Die Wirtschaftliche Entwicklung in den sozialistischen Ländern Osteuropas.* Each annual volume features a chapter on the economic situation in Romania.

9. Education, Research & Libraries

327. Ardoino, Jacques. *Éducation et Relations: Introduction à une Analyse Plurielle des Situations Éducatives [Education and Relations: Introduction to a Plural Analysis of Educational Situations]*. Paris: Gauthier-Villars: UNESCO, 1980.
The sub-chapter, "Roumanie" (pp. 112-125), describes research on teacher-pupil relations conducted at the Romanian Institute of Pedagogical Research.

328. Braham, Randolph L. *Education in Romania: A Decade of Change*. Washington, D.C.: U.S. Department of Health, Education, and Welfare, 1972. HE5.214:14161.
In 1968 Romania implemented a series of reforms, designed to support its rapid industrialization efforts. Discusses goals, administration, organization, and financing of education from preprimary to higher education, as well as the system of teacher education. Despite reforms, the Romanian educational system maintains its rigid framework, with no room for experimentation.

329. Cheng, David K. "An Overview of Electronics Education in Poland and Rumania." *IEEE Transactions on Education* E-22, no. 1 (1979): 14-17.
Reports on engineering and electronics education. Describes types of degrees conferred, faculty hierarchy, and existing schools and comments on library and laboratory facilities.

330. Croghan, Martin J. "Ideological Training in the Romanian School System." Ph.D. diss., Northwestern University, 1978. Ann Arbor: UMI, 1978. AAD79-03242.
Studies contents and methods of communist youth education, from kindergarten to university training, including the ideological preparation of faculty.

331. Croghan, Martin J., and Penelope P. Croghan. *Ideological Training in Communist Education: A Case Study of Romania*. Washington, D.C.: University Press of America, 1980.
Presents results of research conducted between 1971-1976 on ideological training and behavior of students, from kindergarten through high school and university years, as well as the ideological training of teachers.

332. Deligiannis, Emmanuel Alexander Dima. "Education in the Socialist Republic of Romania." Ph.D. diss., University of Southern California, 1971. Ann Arbor: UMI, 1971. AAD:71-27917.
Describes the educational system since its reform in 1968 and the type of individuals it seeks to create.

333. Deubler, Hans. "Wege zur Verwirklichung der Zehnjährigen Bildung in Rumänien [Towards the Realization of the Ten Grade Education in Romania]." *Vergleichende Pädagogik* 9, no. 1 (1973): 87-89.

Examines the guidelines issued by the 1972 conference concerning the introduction of ten years of compulsory education.

334. Dima, Nicholas. "University Education in Eastern Europe: The Case of Geography in Romania." *Journal of Geography* 77, no. 4 (1978): 149-151.
Compares the geography program at the University of Bucharest with education in the U.S. Romanian higher education is centrally planned, rigid and mechanical. Geography students learn facts and do not have an opportunity to develop or learn principles. The major goal is to train youth to become loyal party adherents.

335. Grant, Nigel. "The Changing School in Rumania." *Comparative Education* 2, no. 3 (1966): 167-179.
At the 9th Party Congress (1965), Ceauşescu called for a revision of education. Offers an overview of the pre-1948 school system, post-war developments, the existing system, and ongoing changes.

336. Grant, Nigel. *Society, Schools and Progress in Eastern Europe*. Oxford: Pergamon, 1969.
Chapter five, "Romania" (pp.282-299), describes basic features of the education system.

337. Gulutsan, Metro. "National Identity, Politics and Education in Romania." *Canadian and International Education* 1, no. 1 (1972): 59-77.
Reform in education reflects Romania's national communism. Describes the party-school relationship, the reform of 1968, and the role of teachers in the "pioneer movement."

338. Harrison, K. C. "The Library Situation in Romania." *Library Association Record* 74, no. 10 (1972): 183-186.
Types of libraries and services, the organization of librarianship, and the many problems that remain to be solved.

339. Hawkins, David R. "Psychiatric Education in Eastern Europe." *American Journal of Psychiatry* 138, no. 12 (1981): 1576-1581.
Comparative study of psychiatric education in the USSR, Romania, East Germany, Hungary and Poland. Concludes that training lags behind Western Europe and the U.S., apparently as a function of Soviet ideology, lack of economic resources, and isolation from the rest of the world.

340. Jackson, Marvin R. "Report on Economic Education and Research in Rumania." *ACES Bulletin* 14, no. 1 (1972): 1-17.
Detailed description of the system of higher education in economics and of the institutions involved in economics research.

341. Lebel, Germaine. "Trois Bibliothèques Bucarestoises: Trois Types de Réalisations [Three Bucharest Libraries: Three Types of Achievement]." *Bulletin des Bibliothèques de France* 16, no. 4 (1971): 187-205.
History, organization, and services of the Academy Library, the Central State Library, and the Central University Library.

342. Mayer, Peter. "A Study of the Role of Contemporary Universities in Relation to the Objectives of the Romanian Socialist Republic." Ph.D. diss., New York University, 1972. Ann Arbor: UMI, 1972. AAD73-08184.
Discusses administrative structure of higher education, role of faculty, design of curriculum, and characteristics of student body within the framework of Romania's social, economic and political development, 1948 to 1968.

343. Meder, Zoltan. "The Development of Rumanian Education in a Political Context." Ph.D. diss., University of California, Berkeley, March 1968. Ann Arbor: UMI, 1968. Order No.: 68-13,936.

Studies the interaction between education and political development (1919-1967) and concludes that educational institutions closely reflect the stages of development of Romanian society.

344. Mitchell, Gertrude E. "Glimpses of Education in Poland and Romania." *American Education* 13, no. 3 (1977): 16-24.
Observes how the two countries address issues of socialization and learning from kindergarten to higher education.

345. Neag, Marie. "The Historical Development of the Romanian Educational System with a Comparison of the Organizational Structure and Curricula During the Pre-Socialist (1800-1948) and Post-Socialist (1948-1974) Eras." Ph.D. diss., University of Akron, 1974. Ann Arbor: UMI, 1974. AAD75-10094.
Analyzes the influence of historical events and political, economic, and social forces on the educational system of pre- and post-socialist Romania.

346. Neuman-Steinhart, Gertrude. "La Réforme de l'Enseignement en Roumanie [Educational Reform in Romania]." *Revue du Centre d'Études des Pays de l'Est et du Centre National Pour l'Étude des États de l'Est* 11, no. 1 (1970): 73-101.
An analysis of the reform of 1968 follows a historical overview of the educational system in Romania.

347. Oldson, William O. "The Research Libraries of Romania." *International Library Review* 11, no. 3 (1979): 373-385.
Describes the difficulties encountered by exchange scholars in the social sciences while attempting to use Romania's archives and research libraries. Discusses collections in Bucharest, Cluj, and Iaşi, considered to be some of the most interesting and richly endowed in the world.

348. Oschlies, Wolf. "Deutsch in Rumänien [German in Romania]." *Deutschland Archiv* 7, no. 7 (1974): 729-733.
Since 1968, Ceauşescu emphasized the importance of foreign language skills for scientific-technical information exchange. Describes the place of German language study in education.

349. Oschlies, Wolf. "Gegenwartsprobleme der Jugend- und Bildungspolitik Rumäniens [Current Problems of Youth and Education Policy in Romania]." *Pädagogische Rundschau* 28, no. 4 (1974): 289-320.
Historical review of Romania's educational system, discussing the 1948 reform and the 1968 and 1973 Communist Party directives.

350. Rady, Martyn. "Transylvanian Libraries and Archives in Contemporary Romania." *Journal of the Society of Archivists* 12, no. 2 (1991): 123-126.
Discusses the neglect of rare manuscipts and incunabula during the Ceauşescu years and current efforts to save and inventory collections.

351. Rahmani, Levy. *Psychology in Romania: History and Recent Trends.* Berichte, 15. Köln: Bundesinstitut für Ostwissenschaftliche und Internationale Studien, 1986.
Under the leadership of a small, but active group, theoretical as well as methodological psychology has registered a remarkable development.

352. Ratner, Mitchell S. "Choose and be Chosen: The Transition from Primary to Secondary Education in Contemporary Romania." In *Economy, Society, and Culture in Contemporary Romania*, edited by John W. Cole, 139-155. Research Report, 24. Amherst: University of Massachusetts, Department of Anthropology, 1984.
Studies occupational distribution in the context of equal educational opportunities and concludes that career paths are firmly set at age 14. In the existing system young people in working class schools are at a disadvantage.

353. Ratner, Mitchell Stewart. "Educational and Occupational Selection in Contemporary Romania: A Social Anthropological Account." Ph.D. diss., American University,

1980. Ann Arbor: UMI, 1980. AAD8029026.

Study of the three educational transition points (high school entry, high school continuation examination, higher education entry examination) that determine an adolescent's occupational future, based on Frederik Barth's social interaction approach.

354. Sadlak, Jan. *Higher Education in Romania, 1860-1990: Between Academic Mission, Economic Demands and Political Control.* Special Studies in Comparative Education, 27. Buffalo, New York: State University of New York at Buffalo, 1990.

Traces the history of the academic system to the Ceaușescu era, characterized by intellectual isolationism and the replacement of academic autonomy with ideological and administrative control.

355. Sadlak, Jan. "Legacy and Change: Higher Education and Restoration of Academic Work in Romania." *Technology in Society* 15, no. 1 (1993): 75-100.

Describes the Ceaușescu legacy and post-communist organization of higher education and conditions of academic work.

356. Sadlak, Jan. "Planning of Higher Education in Countries with a Centrally Planned Socioeconomic System: Case Study of Poland and Romania." Ph.D. diss., State University of New York at Buffalo, 1988. Ann Arbor: UMI, 1988. AAD8905472.

Compares the two countries' higher education planning process at the stages of initiation, development, and implementation, as well as their political, legislative, and institutional provisions.

357. Sadlak, Jan. "The Use and Abuse of the University: Higher Education in Romania, 1860-1990." *Minerva (London)* 29, no. 2 (1991): 195-225.

Describes the emergence and development of higher education in Romania, its organization and internal structure. Discusses Nicolae and Elena Ceaușescu's role in the deterioration of university life and prospects for its future.

358. Smith, Mihaela Y. "Romania: Forecasting and Development." *Futures* 12, no. 5 (1980): 430-433.

The Laboratory of Prospective Research at the University of Bucharest, created in 1970, was the first group in Romania with a multidisciplinary structure and a charge for scientific exploration for the future. Because it may have been perceived as a potential focus for intellectual opposition, the Laboratory was closed down in 1978. Nonetheless, years after its demise, publications continued to be attributed to the defunct organization.

359. Thiel, N. "Die Tierärztliche Ausbildung und Tätigkeit in den Ost- und Südosteuropäischen Ländern 5. Mitteilung: In Rumänien [Veterinary Education and Employment in Eastern and Southeastern European Countries. 5th Contribution: Romania]." *Tierärtztliche Umschau* 36, no. 4 (1981): 260-276.

Data on the number of veterinary schools, enrollment, and registered veterinarians. Compares results with similar data from other COMECON countries.

10. Ethnic Relations & Human Rights

See also the following chapters: Most Favored Nation Status; Protest, Dissent & Revolution; Religion

360. Acker, Simon. "Die Rumäniendeutsche Minderheit: Im Rahmen der Beziehungen zwischen der BR Deutschland und der SR Rumänien [The Romanian-German Minority: Within the Framework of West German-Romanian Relations]." *Südosteuropa Mitteilungen* 27, no. 3/4 (1987): 229-238.
   Reviews Bonn-Bucharest diplomatic activities affecting the status of the German minority in Romania.

361. Alder, Nanci, Gerard O. W. Mueller, and Mohammed Ayat. "Psychiatry under Tyranny: A Report on the Political Abuse of Romanian Psychiatry During the Ceauşescu Years." *Current Psychology* 12, no. 1 (1993): 3-17.
   Abusive legislation enforced by the secret police helped turn psychiatric hospitals into detention centers and allowed psychiatrists to engage in false diagnosis and treatment of dissidents. Currently a draft law is trying to redress these abuses.

362. Amnesty International. *Romania.* Amnesty International Briefing Paper, 17. [London]: Amnesty International, 1980.
   Presents the constitutional, legal, and political framework that breeds continuous human rights violations. Notes existing number of prisoners, prison conditions and locations, and gives specific examples of abuses.

363. Amnesty International. *Romania: Human Rights Violations in the Eighties.* London: Amnesty International, 1987.
   Examines patterns of human rights abuses since the communist takeover and illustrates violations occuring throughout the 1980's.

364. Amnesty International, USA. *Romania: Forced Labor, Psychiatric Repression of Dissent, Persecution of Religious Believers, Ethnic Discrimination and Persecution, Law and the Suppression of Human Rights in Romania.* New York: Amnesty International USA, 1978.

365. Beck, Sam. "Ethnicity, Class, and Public Policy: Ţiganii/ Gypsies in Socialist Romania." In *Papers for the V. Congress of Southeast European Studies, Belgrade, September 1984,* edited by Kot K. Shangriladze and Erica W. Townsend, 19-38. Columbus, OH: Slavica, 1984.
   Gypsies are seen as the lowest social class and are treated with racial hostility. Offers suggestions that could lead to a better definition of group identity, recognition of Gypsies as a "cohabiting nationality," and ultimately reduce descrimination.

366. Beck, Sam. "The Romanian Gypsy Problem." In *Papers from the Fourth and Fifth Annual Meetings, Gypsy Lore Society, North American Chapter*, edited by Joanne Grumet, 100-109. New York: The Society, 1985.
The term "Ţigan" (Gypsy) refers to a person with low class identity, who lives in poverty, does not subscribe to accepted norms of work ethic, and is a burden on public resources. Gypsies believe that prejudice against them is on the increase.

367. Beck, Sam, and Marilyn McArthur. "Romania: Ethnicity, Nationalism and Development." In *Ethnicity and Nationalism in Southeastern Europe*, edited by Sam Beck and John W. Cole, 29-69. Papers on European and Mediterranean Societies, 14. Amsterdam: Universiteit van Amsterdam, 1981.
Explains why inter-ethnic tensions exist among Magyars, Germans, and Romanians in Transylvania after more than thirty years of socialism and Marxist-Leninist education.

368. Bergel, Hans. "Die Entwicklung der Siebenbürger Sachsen seit 1945 als Problem der Volksgruppen im Donauraum [Development of the Transylvanian Saxons Since 1945 as a Problem of the Ethnic Groups of the Danube Region]." *Donauraum* 21, no. 3/4 (1976): 151-160.
Gives reasons for the disappearance of Saxon communities and calls on Western governments to intervene with the Romanian government to stop the process of rapid assimilation of Transylvanian Saxons.

369. Bergel, Hans. *Die Sachsen in Siebenbürgen Nach Dreissig Jahren Kommunismus [The Transylvanian Saxons after Thirty Years of Communism]*. Innsbruck: Wort und Welt, 1976.
The Saxons are being systematically destroyed by Romania's nationalistic policies.

370. Braun, Aurel. "Structural Change and its Consequences for the Nationalities in Romania." *Südost-Europa: Zeitschrift für Gegenwartsforschung* 35, no. 7/8 (1986): 422-436.
Reprinted under the same title in *Nationalitätenprobleme in Südosteuropa*, edited by Roland Schönfeld, 181-196. Untersuchungen zur Gegenwartskunde Südosteuropas, 25. München: Oldenbourg, 1987.
Focuses on Hungarian, German, Jewish, and Gypsy minority groups and shows how the Ceauşescu government systematically restricts their rights and attempts to assimilate them into the dominant population.

371. Cartner, Holly. *Destroying Ethnic Identity: The Persecution of Gypsies in Romania*. New York: The Helsinki Watch Committee, 1991.
Reviews the history of Gypsies in Romania and discusses housing, education, employment, culture, and relations of this minority group to authorities during and after the Ceauşescu regime.

372. Castellan, Georges. "The Germans of Rumania." *Journal of Contemporary History* 6, no. 1 (1971): 52-75.
Historical account of settlement distribution and socio-political activities of the German population groups. Ceauşescu's policy of "equality and free cultural development of minorities" is viewed with reservation and skepticism in West Germany.

373. Cole, John W. "Reflections on Political Economy and Ethnicity: South Tyrol and Transylvania." In *Ethnic Challenge: The Politics of Ethnicity in Europe*, edited by Hans Vermeulen and Jeremy Boissevain, 84-99. Forum, 8. Göttingen: Herodot, 1984.
Using the example of Southern Transylvania, studies ethnic relations as a product of social, economic, and political development.

374. Comité pour la Défense des Détenus Politiques Roumains. *Livre Noir de la Roumanie (1944-1983) [Black Paper on Romania (1944-1983)]*. Freiburg: Coresi, 1983.
A brief history of communist terror is followed by a description of human rights abuses in the post-Helsinki era. Appendices list prominent Romanians incarcer-

ated, location of prisons and extermination camps, and names of collaborationists and people directly responsible for torture and abuses.

375. Comité pour la Défense des Minorités en Europe Centrale. "Destruction de 8000 Villages? [Destruction of 8,000 Villages?]." *Temps Modernes* 44, no. 512 (1989): 131-134.
Appeal to the international community describing the destruction of villages as an operation aimed at forced assimilation of minorities.

376. Crowe, David. "The Gypsy Historical Experience in Romania." In *The Gypsies of Eastern Europe*, edited by David Crowe and John Kolsti, 61-79. Armonk, N.Y.: M.E. Sharpe, 1991.
Presents relevant features of Gypsy history in Romania and contends that Ceauşescu's nationalism has encouraged the persecution and stereotyping of Gypsies.

377. Custred, Glynn. "Dual Ethnic Identity of the Transylvanian Saxons." *East European Quarterly* 25, no. 4 (1992): 483-491.
Based on historically granted administrative and ecclesiastic privileges and their linguistic and cultural identity with Germans, Saxons perceive themselves as a distinctive ethnic group. Concludes that Transylvanian Saxons as well as those who emigrated will eventually merge into local dominant cultures.

378. Dima, Nicholas. *Journey to Freedom*. Washington, D.C.: Selous Foundation Press, 1990.
Autobiographical study of life in communist labor camps and under Ceauşescu.

379. Durandin, Catherine. "À Propos du Conflit Roumano-Hongrois [On the Romanian-Hungarian Conflict]." *Défense Nationale* 45 (April 1989): 109-125.
Repressive measures against the Hungarian minority have resulted in the flight of Transylvanian Hungarians to Hungary and in widespread demonstrations in Hungary against Ceauşescu. Moscow does not intervene in this "brotherly" conflict.

380. Durandin, Catherine. "À Propos du Conflict Roumano-Hongrois [On the Romanian-Hungarian Conflict]." *Les Temps Modernes* 45, no. 522 (1990): 96-126.
During 1988-89, Bucharest and Budapest have been at odds over overt persecution of the Hungarian minority by the Ceauşescu regime.

381. Fischer, Mary Ellen. "Nation and Nationality in Romania." In *Nationalism in the USSR & Eastern Europe in the Era of Brezhnev & Kosygin*, edited by George W. Simmonds, 504-521. Detroit: University of Detroit Press, 1977. **Proceedings of the Symposium held at the University of Detroit, October 3-4, 1975**.
Argues that Romanian nationalism, as a strategy to consolidate support for the regime, negatively affects all citizens. While legitimate grievances exist, minorities under Ceau escu fare better than under any previous regime.

382. Fischer, Mary Ellen. "The Politics of National Inequality in Romania." In *Communism and the Politics of Inequalities*, edited by Daniel N. Nelson, 189-220. Lexington, MA: Lexington Books, 1983.
Minority demographics are declining relative to Romanian population statistics. Nationalistic policies are perceived by minority groups as persecution, and their grievances have found renewed echo in the West. Predicts a rise in ethnic tensions in Transylvania in the 1980's.

383. Fleischman, Janet. *Destroying Ethnic Identity: The Hungarians of Romania*. New York: U.S. Helsinki Watch Committee, 1989.
Violation of internationally recognized human rights in Transylvania are evident in education, language, media and publishing, culture, religion, employment, and urban policies. Discusses Hungarian and U.S. government positions.

384. Fleischman, Janet. *Human Rights in Romania: A Report Prepared for the Most Favored Nation Hearings in the U.S. Congress*. New York: Amnesty International,

August 1985.
Describes human rights violations in a country that professes independence in foreign policy.

385. Fleischman, Janet. *Violations of the Helsinki Accords: Romania.* New York: U.S. Helsinki Watch Committee, 1986.
A Report prepared for the Helsinki Review Conference, Vienna 1986.
Discusses the 1966 amnesty for political prisoners and various human rights abuses.

386. Ghermani, Dionisie. "Die Historische Legitimierung der Rumänischen Nationalitätenpolitik [The Historical Legitimation of Romania's Nationalities Policy]." In *Nationalitätenprobleme in Südosteuropa,* edited by Roland Schönfeld, 197-212. Untersuchungen zur Gegenwartskunde Südosteuropas, 25. München: Oldenbourg, 1987.
Surveys Ceauşescu's policies towards Hungarian, Jewish, and Tschangos minority groups and historical arguments concerning territorial rights.

387. Gilberg, Trond. "Ethnic Minorities in Romania under Socialism." *East European Quarterly* 7, no. 4 (1974): 435-464.
Reprinted under the same title in *The Social Structure of Eastern Europe: Transition and Process in Czechoslovakia, Hungary, Poland, Romania, and Yugoslavia,* edited by Bernard Lewis Faber, 195-224. New York: Praeger, 1976.
Examines the effects of urbanization, occupations, and education on five ethnic groups (Romanians, Hungarians, Germans, Gypsies, and Jews). While all groups experience socioeconomic changes, no massive cultural assimilation into the dominant Romanian culture is apparent.

388. Gilberg, Trond. "Romanian Reform Movement in the 1980's: Fundamental Changes in the Making?" *Nationalities Papers* 11, no. 1 (1983): 41-61.
Minorities are opposing unfavorable economic policies, discrimination in education, the arts and culture, and persistent human rights violations.

389. Girtler, Roland. *Verbannt und Vergessen: Eine Untergehende Deutschsprachige Kultur in Rumänien [Exiled and Forgotten: A Disappearing German-Speaking Culture in Romania].* Linz: Veritas, 1992.
The Landler, an Upper-Austrian peasant community, exiled for religious reasons to Romania some 200 years ago, have struggled to maintain their dialect, religion, and traditions. Describes their life in the three existing villages of Grosspold, Neppendorf and Grossau, their interaction with other ethnic groups, and their cultural extinction.

390. Goussev, Catherine. "Impressions de Roumanie [Impressions from Romania]." *Temps Modernes* 44, no. 512 (1989): 111-125.
Describes the Romanian refugees in Hungary and suggests venues of assistance.

391. Haraszti, Endre. *The Ethnic History of Transylvania.* Astor Park, FL: Danubian, 1971.
Overview of the history of Transylvania and analysis of the impact of Ceauşescu's policies of "national communism" on minorities.

392. Hartl, Hans. *Nationalitätenprobleme im Heutigen Südosteuropa [Problems of Nationalities in Today's South-Eastern Europe].* Untersuchungn zur Gegenwartskunde Südosteuropas, 7. München: Oldenbourg, 1973.
Addresses three aspects: Ceauşescu's campaign to gain the support of Transylvania's Hungarians following the invasion of Czechoslovakia; the decline of the German population due to emigration, low birthrates, and assimilation; and the dispute over the annexation of Bessarabia by the Soviets.

393. Hartl, Hans. "Zum Exodus der Deutschen aus Rumänien [About the Exodus of Germans from Romania]." *Südosteuropa-Mitteilungen* 27, no. 3/4 (1987): 220-228.
Causes of the mass-exodus are the low standard of living, the yearning to be free, and especially Ceauşescu's aggressive policy of national homogenization.

394. *Human Rights Issues in United States Relations with Romania and Czechoslovakia: A Staff Report.* Washington: U.S. G.P.O., 1983. Committee Print. Y4.F76/2:S.prt.98-38.
Reports on issues discussed with Romanian Ministry representatives regarding trade, emigration, the Education Repayment Decree, and treatment of ethnic groups and minorities within Romania including Jews, Baptists, Germans, and Roman Catholics. Appendix A contains the text of the "Romanian Decree on Emigrants Reimbursing the State of Educational Costs Incurred While Living in Romania."

395. Illyés, Elemér. "Education and National Minorities in Contemporary Romania." In *Transylvania: The Roots of Ethnic Conflict,* edited by John F. Cadzow, Andrew Ludányi, and Louis J. Elteto, 245-268. Kent, OH: Kent State University Press, 1983.
A collection of papers, some of which were presented at the Symposium on Transylvania, held on May 18-20, 1979, at Kent State University.
Traces educational policies to the 1970's and discusses compulsory teaching of Romanian in the minority schools and the lack of educational oportunities for Hungarian minorities.

396. Illyés, Elemér. *National Minorities in Romania: Change in Transylvania.* East European Monographs, 112. New York: Columbia University Press, 1982.
Updated translation of the author's *Nationale Minderheiten in Rumänien: Siebenbürgen im Wandel.* Vienna: Braumüller, 1981.
Historical survey of national minority education, religion and media, through the late 1970's.

397. Kaplan, Robert D. "Where History and People Get Mangled: Bloody Romania." *New Republic* 203, no. 5-6 (1990): 12-15.
Overview of historical prejudices, including anti-Semitism, and their re-emergence in post-Ceauşescu Romania.

398. King, Robert R. *Minorities under Communism: Nationalities as a Source of Tension among Balkan Communist States.* Cambridge, MA: Harvard University Press, 1973.
Chapter eight, "Territorial Autonomy and Cultural Rights: Rumania" (pp. 146-169), explores the history of the Hungarian and German minority in Transylvania since World War II and looks at Gheorghiu-Dej's and especially Ceauşescu's policies in light of the revival of nationalism. Chapter 11, "Historical Debates: Bessarabia," summarizes the scholarly dispute over the annexation of Bessarabia and Northern Bukovina, as a means to further Ceauşescu's foreign policy aims and gain popular support at home.

399. Klaube, Manfred. *Deutschböhmische Siedlungen im Karpatenraum [German-Bohemian Settlements in the Carpathian Region].* Wissenschaftliche Beiträge zur Geschichte und Landeskunde Ostmitteleuropas, 120. Marburg/Lahn: Herder-Institut, 1984.
Studies life and customs of German-Bohemian villages in the Banat and Bukovina from the 19th century to the end of the 1970's.

400. Klaube, Manfred. *Das Sächsische Minderheitensiedlungsgebiet im Südsiebenbürgen [The Saxon Settlements in Southern Transylvania].* Schriftreihe der Siebenbürger Sachsen, 1-2. München: Hans Meschendörfer, 1971.
Describes the Saxons, their settlement patterns and socio-cultural organization within socialist Romania.

401. Kovrig, Bennett. "The Magyars in Rumania: Problems of a 'Coinhabiting' Nationality." In *Nationalitätenprobleme in Südosteuropa,* edited by Roland Schönfeld, 213-230. Untersuchungen zur Gegenwartskunde Südosteuropas, 25. München: Oldenbourg, 1987.
Examines the historical background, current population size, and socioeconomic and political status of the Hungarian population. Discusses Ceauşescu's educational and cultural policy toward the Magyars, forms of dissent and repressive responses, the attitude of the Hungarian government, and Western opinion concerning violations of human rights.

402. Kŭrti, László. "Transylvania, Land Beyond Reason: Toward an Anthropological Analysis of a Contested Terrain." *Dialectical Anthropology* 14, no. 1 (1989): 21-52.
     Discusses the background of interethnic tensions and the attitude of the Hungarian government regarding the treatment of Hungarians in Romania.

403. Lendvai, Paul. *Anti-Semitism Without Jews: Communist Eastern Europe.* Garden City, NY: Doubleday, 1971.
     The chapter, "The Surprise of Rumania," (pp.327-349), contends that the country's independent stance and proclaimed nationalism have neither inflamed nor perpetuated historic anti-Semitic, anti-Zionist sentiments. Under Ceauşescu, relations with the Jewish community have improved and Israeli-Romanian cooperation has flourished.

404. Ludányi, Andrew. "Hungarians in Rumania and Yugoslavia: A Comparative Study of Communist Nationality Policies." Ph.D. diss., Louisiana State University, 1971. Ann Arbor: UMI, 1971. AAD72-03507.
     Studies nationality policies as applied to Hungarians living in Transylvania and Vojvodina and concludes that political considerations rather than ideology forms the basis of policy decisions.

405. Ludányi, Andrew. "Ideology and Political Culture in Romania: The Daco-Roman Theory and the Place of Minorities." In *Transylvania: The Roots of Ethnic Conflict,* edited by John F. Cadzow, Andrew Ludányi, and Louis J. Elteto, 229-244. Kent, OH: Kent State University Press, 1983.
     A collection of papers, some of which where presented at the Symposium on Transylvania, May 18-20, 1979, at Kent State University.
     Presents the Romanian continuity theory as legitimization for territorial claims and discriminatory policies.

406. McArthur, Marilyn. "The Politics of Identity: Transylvanian Saxons in Socialist Romania." Ph.D. diss., University of Massachusetts, 1981. Ann Arbor: UMI, 1981. AAD8201361.
     historical review of Transylvanian Saxons, followed by a study of their participation in socialist development. Saxons' life in the village of Marienburg (Feldioara), Braşov County, is characterized by demographic disruptions, errosion of time-honored principles of solidarity, tolerance, and inter-ethnic harmony, and confused loyalties for East and West.

407. McArthur, Marilyn. "The Saxon Germans: Political Fate of an Ethnic Identity." *Dialectical Anthropology* 1, no. 4 (1976): 349-364.
     Discusses the adaptation of ethnic Germans (Saxons) to socialist transformation in Romania, using the village of Marienburg (Feldioara). Post World War II Romania adhered to a policy of ethnic autonomy and protection of the cultural tradition of minorities. Nonetheless, the Saxons have not adapted well to the policy of cultural pluralism and show signs of disintegrating as an ethnic group. They are decreasing rapidly and their ethnic identity faces a crisis of values. The expected ethnic coexistence of different cultural traditions has not been achieved.

408. McArthur, Marilyn. "Les 'Vrais Allemands' àpres Hitler: Racisme et Identité Culturelle chez les Allemands de Transylvanie [The 'True Germans' after Hitler: Racism and Cultural Identity of the Transylvanian Germans]." In *Paysans et Nations d'Europe Centrale & Balkanique,* 269-279. Paris: Maisonneuve et Larose, 1985.
     Saxons, who consider themselves more German than West Germans, display racist attitudes and reject Romanian socialism. After emigrating however, they long for their Transylvanian homeland.

409. Nanay, Julia. *Transylvania: The Hungarian Minority in Romania.* Problems behind the Iron Curtain Series, 10. Astor, FL: Danubian, 1976.
     Chapter four, "Nicolae Ceauşescu Slips Into Leadership" (pp. 49-55), discusses the abolition of the Mureş-Magyar Autonomous Region, the statistical misrepresenta-

tion of minorities, and the impact of the "Prague Spring" on Transylvania. Contends that Ceauşescu's policy leads to cultural anihilation.

410. Oschlies, Wolf. *Die Deutschen in Rumänien. Teil I: Nachbarn seit Jahrhunderten [Germans in Romania. Part I: Neighbors for Centuries].* Berichte des Bundesinstituts für Ostwissenschaftliche und Internationale Studien, 15. Köln: Bundesinstitut für Ostwissenschaftliche und Internationale Studien, 1980.
The Romanian-Germans have fared far better than the Germans in other socialist countries. Yet Germans are leaving Romania in large numbers. Presents a history of German minority groups in Transylvania, Banat, Bukovina, and Dobrogea.

411. Oschlies, Wolf. *Rumäniendeutsches Schicksal 1918-1988: Wo Deutsch zur Sprache der Grabsteine wird...[Fate of Romanian-Germans, 1918-1988: Where German becomes the Language of Tombstones...].* Köln: Böhlau, 1988.
Following a discussion of social life of Romanian-Germans before and after World War II, part two (pp.113-200) focuses on life under Ceauşescu and on the mass emigration of the German minority to West-Germany.

412. Peyfuss, Max Demeter. "Aromunen in Rumänien [Aromanians in Romania]." *Österreichische Osthefte* 26, no. 2 (1984): 313-319.
No research on Aromanian history, language or literature has been published in Romania since World War II, largely for political reasons. Documents the resurgence of interest in the Aromanian minority and its place in the Romanian ethnogeny.

413. Pilisi, Paul. "Hungarian Minority in Romania." *International Perspectives* January/February 1979: 24-28.
Addresses restrictive measures taken by the Romanian government against individual and collective rights of the Hungarian minority.

414. Romanian Research Group, Department of Anthropology, University of Massachusetts, Amherst. "On Transylvanian Ethnicity." *Current Anthropology* 20, no. 1 (1979): 135-140.
Reply to Michael Sozan's claim of ethnocide of Szeklers under Ceauşescu, followed by the history of ethnic relations in Transylvania.

415. Sanborn, Anne Fay, and Géza Wass de Czege, eds. *Transylvania and the Hungarian-Romanian Problem: A Symposium.* Astor, FL: Danubian, 1979.
Discusses Romania's discriminatory policies towards its Hungarian minority.

416. Scarfe, Alan. "Dismantling a Human Rights Movement: A Romanian Solution." *Religion in Communist Lands* 7, no. 3 (1979): 166-177.
The government uses arrests and forced emigration to undermine the human rights movement promoted by religious believers.

417. Schenk, Annemie. *Familie und Wohnung in Stolzenburg: Eine Untersuchung bei Sachsen und Rumänen in einem Siebenbürgischen Dorf [Family and Housing in Stolzenburg: Observations on Saxons and Romanians in a Transylvanian Village].* Köln: Böhlau, 1984.
Describes traditional family life and work and the changes brought about by industrialization.

418. Schenk, Annemie, and Ingeborg Weber-Kellermann. *Interethnik und Sozialer Wandel in einem Mehrsprachigen Dorf des Rumänischen Banats [Inter-Ethnic and Social Transformations in a Multilingual Village in Banat, Romania].* Marburger Studien zur Vergleichenden Ethnosoziologie, 3. Marburg: Marburger Studienkreis für Europäische Ethnologie, 1973.
Studies ethnic interaction among German, Romanian, and Serb villagers of Becicherecul-Mic and their adaptation to socioeconomic and cultural changes brought about by collectivization and socialist industrialization.

419. Schöpflin, George. "National Minorities under Communism in Eastern Europe." In *Eastern Europe in Transition*, edited by Kurt London, 117-141. Baltimore: Johns Hopkins Press, 1966.
   Shows country by country statistics on population by nationality and discusses discriminatory policies and practices against Romania's Hungarian and German minorities.

420. Schöpflin, George. "Rumänien, Ungarn und Siebenbürgen [Romania, Hungary and Transylvania]." *Europäische Rundschau* 11, no. 1 (1983): 79-91.
   Tensions are rising in Transylvania due to nationalism. Contends that from a Romanian perspective, the disappearance of the Hungarian minority would solve existing problems, a solution that remains unacceptable to the Hungarian minority and Hungary.

421. Schöpflin, George, and Hugh Poulton. *Romania's Ethnic Hungarians*. Rev. ed. London: Minority Rights Group, 1990.
   Previously published in 1978 as *The Hungarians of Rumania*.
   Study of the Magyars under the final years of the Ceauşescu regime.

422. Sick, Wolf Dieter. "Die Siebenbürger Sachsen in Rumänien: Heutige Siedlungs-, Wirtschafts- und Sozialverhältnisse einer Deutschen Volksgruppe [The Transylvanian Saxons in Romania: Current Settlement Patterns, and Socioeconomic Conditions of a German Population Group]." *Geographische Rundschau* 20, no. 1 (1968): 12-22.
   Studies the Saxons and their place as a minority in a socialist state.

423. Sozan, Michael. "Ethnocide in Rumania." *Current Anthropology* 18, no. 4 (1977): 781-782.
   Claims that Ceauşescu's policies are meant to exterminate the Transylvanian Szeklers.

424. Sozan, Michael. "Reply." *Current Anthropology* 20, no. 1 (1979): 140-148.
   Response to the Romanian Research Group, University of Massachusetts, Amherst on their assessment of ethnic relations in Transylvania, with special emphasis on the situation of the Szeklers.

425. Steigerwald, Jacob. *Tracing Romania's Heterogeneous German Minority From its Origins to the Diaspora*. Winona, MN: Winona State University Press, 1985.
   Presents the eleven German minority groups in historical perspective and demonstrates that recent constitutional changes mandate their assimilation into the dominant culture. The passive and inept are assimilated. The resourceful and better educated usually emigrate.

426. Steinke, K. "Les Minorités Hongroise et Allemande de Roumanie. Données de Base d'une Description Sociolinguistique [Hungarian and German Minorities in Romania. Basic Data of a Sociolinguistic Description]." *Recherches Sociologiques* 8, no. 1 (1977): 51-74.
   Following a historical introduction, presents a statistical analysis of Hungarian and German minorities in the Romanian sociolinguistic space.

427. Suga, Alexander. "Die Volkszählung in Rumänien und die Entwicklung der Deutschen Volksgruppe [Population Census in Romania and the Development of the German Minority Group]." *Osteuropa* 28, no. 3 (1978): 229-235.
   The decrease in the German minority group may be attributed to an aggressive governmental policy of assimilation and to the increased emigration to West Germany.

428. Szaz, Z. Michael. "Contemporary Educational Policies in Transylvania." *East European Quarterly* 11, no. 4 (1977): 493-501.
   The need of skilled manpower in Transylvania lead to a temporary expansion of vocational education in Hungarian. Overall, however, education in Hungarian and German is declining and the value of minorities' contributions to Transylvanian history continues to be minimized.

429. Szaz, Z. Michael. "Oppression of the National Minorities in Romania." In *Sources of "Human Rights Violations in Romania,"* edited by Philip S. Cox, 60-80. Washington, D.C.: American Foreign Policy Institute, 1986.
Repression is evident in the school system, in human rights abuses, and in the denial of cultural expression. Calls for respect for human and cultural rights of minorities.

430. Tamás, Gáspár Miklós. *Censorship, Ethnic Discrimination and the Culture of the Hungarians in Romania.* New York: Helsinki Watch Committee, 1985.
Assesses the situation of the Hungarian ethnic minority.

431. "Ukrainians Abroad: In Romania." In *Ukraine: A Concise Encyclopedia*, edited by Volodymyr Kubijovyc, 163-167. Toronto: University of Toronto Press, 1971.
Assessment of the Ukrainian minority in Romania.

432. U.S. Commission on Security and Cooperation in Europe. *Reform and Human Rights in Eastern Europe.* Washington: U.S. G.P.O., December 1988. Committee Print. Y4.Se.2:100-2-39.
Ceaușescu has rejected reforms. The rotation of cadres helps him maintain centralized control. Cultural life and the media remain under tight Party scrutiny. In spite of repeated human rights violations, activism is on the increase.

433. U.S. Commission on Security and Cooperation in Europe. *The State of Human Rights in Romania (An Update).* Washington: U.S. G.P.O., December 1988. Committee Print. Y4.Se2:100-2-38.
Reports on the destruction of Bucharest and the systematization of the countryside. Political activism and dissent are on the increase.

434. U.S. Congress. House. Committee on Foreign Affairs. *Consideration of Miscellaneous Bills and Resolutions: Markup Before the Committee on Foreign Affairs....*, v.3, pp. 368-371. Washington: U.S. G.P.O., 1989. Y4.F76/1:B49/2/989/v.3.
Reprints House Resolution 505, amended and favorably reported, condemning the Romanian government for human rights violations.

435. U.S. Congress. House. Committee on Foreign Affairs. Subcommittee on Europe and the Middle East. *Developments in Europe, June 1986: Hearing....June 19, 1986.* Washington: U.S. G.P.O., 1986. House Hearing. Y4.F76/1:Eu7/25/986-4.
Provides an overview of relations between church and state in Romania. Rozanne L. Ridgway, Bureau of European and Canadian Affairs, testifies on levels of Romanian emigration to the United States, West Germany, and Israel.

436. U.S. Congress. House. Committee on Foreign Affairs. Subcommittee on Europe and the Middle East. *Human Rights in Romania: Hearing....May 14, 1985.* Washington: U.S. G.P.O., 1985. House Hearing. Y4.F76/1:H88/37.
Contains reports on aspects of human rights violations from Jeri Laber, U.S. Helsinki Watch Committee; Nina Shea, Program Director, International League of Human Rights; Robert Sharlet, Amnesty International U.S.A.; and Gary Matthews, Deputy Assistant Secretary of State, Human Rights and Humanitarian Affairs. Appendices include: Country Reports on Human Rights Practices for 1984, Section Romania; Annual Romanian Emigration to the United States, Israel and the Federal Republic of Germany, 1971-1984, prepared by the Department of State; a statement of Ion Vardala, Vice-President, Truth About Romania Committee; "The Bible as Romanian Toilet Paper," *Wall Street Journal* (June 14, 1985); "Press Romania on Rights," *New York Times* (June 12, 1985); and "Romanians Accused," *New York Times* (June 10, 1985).

437. U.S. Helsinki Watch Committee. *Romania: Human Rights in a "Most Favored Nation."* New York: Helsinki Watch, 1983.
Documents human rights abuses against applicants for emigration, political prisoners, religious believers, minorities, as well as against Romanian emigrants abroad.

438. Váli, Ferenc A. "Transylvania and the Hungarian Minority." *Journal of International Affairs* 20, no. 1 (1966): 32-44.
Focuses on the policy of discrimination and absorption against the Hungarian minority and on Soviet attempts to use the Transylvanian question as a political lever.

439. Verdery, Katherine. "The Unmaking of an Ethnic Collectivity: Transylvania's Germans." *American Ethnologist* 12, no. 1 (1985): 62-83.
Compares ethnic identification under socialism in two Transylvanian minority groups: Hungarians and Germans.

440. Wagner, Ernst. *Geschichte der Siebenbürger Sachsen: Ein Überblick [History of the Transylvanian Saxons: An Overview]*. Innsbruck: Wort und Welt, 1981.
Highlights relevant events in the historical development of the Saxons.

441. Waldmann, Dietger. *Die Deutschen im Rumänien von Heute: Bericht zur Lage der Deutschen Minderheit [Germans in Today's Romania: Report on the Situation of the German Minority]*. Eckart-Schriften, 34. Vienna: Österreichische Landsmannschaft, 1970.
Discusses the history of German settlements in Romania and their contemporary social, economic, and cultural life. Contemplates their relationship to Germany and Austria and their future in Romania.

442. Weber, George, and Renate Weber. *Zendersch: Eine Siebenbürgische Gemeinde im Wandel [Zendersch: A Changing Transylvanian Community]*. Münster: Delp, 1985.
Describes geography, social life, and customs of Saxons in the community of Zendersch (Senereus), in present-day Romania.

11. Foreign Affairs

443. Accoce, Pierre, and Jean Daniel Pouget. *Le Réseau Caraman: 13 Roumains Font Trembler l'OTAN [The Caraman Spy-Ring: 13 Romanians Terrify NATO].* [Paris]: Fayard, 1972.
Describes the Romanian espionage activities in France in the 1960's and the events that led to dismantling the powerful Caraman spy-ring.

444. Alpern, Joseph. "Les Relations entre Israël et la Roumanie: De la Guerre des Six Jours à la Guerre du Kippour (1967-1973) [The Israeli-Romanian Relations: From the Six-Day War to the Yom Kippur War (1967-1973)]." *Politique Étrangère* 38, no. 6 (1973): 725-752.
Highlights the diplomatic and economic benefits derived by Romania from its special relation to Israel and the political and moral advantages derived by Israel from this cooperation.

445. Barnes, Harry G., Jr. "Impressions of Romania." In *The United States and Romania: American-Romanian Relations in the Twentieth Century*, edited by Paul D. Quinlan, 124-128. American-Romanian Academy of Arts and Sciences, 6. Woodland Hills, CA: ARA, 1988.
An American diplomat remembers events dating from 1968 to 1977.

446. Barnett, Thomas P. M. *Romanian and East German Policies in the Third World: Comparing the Strategies of Ceaușescu and Honecker*. Westport, CT: Praeger, 1992.
Analyzes strategies used by Romania and East Germany in the Third World.

447. Barnett, Thomas P. M. "Warsaw Pact - Third World Relations, 1968-1987: Explaining the Special Roles of Romania and East Germany (Third World)." Ph.D. diss., Harvard University, 1990. Ann Arbor: UMI, 1990. AAD9035435.
Analyzes the reasons, successes and failures of Romania and East Germany's involvement with the Third World region and the role played by the Soviet Union in the adoption of their policies.

448. Bender, Peter. *East Europe in Search of Security*. Translated by S. Z. Young. London: Chatto & Windus, 1972.
Analyzes potential military threats from East and West. Concludes that Romania's foreign policy exhibits tendencies toward neutrality and non-alignment.

449. Bianchini, Stefano. "The Adriatic Southern European Area: The Balkans." *International Spectator* 25, no. 4 (1990): 310-329.
The Balkans are a critical area for Western Europe, especially for Italy. Military conflicts could draw in many countries from the region. Summarizes Romania's recent history under Ceaușescu, the problem of Bessarabia, and the country's policy

toward minorities. Discusses Italy's role in the pacification, integration, and development of the area.

450. Braun, Aurel. *Romanian Foreign Policy Since 1965: The Political and Military Limits of Autonomy.* New York: Praeger, 1978.
Discusses Romania's policy of autonomy in foreign affairs, its utilization of principles of international law, its concept of security and military defenses, and its relations to countries of Eastern Europe and the Soviet Union.

451. Braun, Aurel. "Romania's Travails." *Problems of Communism* 31, no. 3 (1982): 49-55.
Questions the limits of Romania's independence and the degree of legitimacy it conferred to the regime and notes the trivial and grotesque character of some of its foreign policy initiatives.

452. Breitenstein, Rolf. "Nixons Reise nach Rumänien [Nixon's Trip to Romania]." *Europa Archiv* 24, no. 16 (1969): 559-562.
Assesses the importance of this visit by examining Soviet reactions to Romania and the United States.

453. Brown, J. F. "Rumania Today: II. The Strategy of Defiance." *Problems of Communism* 18, no. 2 (March 1969): 32-38.
Romania's independent course places the country in imminent danger of Soviet retaliation. Its only safeguard against invasion is unity.

454. Brown, J. F. "Rumania's Uphill Struggle for an Independent Role." *The World Today* 29, no. 3 (1973): 126-133.
In the 1970's, Romania's importance in international politics is declining while internally Ceauşescu's popular support is eroding.

455. Brown, J. F. "Rumänien - der Unbotmässige Verbündete: Die Rumänische Aussenpolitik im Jahre 1967 [Romania - the Unsubmissive Ally: Romania's Foreign Policy in 1967]." *Europa-Archiv* 22, no. 1 (1967): 875-885.
After estabishing diplomatic relations with West Germany and declaring neutrality in the Middle East conflict, Romania is isolated and experiences Soviet political pressure.

456. Buchan, David. "Romania's Policy Gamble." *Washington Quarterly* 5, no. 3 (1982): 148-150.
Ceauşescu's dismal record on human rights and his doubtful economic practices makes Western support difficult. Similarly, Moscow understands that no amount of favors will appease Ceauşescu. Romania appears to have run out of allies and political options.

457. Burks, Richard V. "The Rumanian National Deviation: An Accounting." In *Eastern Europe in Transition*, edited by Kurt London, 93-113. Baltimore: Johns Hopkins Press, 1966.
Also published in German in *Osteuropa* 16, no. 1 (1966): 314-328.
Discusses Romania's deviation from bloc policies, its autonomous foreign policy, and the "romanization" of its party and culture. Questions the ability of Western experts to recognize changes as they occur.

458. Chalet, Jean Anne. *La Roumanie Alliée Rebelle [Allied and Rebellious Romania].* Collection PH, 5. N.p.: Casterman, 1972.
Journalistic sketch of events in Romania in the sixties, with special emphasis on the political balancing act during the invasion of Czechoslovakia. Affirms that Ceauşescu's rare quality is that of moral honesty.

459. Ciorănescu, George. *Bessarabia: Disputed Land Between East and West.* München: Dumitru, 1985.

Sixteen articles written in most part as a response to Soviet claims to Bessarabia and Northern Bukovina.

460. Cioranescu, George. "Reviriment Politique [Political Rebirth]." In *Aspects des Relations Russo-Roumaines: Rétrospectives et Orientations*, by George Cioranescu [et al.], 227-239. Paris: Minard, 1967.
Examines China's role in the Soviet-Romanian dispute over Bessarabia.

461. Cioranescu, George. "Rumania After Czechoslovakia: Ceausescu Walks the Tightrope." *East Europe* 18, no. 6 (1969): 2-7.
Ceausescu uses a blend of "orthodoxy and revisionism" to preserve his independent course. His diplomatic maneuvers have earned him a measure of respect both internally and abroad.

462. Clark, Cal, and Robert L. Farlow. *Comparative Patterns of Foreign Policy and Trade: The Communist Balkans and International Politics.* Studies in East European and Soviet Planning, Development and Trade, 23. Bloomington: International Development Research Center, Indiana University, 1976.
The chapter on Romania (pp.49-65) focuses on three evolutionary stages of Romanian foreign policy and trade: 1958-1963, when Romania articulates its policy of partial alignment; 1964-1968, when it develops stronger ties to the West and consolidates its autonomy; and 1969-1972, an era marked by economic difficulties and fluctuations between resistance and compromise.

463. Crowther, William E. "Romanian Politics and the International Economy." *Orbis* 28, no. 3 (1984): 553-574.
Explores the political reasons that lead Romania into economic relations with the West and the impact of world market forces on its domestic policies.

464. D'Encausse, Hélène Carrère. "La Fin du Mythe Unitaire: Vingt Ans de Conflits dans l'Europe Socialiste [End of the Unity Myth: Twenty Years of Conflicts in Socialist Europe]." *Revue Française de Science Politique* 18, no. 6 (1968): 1155-1189.
Examines the Romanian independence stance among other conflicts occuring in the Soviet bloc countries. These conflicts paved the way for the "Prague Spring."

465. Dima, Nicholas. *Bessarabia and Bukovina: The Soviet-Romanian Territorial Dispute.* East European Monographs, 108. New York: Columbia University Press, 1982.
For updated, enriched edition, see *From Moldavia to Moldova: the Soviet-Romanian Territorial Dispute.* New York: Columbia University Press, 1991.

466. Dima, Nicholas. *From Moldavia to Moldova: The Soviet-Romanian Territorial Dispute.* East European Monographs, 309. New York: Columbia University Press, 1991.
Enriched and updated edition of *Bessarabia and Bukovina: The Soviet-Romanian Territorial Dispute.* New York: Columbia University Press, 1982.
Charts the history of the disputed territory, and discusses Ceausescu's "academic" polemic with Moscow.

467. Durandin, Catherine. "La Roumanie et les Enjeux Contemporains [Romania and the Current Stakes]." *Défense Nationale* 44 (April 1988): 75-89.
Romania remains non-aligned, striving to create a nuclear-free zone in the Balkans. Its concept of change and restructuring differs from Gorbachev's *perestroika*.

468. Durandin, Catherine. "Le Système Ceausescu: Utopie Totalitaire et Nationalisme Insulaire [The Ceausescu System: Totalitarian Utopia and Insular Nationalism]." *Vingtième Siècle* 25 (January-March 1990): 85-96.
Reviews Ceausescu's policies and ideology. Over time, international opinion has fluctuated between seduction/admiration and condemnation/indignation.

469. Dziewanowski, M. K. "The 1970 Romanian-Soviet Treaty." *East Europe* 20, no. 1 (1971): 19-22.

Explores the background against which the twenty-year Romanian-Soviet Friendship Treaty was signed. Compares it with the Czech-Soviet treaty and underscores advantages and disadvantages for Romania.

470. Dziewanowski, M. K. "The Pattern of Rumanian Independence." *East Europe* 18, no. 6 (1969): 8-12.
Discusses the origins and path of Romania's independence. The autonomous foreign policy runs the risk of unleashing nationalism or unwanted liberalization.

471. Eissner, Albin. "Rumäniens Anspruch auf Bessarabien und Bukowina [Romania's Claim on Bessarabia and Bukovina]." *Aussenpolitik* 17, no. 8 (1966): 496-502.
Moscow respondes to Romania's renewed claim to its northern provinces by organizing a lavish celebration of the "liberation" of the Moldavian Soviet Socialist Republic.

472. Eyal, Jonathan. "Transylvanian Discords." *The World Today* 44, no. 8/9 (1988): 130-132.
Relations between Hungary and Romania are tense. More and more Romanians are crossing the border into Hungary.

473. Farlow, Robert L. "Alignment and Conflict: Romanian Foreign Policy." Ph.D. diss., Case Western Reserve University, 1971. Ann Arbor: UMI, 1971. AAD71-22799.
Looks at two time periods 1958-63 (the leadership of Gheorghiu-Dej) and 1964-1969 (the Ceauşescu period) and analyzes Romania's partial alignment to the communist bloc.

474. Farlow, Robert L. "Romania and the Policy of Partial Alignment." In *The Foreign Policies of Eastern Europe: Domestic and International Determinants*, edited by James A. Kuhlman, 191-207. East-West Perspectives, 4. Leyden: Sijthoff, 1978.
Studies Romania's foreign policy of partial alignment and explores its idiosyncratic, systemic, governmental, and societal determinants.

475. Farlow, Robert L. "Romanian Foreign Policy: A Case of Partial Alignment." *Problems of Communism* 20, no. 6 (1971): 54-63.
Summarizes foreign policy in general and developments since 1965 in particular and analyzes Romania's posture and determinants of partial alignment.

476. Fenyvesi, Charles. "Romania and Hungary Compete to be America's Favorite Communist Pet: The Middleman Cometh." *New Republic* 178, no. 18 (1978): 11-12.
Nicolae Ceauşescu is a cowardly opportunistic broker in international relations in contrast to Hungarian leaders' sophisticated diplomatic efforts in vying for Western favors.

477. Filiti, Gregoire. "La Lois du Vainqueur [The Law of the Conqueror]." In *Aspects des Relations Russo-Roumaines: Rétrospectives et Orientations*, by George Cioranescu [et al.], 188-217. Paris: Minard, 1967.
Chronicles Soviet-Romanian relations from 1947 to 1967.

478. Fischer-Galaţi, Stephen. "The Moldavian Soviet Republic in Soviet Domestic and Foreign Policy." In *The Influence of East Europe and the Soviet West on the USSR*, edited by Roman Szporluk, 229-250. New York: Praeger, 1975.
Based on papers presented at a conference, University of Michigan, May 1970..
Charts the history of the Moldavian Socialist Soviet Republic since its establishment and discusses the overt challenge issued to the Soviets by Gheorghiu-Dej and his successor Ceauşescu, marking the reopening of the territorial dispute over Bessarabia.

479. Fischer-Galaţi, Stephen. "Romania and the Sino-Soviet Conflict." In *Eastern Europe in Transition*, edited by Kurt London, 261-306. Baltimore: Johns Hopkins Press, 1966.

Reviews the history of Romania's non-alignment and shows how it has masterfully exploited the Sino-Soviet conflict.

480. Fischer-Galați, Stephen. "Romania's 'Independent Course': Retrospect and Prospects." *Harvard International Review* 7 (September/October 1984): 9-12.
     Argues that Ceaușescu's merit lies within his cunning ability to mediate in international conflicts, thus claiming a role for Romania in international affairs, a wise policy that ought to be emulated by his successor.

481. Fischer-Galați, Stephen. "Smokescreen and Iron Curtain: A Reassessment of Territorial Revisionism vis-à-vis Romania Since World War I." *East European Quarterly* 22, no. 1 (1988): 37-53.
     A detailed discussion of Moscow's revisionist politics aimed at securing hegemony in Eastern Europe, its own claim over Bessarabia and Bukovina, and its exploitation of historical territorial disputes among Romania, Hungary, and Bulgaria.

482. Fischer-Galați, Stephen. "The Socialist Republic of Rumania." In *The Changing Face of Communism in Eastern Europe*, edited by Peter A. Toma, 14-37. Tucson: University of Arizona Press, 1970.
     Examines foreign policy changes since Romania proclaimed its independence from the Soviet Union and their impact on the country's relations to East and West.

483. Funderburk, David B. *Betrayal of America: Bush's Appeasement of Communist Dictators Betrays American Principles*. Dunn, NC: Larry McDonald Foundation, 1991.
     In chapter nine, "Appeasement of Nicolae Ceaușescu in Romania" (pp. 83-109), contends that George Bush and the foreign policy establishment, in full knowledge of Ceaușescu's disregard for human rights and "Orwellian politics," openly praised and supported the dictator with foreign aid.

484. Funderburk, David B. *Pinstripes and Reds: An American Ambassador Caught Between the State Department and the Romanian Communists, 1981-1985*. Washington, D. C.: Selous Foundation, 1987.
     Exposes the ill-conceived State Department policy that allowed Ceaușescu to receive substantial economic advantages from the United States in the erroneous belief that such assistance would advance Western objectives in Romania.

485. Funderburk, David B. "Relations Between the United States and Romania during the First Half of the 1980's." In *The United States and Romania: American-Romanian Relations in the Twentieth Century*, edited by Paul D. Quinlan, 147-160. American-Romanian Academy of Arts and Sciences, 6. Woodland Hills, CA: ARA, 1988.
     Since the late 1960's, U.S. policy has worked against the interests of the Romanian people. Advocates humanitarian assistance and continued pressure against human rights violations.

486. Gabanyi, Anneli Ute. "Bukarest Schert Wieder Aus: Rumänien und das Moskauer Gipfeltreffen des Warschauer Pakts [Bucharest Moves Farther Away: Romania and the Warsaw Pact Summit Meeting in Moscow]." *Osteuropa* 29, no. 3 (1979): 197-202.
     Romania resists Warsaw Pact pressures to increase its defense budget and condemn China or the Middle East peace efforts.

487. Gabanyi, Anneli Ute. "Rumänien: Ceaușescu Bleibt Widerspenstig [Romania: Ceaușescu Remains Obstinate]." *Osteuropa* 33, no. 3-4 (1983): 214-215.
     The official reaction to Breshnev's death and Andropov's election is chilly. Despite economic difficulties and political isolation, Romania ignores Soviet pressure for closer cooperation within CMEA.

488. Gabanyi, Anneli Ute. *Rumäniens Eigenwillige Positionen auf der Madrider KSZE-Folgetreffen und auf der KVAE [Romania's Individualistic Positions at the Madrid CSCE Follow-Up Conference and at the CDE]*. Berichte, 47. Köln: Bundesinstitut

für Ostwissenschaftliche und Internationale Studien, 1984.
Analyzes Romania's stand on policies concerning security and disarmament in the 1980's.

489. Gati, Charles. *The Bloc That Failed: Soviet-East European Relations in Transition.* Bloomington: Indiana University Press, 1990.
Addresses Romania's position during the "Prague Spring" and its subsequent resistance to *perestroika* and *glasnost*. Discusses its precarious economic conditions in the 1980's and the overthrow of its repressive and corrupt regime by the 1989 revolution.

490. Gati, Charles, ed. *The International Politics of Eastern Europe.* New York: Praeger, 1976.
Discusses Romania within the framework of Eastern Europe. Questions if, in the post-1968 era, Eastern Europe is still an asset to the Soviet Union. Examines Western influence in, and its political objectives for, the region and the role of small states in the European system.

491. Ghermani, Dionisie. "Aussen- und Sicherheitspolitische Konzepte Rumäniens [Romanian Foreign and Security Policy Concepts]." In *Reform und Wandel in Südosteuropa*, edited by Roland Schönfeld, 61-72. Untersuchungen zur Gegenwartskunde Südosteuropas, 26. München: Oldenbourg, 1985.
The 1984 Congress of the Romanian Communist Party's report on security and foreign policy lacked any surprises. The time when Ceauşescu played an important role as mediator of international conflicts is long gone.

492. Ghermani, Dionisie. *Die Nationale Souveranitätspolitik der SR Rumänien. 1.Teil: Im Rahmen des Sowjetischen Bündnissystems [The National Sovereignty of the Romanian Socialist Republic. Part 1: Within the Framework of the Soviet Coalition System].* Untersuchungen zur Gegenwartskunde Südosteuropas, 17. München: Oldenbourg, 1981.
Describes the Romanian Communist Party from its beginnings in 1921 to 1981 and analyzes the theoretical foundations of its independence policy, its role as intermediary between Moscow and Peking, and its political, economic, and ethnic relations to socialist neighbors.

493. Ghermani, Dionisie. "Rumänien und die Deutsche Frage [Romania and the German Question]." In *Die Deutsche Frage und die Internationale Sicherheit*, edited by Günther Wagenlehner, 192-198. Koblenz: Bernard & Graefe, 1988.
Romania remains neutral on the question of German reunification, even though political, economic and, ideological interests influence its position toward East and West Germany.

494. Ghermani, Dionisie. "Rumänien und die Europäische Sicherheit [Romania and European Security]." *Zeitschrift für Politik* 20, no. 4 (1973): 375-400.
Study of Romania's independent stand during the preparations for the Conference on European Security and Cooperation (1966-1973).

495. Ghermani, Dionisie. "Rumäniens Problematische Beziehungen zum RGW [Romania's Problematic Relations to COMECON]." In *RGW-Integration und Südosteuropa*, edited by Roland Schönfeld, 143-161. Untersuchungen zur Gegenwartskunde Südosteuropas, 24. München: Oldenbourg, 1984.
With mounting economic problems, Romania's independence from the Soviet Union is increasing.

496. Ghermani, Dionisie. "Die Rumänische Aussenpolitik im Spannungsfeld von Autonomie und Blocktreue [The Romanian Foreign Policy Between Independence and Bloc Loyalty]." In *Südosteuropa in Weltpolitik und Weltwirtschaft der Achtziger Jahre*, edited by Roland Schönfeld, 65-74. Untersuchungen zur Gegenwartskunde Südosteuropas, 21. München: Oldenbourg, 1983.

As economic and political relations with the West deteriorate, Romania turns more and more to COMECON partners for support. Neither Western countries nor former Eastern allies are inclined to assist Romania. The end of the Ceauşescu era appears to be near.

497. Gill, Graeme J. "Rumania: Background to Autonomy." *Survey (London)* 21, no. 3 (1975): 94-113.
Romania's opposition to Soviet attempts to "excommunicate" the Chinese Communist Party or bring about a closer economic and military integration of bloc members was the cornerstone of its independence policy. With the 1970's economic decline, détente, and change in China's political position, Ceauşescu is forced to soften his stance on autonomy.

498. Gold, Jack. "Bessarabia: The Thorny 'Non-Existent' Problem." *East European Quarterly* 13, no. 1 (1979): 47-74.
Analyzes A. M. Lazarev's work claiming Moldavia as a territory historically belonging to the Soviet Union and condemning Romanian historians for their "nationalistic" orientations.

499. Gross, George. "Rumania: The Fruits of Autonomy." *Problems of Communism* 15, no. 1 (1966): 16-27.
Traces Romania's independent course under Gheorghiu-Dej and speculates that Ceauşescu will adopt and develop the policies of his predecessor.

500. Hacker, Jens. "Rumänien: Die Unschätzbaren Vorteile der Geographie [Romania: The Invaluable Advantages of Geography]." In *Der Ostblock: Entstehung, Entwicklung und Strucktur, 1939-1980*, 739-744. Baden-Baden: Nomos, 1983.
Identifies two determining factors in Romania's successful pursuit of independence: its geographic position (being surrounded by communist states is reassuring to the Soviets) and a popular leader at the right political time.

501. Haiducu, Matei Pavel. *J'ai Refusé de Tuer: Un Agent Secret Roumain Relève les Dessous de l'Affaire [I Refused to Kill: A Romanian Secret Agent Reveals the Details of the Incident]*. Paris: Plon, 1984.
Haiducu, who defected to the French authorities, recounts his mission to assassinate dissidents Goma and Tănase.

502. Harrington, Joseph F., and Bruce J. Courtney. "Romanian-American Relations During the Johnson Administration." *East European Quarterly* 22, no. 2 (1988): 213-232.
Describes President Johnson's policy of "building bridges" and the efforts that led to educational, scientific, and cultural accords and progress in trade initiatives between Romania and the U.S.

503. Harrington, Joseph F., and Bruce J. Courtney. *Tweaking the Nose of the Russians: Fifty Years of American-Romanian Relations, 1940-1990*. East European Monographs, 296. New York: Columbia University Press, 1991.
Following a historical review of Bucharest-Washington relations, chapters nine to twenty discuss Ceauşescu's Romania and its relations with the U.S., beginning with Nixon's visit, through the MFN-status debates in Congress, and ending with the demise of communism.

504. Hartl, Hans. "Rumänien: Nationale Autonomie und Innere Erstarrung [Romania: National Autonomy and Internal Ossification]." In *Der Sowjetblock Zwischen Vormachtkontrolle und Autonomie*, edited by Richard Löwenthal and Boris Meissner, 227-250. Köln: Markus, 1984.
Outlines Romanian history since World War II, with special emphasis on Gheorghiu-Dej's and Ceauşescu's quest for independence. In light of current economic difficulties, forcing Romania to turn to the Soviets for help, Hungary's quiet yet effective policies compare favorably to Ceauşescu's spectacular successes and even more dramatic failures.

505. Haupt, Georges. "La Genèse du Conflit Sovieto-Roumain [Genesis of the Soviet-Romanian Conflict]." *Revue Française de Science Politique* 18, no. 4 (1968): 669-684.
     Analyzes the origins of the dispute and questions if the Romanian quest for independence represents an isolated case or a step on the developmental path of all socialist countries.

506. Heiman, Leo. "Politics or Economics? Rumania's Trade Agreement with Israel." *East Europe* 17, no. 2 (1988): 9-13.
     The trade pact with Israel, bringing both political and economic benefits to Romania, is not without risk of increasing Soviet irritation.

507. Holtermann, Rudolf. "Rumäniens Neue Linie [Romania's New Direction]." *Der Europäische Osten* 13, no. 145 (1967): 205-211.
     Ceauşescu continues his predecessor's path towards independence. Romania's example may lead to better East-West relations.

508. Ionescu, Ghiţă. "Rumäniens Aussenpolitische Position [Romania's Foreign Policy Position]." *Europa Archiv* 24, no. 17 (1969): 609-618.
     Following Nixon's visit to Romania, reviews main themes of Romanian foreign policy rhetoric, and assesses its vulnerable position vis-à-vis the Soviet Union.

509. Jordan, Lloyd. "R & D in Bucharest." *Survey (London)*, no. 76 (Summer 1970): 122-136.
     In 1965/1967 Romania launched an ambitious program to develop and upgrade science and technology. Explores the political and economic reasons for Romania's all-out drive.

510. Kaplan, Robert D. "Ceauşescu Looks West But Acts East: Rumanian Gymnastics." *New Republic* 191, no. 25 (1984): 10-12.
     Romania seems to be individualistic in terms of foreign affairs, but, in fact, is increasingly connected to the Soviet Union. 1980's Romania is compared with 1930's Soviet Union, with massive construction occurring that has little long-term value and great human cost. Ceauşescu's regime is one of Eastern Europe's most nepotic and corrupt.

511. King, Robert R. "Autonomy and Détente: The Problems of Rumanian Foreign Policy." *Survey (London)* 20, no. 2-3 (1974): 105-120.
     Western and Chinese support for Romania's independence policy is weakening. It is uncertain if European détente will strengthen Romania's autonomy.

512. King, Robert R. "The Future of Romanian-Soviet Relations in the Post-Ceauşescu Era." In *East-Central Europe and the USSR*, edited by Richard F. Staar, 229-247. New York: St. Martin, 1991.
     Summarizes Romania's claim to autonomy from the Soviet Union and its policy of sovereignty and independence initiated by Gheorghiu-Dej and expanded by Ceauşescu. Outlines the country's relations with Moscow after the revolution with special emphasis on Bessarabia and Transylvania.

513. King, Robert R. "Romania and the Soviet Union: Toward a Rapprochement?" In *Eastern Europe's Uncertain Future: A Selection of Radio Free Europe Research Reports*, edited by Robert R. King and James F. Brown, 46-63. New York: Praeger, 1977.
     Outlines changes in Bucharest-Moscow relations since 1976, suggesting a reduction in friction.

514. King, Robert R. "Romania and the Third World." *Orbis* 21, no. 4 (1978): 875-892.
     Examines the political circumstances of the 1960's and beyond that permitted Romania to achieve a degree of independence from Moscow. Romania's strategy to develop closer relations to Third World countries was motivated by economic as

well as by political considerations. A decade later, however, its successes are limited due to fear of Soviet repercussions.

515. King, Robert R. "Romania's Struggle for an Autonomous Foreign Policy." *The World Today* 35, no. 8 (1979): 340-348.
Romanian leaders are sensitive to what the Soviet leadership will tolerate with regard to deviance in foreign policy issues. Romania does not challenge Soviet security interests. Predicts that the pattern of relative stability between the two countries will continue with periodic confrontations and reconciliations.

516. King, Robert R. "Rumania and the Sino-Soviet Conflict." *Studies in Comparative Communism* 5, no. 4 (1972): 373-393.
Discusses Romania's position towards Sino-Soviet differences and the effects of this policy on Romania's relationship with the Soviet Union. The strong Romanian-Chinese alliance has weakened of late, but the bond stems from a common perception of Soviet threat to their independence.

517. King, Robert R. "Rumania: The Difficulty of Maintaining an Autonomous Foreign Policy." In *East European Perspectives on European Security and Cooperation*, edited by Robert R. King and Robert W. Dean, 168-190. New York: Praeger, 1974.
The Romanian government considers the Conference on Security and Cooperation in Europe an opportunity to bolster its fight for independence and a means to increase international economic cooperation.

518. King, Robert R. "Rumänien und die Europäische Sicherheit [Romania and European Security]." *Europa Archiv* 27, no. 22 (1972): 775-784.
Discusses differences in positions adopted by a majority of Warsaw Pact countries on European security and those represented by Romania. A conference on European security may serve as a vehicle for Romania to reiterate its principles of sovereignty, equality, independence, and non-interference in internal affairs.

519. King, Robert R. "Verschärfter Disput um Bessarabien: Zur Auseinandersetzung Zwischen Rumänischen und Sowjetischen Historikern [Heightened Argument Over Bessarabia: Altercation Between Romanian and Soviet Historians]." *Osteuropa* 26, no. 12 (1976): 1079-1087.
In the Lazarev polemic over Bessarabia, the Romanian government uses nationalistic fervor to gain popularity and historical legitimacy. In its responses the Soviet Union reminds the Romanians that, in territorial questions, it remains judge and jury.

520. König, Helmut. "Drahtseilakt Ohne Netz: Rumäniens Standort in der Kommunistischen Weltbewegung [High Wire Routine without a Net: Romania's Place in the World Communist Movement]." *Osteuropa* 20, no. 2 (1970): 77-94.
Romania's independence rests on its loose military ties to the Warsaw Pact, an understanding with Tito and China, and cordial relations to capitalist countries. The country's uncertain future is defined by this unique foreign policy balancing act.

521. Kun, Joseph C. "Nordkorea - Das Rumänien des Fernen Ostens? [North Korea - Is it the Romania of East Asia?]." *Osteuropa* 17, no. 4 (1967): 259-263.
Focuses on similarities and differences between Bucharest's and Pyongyang's foreign policy.

522. Larrabee, F. Stephen. *The Challenge to Soviet Interests in Eastern Europe: Romania, Hungary, East Germany*. Rand Report, R-3190-AF. Santa Monica, CA: Rand, 1984.
In the chapter "Romania" (pp. 23-550) the author argues that economic difficulties compel Romania to turn more and more to Moscow for help. The country no longer represents a challenge to the USSR. Concludes that the status quo is likely to continue and that a change in leadership is unlikely.

523. Larrabee, F. Stephen. "Changing Russian Perspectives in the Balkans." *Survey (London)* 18, no. 3 (1972): 16-35.

Argues that the Soviet Union has historically regarded the Balkans as essential to its national interests. Reviews current relations and prospects of future developments with Romania, Bulgaria, and Yugoslavia.

524. Larrabee, F. Stephen. "Europäische Sicherheit und Sicherheitsprobleme auf dem Balkan [European Security and Problems of Security in the Balkans]." *Osteuropa* 24, no. 3 (1974): 167-179.
Better relations and regional cooperation reduces tensions in the Balkans and decreases chances of confrontation in Southeastern Europe. Superpowers are vitally interested in a stable Mediterranean region.

525. Larrabee, F. Stephen. "The Rumanian Challenge to Soviet Hegemony." *Orbis* 17, no. 1 (1973): 227-246.
Describes four evolutionary phases of the challenge. Romania never suffered punitive retaliation due to its precise sense of "permissible deviation."

526. Laux, Jeanne Kirk. "Intra-Alliance Politics and European Détente: The Case of Poland and Romania." *Studies in Comparative Communism* 8, no. 1/2 (1975): 98-122.
Uses content analysis of speeches by heads of the Party and government in Poland and Romania to identify how significant changes in the external environment are reflected in the official foreign policy doctrine at home.

527. Laux, Jeanne Kirk. "The Limits of Autonomy: Romania in the 1980's." In *East European Economic Assessment. Part 2 - Regional Assessments,* submitted to U.S. Congress, Joint Economic Committee, 107-127. Washington, D.C.: U.S. G.P.O., 1981. Committee Print. Y4.Ec7:Eu7/9/pt.2.
Discusses Romania's participation in Warsaw Pact activities, its diplomatic initiatives, its economic strategy within and outside CMEA, and interprets its foreign economic policy as "less deviant" than in the past.

528. Laux, Jeanne Kirk. "Socialism, Nationalism, and Underdevelopment: Research on Romanian Foreign Policy Making." In *Foreign Policy Making in Communist Countries: A Comparative Approach,* edited by Hannes Adomeit and Robert Boardman, 49-78. New York: Praeger, 1979.
Reviews Romania's divergent foreign policy and its change from "militant nationalism" in 1966-1969, to "selective cooperation" in 1970-1971.

529. Lee, Sookja. "A Comparative Study of Eastern European States' Foreign Policies with the USSR: The Albanian, Romanian, and Yugoslav Cases." Ph.D. diss., University of South Carolina, 1982. Ann Arbor: UMI, 1982. AAD8220208.
Describes and compares contributing factors, e.g. political leadership, foreign trade, foreign aid, in achieving and sustaining autonomy.

530. Lepage, Françoise Odette. "Romanian Perspectives on the International System During the Ceauşescu Era." Ph.D. diss., The Catholic University of America, 1979. Ann Arbor: UMI, 1979. AAD79-20558.
Examines foreign policy decisions to determine if these were based on a coherent theory of international relations or were simply reactions to evolving events.

531. Levesque, Jacques. *Le Conflit Sino-Soviétique et l'Europe de l'Est: Ses Incidences sur les Conflits Soviéto-Polonais et Soviéto-Roumain [The China-Soviet Conflict and Eastern Europe: Its Impact on the Soviet-Polish and Soviet-Romanian Conflicts].* Montréal: Presses de l'Université de Montréal, 1970.
Discusses the effects of the Sino-Soviet conflict on Soviet-Polish relations between 1956 and 1959 and on Soviet-Romanian relations between 1960 and 1968 (p. 97-190). Includes a brief biographical sketch of political leaders, including one on Ceauşescu (p. 290-292).

532. Lhomel, Edith. "Gorbatchev Face au Cas Roumain [Gorbachev Faces the Romanian Problem]." *Temps Modernes* 45, no. 522 (1990): 83-95.

The current economic rapprochement with the Soviet Union may lead to changes despite Ceauşescu's resistance to reforms.

533. Library of Congress. Foreign Affairs and National Defense Division. *U.S. Relations with the Countries of Central and Eastern Europe: Report prepared for the Sub-committee on Europe and the Middle East of the Committee on Foreign Affairs, U.S. House of Representatives....* Washington: U.S. G.P.O., 1979. Committee Print. Y4.F 76/1:R 27/4.
Notes (in the Romanian section, pp. 73-80) that Romania has developed the broadest and most diversified ties with the United States among Warsaw Pact member countries and has received preferential trade treatment. Discusses the current status of Romanian trade, emigration, political, foreign, and economic policies.

534. Linden, Ronald H. *Bear and Foxes: The International Relations of the East European States, 1965-1969.* East European Monographs, 50. New York: Columbia University Press, 1979.
Chapter five, "Focus on Romania" (pp. 177-203), analyzes factors enabling and stimulating Romania's deviance from Soviet foreign policy norms.

535. Linden, Ronald H. "Romanian Foreign Policy in the 1980's: Domestic-Foreign Policy Linkages." In *Foreign and Domestic Policy in Eastern Europe in the 1980's: Trends and Prospects*, edited by Michael J. Sodaro and Sharon L. Wolchik, 47-80. New York: St.Martin's Press, 1983.
Examines factors responsible for Romania's deviant foreign policy and questions if the same direction could be sustained in the 1980's. Describes the changing economic and political scene and suggests scenarios for the future.

536. Lindner, Robert. "Rumänien 1973 (I-II.): Stationen der Lateinamerika-Reise Ceauşescus [Romania 1973 (I-II): Ceauşescu's Trip to Latin America]." *Osteuropa* 25 (1975): 879-887, 949-952.
Two part article describing Ceauşescu's visits to other countries and summarizing other events of the year in foreign affairs.

537. Madsen, Mark Hunter. "The Uses of Beijingpolitik: China in Romanian Foreign Policy Since 1953." *East European Quarterly* 16, no. 3 (1982): 277-309.
Studies Romania's efforts for greater political autonomy vis-à-vis the Soviet Union in the light of its policy towards China. Beginning in 1953, five historical phases in the Sino-Romanian relations are examined. Over three decades, the stable link forged between Bucharest and Beijing has served the interests of both regimes.

538. Manea, Ion. "The Romanian Communists on Bassarabia." In *The Tragic Plight of a Border Area: Bassarabia and Bucovina*, edited by Maria Manea-Manoliu, 113-129. American Romanian Academy of Arts and Science Publication, 3. Los Angeles: A.R.A., 1983.
Studies Romanian policy towards Bessarabia with particular emphasis on the time 1964-1976.

539. McGovern, George S. *Perspectives on Détente, Austria, Romania, and Czechoslovakia: A Report to the Committee on Foreign Affairs, United States Senate.* Washington: U.S. G.P.O., 1979. Committee Print. Y4.F76/2:N81 a/7.
Reports on a 1978 trip to Romania. Notes progress in U.S.-Romanian relations since President Nixon's visit (1969), the increased level of trade since granting MFN status, and increased official contacts from cultural and educational exchanges. Describes meetings with political leaders on issues relating to the Middle East and East-West détente.

540. Oschlies, Wolf. "Die Deutsch-Rumänische Wechselseitigkeit: Zum 30. Nationalfeiertag Rumäniens [German-Romanian Cooperation: On the Thirtieth National Anniversary of Romania]." *Deutschland-Archiv* 7, no. 9 (1974): 938-946.
Ceauşescu's policies are based on the belief that what is good for Romania is good

for socialism. Friendly relations and economic collaboration with West Germany benefit the country and thus the regime.

541. Oschlies, Wolf. "Die Deutschen in Rumänien und die DDR [The Germans in Romania and the German Democratic Republic]." *Deutschland-Archiv* 21 (May 1988): 533-535.
Since 1967, when Romania adopted an independent external policy, East Berlin has forgotten the very existence of their ethnic brothers living in Transylvania.

542. Oschlies, Wolf. "Rumänien Zwischen Helsinki und Belgrad [Romania Between Helsinki and Belgrade]." Berichte, 45. Köln: Bundesinstitut für Ostwissenschaftliche und Internationale Studien, 1977.
Discusses Romania's disappointment with the outcome of the 1975 Conference on Security and Cooperation in Europe and its hopes for better results at the follow-up conference in Belgrade.

543. Pacepa, Ion Mihai, and Michael Ledeen. "Romania Reaps Rewards of High-Tech Thefts." *Human Events* 45, no. 11 (16 March 1985): 12-13+.
The Securitate is engaged in technological espionage and covert operations. These activities are meant to reduce dependency on western imports and improve hard currency income.

544. Paul, David W. "Romania's Special Diplomatic Position: A Case Study of China's Role." *East European Quarterly* 7, no. 3 (1973): 311-329.
Ceauşescu has skillfully used the Sino-Soviet conflict to his advantage. His ingenious diplomatic maneuvers have earned Romania a degree of independence from the Soviet Union. China has supported Ceauşescu's policy of relative independence.

545. Radu, Michael. "Romania and the Third World: The Dilemmas of a 'Free Rider'." In *Eastern Europe and the Third World: East vs. South*, edited by Michael Radu, 235-272. New York: Praeger, 1981.
Discusses the historical and ideological background of Romania's economic and political ties to developing countries and the constraints and opportunities that this alliance represents for the country's continued independent foreign policy.

546. Rafael, Edgar R. *'Entwicklungsland' Rumänien: Zur Geschichte der 'Umdefinierung' eines Sozialistischen Staates [Romania - 'a Developing Country': On the History of 'Relabeling' a Socialist State]*. Untersuchungen zur Gegenwartskunde Südosteuropas, 12. München: Oldenbourg, 1977.
Profiles diplomatic initiatives and ideological arguments that secured Romania a membership in the "Group of 77" and thus a place among developing countries.

547. Ratiu, Ion. *Contemporary Romania: Her Place in World Affairs*. Richmond, England: Foreign Affairs Publishing, 1975.
Historical account on the ascension of communism, Gheorghiu-Dej and the COMECON confrontation, life under Ceauşescu, nationalism, the cult of personality, and the quest for internal and external legitimacy.

548. Remington, Robin Alison. "Romania: Boundary Disintegration Between East and South." In *The Soviet Bloc and the Third World: The Political Economy of East-South Relations*, edited by Brigitte H. Schultz and William W. Hansen, 197-211. Boulder: Westview, 1989.
Romania's involvement in the Third World has brought political benefits while creating trade imbalances. Predicts that Ceauşescu will maintain the same course of action.

549. Remington, Robin Alison. *The Warsaw Pact: Case Studies in Communist Conflict Resolution*. Cambridge: MIT Press, 1971.
Chapter four, "Rumania: A Case for Containment" (pp. 56-93), traces Soviet-Romanian differences over economic and foreign policy issues from 1956 to the beginning of the 1970's, a time of normalization of relations.

550. Schaefer, Henry Wilcox. *COMECON and the Politics of Integration.* New York: Praeger, 1972.
     Presents a review of COMECON activities (with ample references to Romania's intra-bloc relations) from the invasion of Czechoslovakia to the adoption of the economic integration program (1968-1971). Notes that Romania, while subscribing to integration, continues to reject supranationalism.

551. Schlegel, Dietrich. "Rumänische Positionen gegenüber Moskau [Romanian Positions towards Moscow]." *Aussenpolitik* 22, no. 9 (1971): 541-552.
     Backed by the Chinese, Ceaușescu continues his independent course while maintaining a firm grip on domestic matters. This way he hopes to avoid repercussions from Moscow.

552. Schönfeld, Roland. "Rumäniens Eigenwillige Politik [Romania's Independent Policies]." *Europa Archiv* 42, no. 18 (1987): 523-532.
     A review of Romania's international relations and economic development. Faced with enormous political pressure, economic difficulties, and criticism on violations of minority rights, Ceaușescu has intensified internal oppression and has taken steps to consolidate his power.

553. Schultz, Lothar. "Der Neue Vertrag Zwischen Rumänien und der Sowjetunion [The New Treaty Between Romania and the Soviet Union]." *Osteuropa* 20, no. 12 (1970): 831-838.
     While the new Soviet-Romanian Friendship Treaty reflects Romania's independent position, an increase in trade with the Soviet Union announced immediately after signing the document signals Romania's willingness to continue its balancing act between East and West.

554. Schweisfurth, Theodor. "Der Freundschaftsvertrag DDR-Rumänien vom 12. Mai 1972 [The Friendship Treaty between GDR and Romania, May 12, 1972]." *Aussenpolitik* 23, no. 8 (1972): 469-479.
     Among Warsaw Pact countries, Romania and East Germany were the last states to sign a treaty of friendship, cooperation, and mutual assistance. Focuses on the treaty sections dealing with international relations and the concept of socialist internationalsm.

555. Shafir, Michael. *Rumanian Policy in the Middle East, 1962-1972.* Research Paper, 7. Jerusalem: Hebrew University of Jerusalem, Soviet and East European Center, April 1974.

556. Simon, Jeffrey. *Cohesion and Dissension in Eastern Europe: Six Crises.* New York: Praeger, 1983.
     Looks at the political reliability of non-Soviet Warsaw Pact countries (with special references to Romania) during various international crises, e.g.: Middle East wars (1967, 1973), Czechoslovakia (1968), Ussuri (1969), and Sadat's visit to Israel (1977).

557. Socianu, Horia. "The Foreign Policies of Rumania in the Thirties and Sixties." Ph.D. diss., George Washington University, 1971. Ann Arbor: UMI, 1971. AAD7127994.
     A two part study of pre- and post-World War II Romanian foreign policy. Part two focuses on the circumstances that allowed for Gheorghiu-Dej's independent foreign policy course and its continuation by Ceaușescu.

558. Socianu, Horia. "The Foreign Policy of Romania in the Sixties." In *The Foreign Policies of Eastern Europe: Domestic and International Determinants*, edited by James A. Kuhlman, 167-189. East-West Perspectives, 4. Leyden: Sijthoff, 1978.
     Analyzes Gheorghiu-Dej's and Ceaușescu's foreign policy course and looks at Soviet tolerance towards Romania's disengagement from the communist bloc.

559. Socor, Vladimir. "The Limits of National Independence in the Soviet Bloc: Rumania's Foreign Policy Reconsidered." *Orbis* 20, no. 3 (1976): 701-732.

Examines the Romanian-Soviet state relations, the Moscow-Bucharest-Peking diplomacy, Romania's position in COMECON and in the Warsaw Pact, its overtures to the West, and finally Romania's contribution to the Soviet campaign for European security. Concludes that Romania's operations have not diverged from Soviet policies. Soviet permissiveness points to "an enlightened comprehension by each side of the advantages to be drawn from such a course" (p. 731).

560. Ströhm, Carl Gustaf. "Der Rumänische Weg [The Romanian Path]." *Der Europäische Osten* 12, no. 141 (1966): 682-687.
Romania resists Soviet attempts to exploit her and embarks on a nationalistic path. A new economic and political partnership with Bonn is emerging.

561. Suga, Alexander. "Die Europäische Sicherheit aus der Sicht der Sozialistischen Republik Rumänien [European Security from the Perspective of the Socialist Republic of Romania]." *Internationales Recht und Diplomatie* (1975/76): 73-91.
Romania is strongly supporting the position of other socialist states and is pressing for the recognition of existing borders and for U.N. representation for both German states.

562. Summerscale, Peter. *The East European Predicament: Changing Patterns in Poland, Czechoslovakia and Romania.* Hants, England: Gower, 1982.
Reviews economic and political developments since World War II and studies benefits and costs of overtures to the West in the mid-1950's, problems in handling competing East-West pulls in the 1970's and 1980's, and internal and external factors of influence in the post-Brezhnev era.

563. Timmermann, Heinz. "'Neue Enheit' im Weltkommunismus? Zur Interessenallianz zwischen Rumänischen und Westeuropäischen Kommunisten ['New Unity' in World Communism? On Common Interests Uniting Communists in Romania and Western Europe]." *Osteuropa* 22, no. 3 (1972): 533-544.
Looks at Romania's role as middleman and discusses reasons bringing together communists in East and West. Considers the impact of such an alliance on future interparty relations.

564. "A Turning Point in United States-Romanian Relations: Round-Table." *Journal of the Romanian-American Academy of Arts and Sciences* 12 (1989): 29-62.
M. Botez, D. B. Funderburk, N. Ratesh and L. K. D. Kristof discuss bilateral relations in light of the rescission of the MFN status for Romania.

565. U.S. Congress. House. Committee on Foreign Affairs. Subcommittee on Europe and the Middle East. *U.S. Policy Toward Eastern Europe, 1985: Hearings.... October 2 and 7, 1985.* Washington: U.S. G.P.O., 1986. House Hearing. Y4.F76/1:Un35/77.
Rozanne L. Ridgway, Bureau of European and Canadian Affairs, presents a statement dealing with policy choices for the United States. Emigration policies and the MFN status, Romanian harassment of Hungarian nationals, its international debt situation, and former Ambassador Funderburk's criticism of U.S. policy towards Romania are discussed. Supplemental questions focus on U.S. foreign policy in light of Romania's Stalinist internal policies, on economic prospects, and the Ceauşescu cult of personality.

566. Uschakow, Alexander. "Die Neuen Bundnisverträge der Sowjetunion mit der Tschechoslowakei und Rumänien [The New Treaties for Cooperation between the Soviet Union and Czechoslovakia and Romania]." *Europa Archiv* 25, no. 21 (1970): 791-800.
Discusses the 1970 bilateral treaties pledging friendship, cooperation, and mutual support signed under Soviet pressure in the aftermath of the Warsaw Pact invasion of Czechoslovakia.

567. Weiner, Robert. "Albanian and Romanian Deviance in the United Nations." *East European Quarterly* 7, no. 1 (1973): 65-90.

Study of polycentric tendencies adopted by Albania and Romania with regard to arms control, peace keeping, the Middle East, colonialism, economics, and international law.

568. Weiner, Robert. "Romania and the United Nations." *Balkanistica* 5 (1979): 140-168. Studies Romanian foreign policy at the U.N. from 1955 to 1977.

569. Weiner, Robert. *Romanian Foreign Policy and the United Nations.* New York: Praeger, 1984.
Contents: "Domestic and External Sources of Romanian Foreign Policy," "Romania and International Organization," "Evolution of Romanian Foreign Policy at the United Nations," "Arms Control, Disarmament, and Peacekeeping," "Europe," "The New International Economic Order," "The Middle East, Africa, and Decolonization," "The Special Agencies," "International Law."

570. Weiner, Robert. "The U.S. Policy of Differentiation Toward Romania." In *The United States and Romania: American-Romanian Relations in the Twentieth Century*, edited by Paul D. Quinlan, 129-146. American-Romanian Academy of Arts and Sciences, 6. Woodland Hills, CA: ARA, 1988.
Until the 1980's, U.S. policy towards Romania was designed to reward its independent path. However, in light of the Bucharest-Moscow rapprochement of the mid 1980's, this policy needs to be revisited.

571. Wolton, Thierry. *Le KGB en France [The KGB in France].* Paris: B. Grasset, 1986. Describes Romanian espionage activities (pp. 159-182 and 384-400).

572. Zimmerman, William. "Soviet Relations with Yugoslavia and Romania." In *Soviet Policy in Eastern Europe*, edited by Sarah Meiklejohn Terry, 125-154. New Haven: Yale University Press, 1984.
Explores the origins of Romania's autonomy, its military and economic position, and the political and ideological challenge it represents to the Soviet Union. Discusses future Soviet options towards Romania.

12. Geography

573. Balzer, Michael, and Bernd Weltin. "Räumliche Disparitäten und die Entwicklung des Siedlungsgefüges in Mittel- und Südosteuropäischen Sozialistischen Staaten seit 1970: Ein Beitrag zur Aktuellen Siedlungs- und Stadtgeographischen Entwicklungstendenzen in der DDR, Polen, der ČSSR, Ungarn, Rumänien und Bulgarien [Spatial Disparities and the Development of the Settlement System in Socialist Countries of Middle Europe and Southeastern Europe Since 1970: Some Remarks About Recent Settlement and Urban Geographical Tendencies in the GDR, Poland, Czechoslovakia, Hungary, Romania, and Bulgaria]." *Geographische Zeitschrift* 70, no. 1 (1982): 35-55.
Eastern Europe exhibits tendencies of urban concentration due to population flight towards industrialized cities. In less developed socialist countries, such as Romania and Poland, strident new regional disparities come into existence.

574. Bethlemont, Jacques. "Le Delta du Danube et son Intégration dans l'Éspace Économique Roumain [The Danube Delta and its Integration into Romanian Economy]." *Revue de Géographie de Lyon* 50, no. 1 (1975): 77-95.
The longest delta in Europe has a rich ecosystem whose balance is threatened by clumsy attempts to harvest its reed.

575. Blanc, André. *L'Europe Socialiste [Socialist Europe]*. Paris: Presses Universitaires de France, 1974.
Studies the geographical characteristics of Eastern European countries with ample references to Romania.

576. Helin, Ronald A. "The Volatile Administrative Map of Rumania." *Annals of the Association of American Geographers* 57, no. 3 (1967): 481-502.
Presents seven major changes in the administrative division of Romania since World War II and argues that communist governments use such changes for political purposes.

577. Heller, Wilfried. "Bevölkerungsgeographische Betrachtungen Rumäniens: Seit dem 2. Weltkrieg [Demographic-Geographical Observations on Romania: Since World War II]." In *Hans Graul-Festschrift*, edited by Horst Eichler and Heinz Musall, 467-488. Heidelberger Geographische Arbeiten, 40. Heidelberg: Geographisches Institut der Universität Heidelberg, 1974.
Demographic growth, age distribution, economic and educational achievement illustrate the socioeconomic development of the country in general and selected regions in particular.

578. Heller, Wilfried. "Räumliche Bevölkerungsentwicklung in Griechenland und Rumänien [Spatial Population Changes in Greece and Romania]." *Erdkunde* 29 (1975): 300-314.

Comparative study of population growth, settlement patterns and regional disparities.

579. Heller, Wilfried. *Regionale Dispäritaten und Urbanisierung in Griechenland und Rumänien: Aspekte eines Vergleichs Ihrer Formen und Entwicklung in Zwei Ländern Unterschiedlicher Gesellschaft- und Wirtschaftsordnung seit dem Ende des 2. Weltkrieges [Regional Disparities and Urbanization in Greece and Romania: Comparative Aspects of Form and Development Since World War II in Two Countries of Different Social and Economic Organization].* Göttinger Geographische Abhandlungen, 74. Göttingen: Erich Goltze, 1979.
     Comparative analysis of agricultural development and of regional economic and social characteristics as indicators of urbanization in the the regions of Argeș, Brașov, and Ilfov in general, and in the rural settlements of Rociu and Suseni in particular.

580. Kosinski, Leszek Antoni. "Geography of Population and Settlements in East-Central Europe." *Annals of the Association of American Geographers* 61 (September 1971): 599-615.
     Review article describing institutional organization, scholarly output, and topics of research in Eastern Europe, including Romania.

581. Matley, Ian M. "The Human Geography of the Western Mountains of Romania." *Scottish Geographical Magazine* 87 (1971): 116-127.
     Description of physical features, settlement, and economy of the Western Mountain region of Transylvania. Planners need to stimulate industrial growth and create a modern infrastructure. Economic subsidies may be the only way to prevent depopulation and land abandonment.

582. Mellor, Roy E. H. *Eastern Europe: A Geography of the COMECON Countries.* London: Macmillan, 1975.
     Presents the historical, demographic and economic framework of countries in East-Central Europe and offers a sketch of national economic geography for developed (GDR, Poland, Czechoslovakia, Hungary) and developing (Romania, Albania, Yugoslavia, Bulgaria) countries.

583. Poncet, Jean. "Les Enseignements des Inondations Catastrophiques du Printemps 1970 en Roumanie [Lessons from the Disastrous Floods of Spring 1970 in Romania]." *Annales de Géographie* 81, no. 445 (1972): 298-315.
     Contends that Romania has succeeded in articulating a complex, long-range program to prevent future environmental disasters.

584. Rey, Violette. "Organisation Régionale et Structure Urbaine de la Roumanie, d'après la Litérature Géographique Roumaine Récente [Regional Organization and Urban Structure in Romania, as Reflected in Recent Romanian Geography Literature]." *Annales de Géographie* 81, no. 448 (1972): 711-729.
     Describes the organization of five major regions and outlines recent research on spatial and economic interrelations.

585. Turnock, David. *The Human Geography of the Romanian Carpathians with Fieldwork Case Studies, 1977.* Geographical Field Group Studies, 22. Nottingham, England: Geographical Field Group, 1980.
     An examination of settlement patterns and economic development of the Carpathian region with special field work case studies in selected urban and rural areas.

13. Government, Politics & Domestic Affairs

586. Almond, Mark. *Decline Without Fall: Romania under Ceauşescu.* European Security Studies, 6. London: Institute for European Defence & Strategic Studies, 1988. Shows the grim results of two decades of Ceauşescu's policies and accuses Western governments of indifference and duplicity in dealing with Romania.

587. Bacon, Walter M., Jr. "Romanian Secret Police." In *Terror and Communist Politics: The Role of the Secret Police in Communist States*, edited by Jonathan R. Adelman, 135-154. Boulder: Westview, 1984. Reviews institutions of repression in pre-communist Romania. After 1945, describes Stalinist purges, the decline of institutionalized terror under Gheorghiu-Dej, and the emergence of the Securitate.

588. Beck, Carl. "Career Characteristics of East European Leadership." In *Political Leadership in Eastern Europe and the Soviet Union*, edited by R. Barry Farrell, 157-194. Chicago: Aldine, 1970. Studies communist leadership in East Europe, including Romania, from the establishment of revolutionary regimes, in 1945, to the "post-New Course" period, extending in Romania to the beginning of the Ceauşescu era.

589. Brown, J. F. "Rumania Today: I. Towards 'Integration'." *Problems of Communism* 18, no. 1 (1969): 8-17. Overview of the first four years of domestic policy under Ceauşescu.

590. Burakow, Nicholas. "Romania and Greece: Socialism vs. Capitalism." *World Development* 9, no. 9-10 (1981): 907-928. Analyzes Romania's development under socialism and compares and contrasts it with Greece under capitalism, using as criteria development strategy, economic performance, basic human needs, and human rights.

591. Caranfil, Adrian C. *Umweltschutz in Rumänien [Environmental Protection in Romania].* Berichte, 58. Köln: Bundesinstitut für Ostwissenschaftliche und Internationale Studien, 1973. Discusses water, air, ground, and noise pollution, coverage of pollution issues in professional and popular media, and measures for environmental protection.

592. Cazacu, Matei. "Quelle 'Voie Roumaine' Vers le Communisme? [What is the "Romanian Path" Toward Communism?]." *Esprit* 147 (February 1989): 15-18. Discusses how a country rich in natural resoures could be reduced to poverty and despair in only four decades.

593. Chirot, Daniel. "Romania: Ceauşescu's Last Folly." *Dissent (New York)* 35 (June 1988): 271-275.

Ceaușescu reigns despotically over a capital in ruins, economic chaos, social dysfunction, and increased dependency on the Soviet Union.

594. Chirot, Daniel. "Social Change in Communist Romania." *Social Forces* 57, no. 2 (1978): 457-499.
Compares the regime's economic achievements with those of other European countries. Analyzes the methods by which communist rule was established in Romania and how it maintains its grip on Romanian society. Concludes that communist rule has not "saved" Romania from economic disaster.

595. Cismarescu, Michael. "Zum Rumänischen Parteitag [About the Romanian Party Congress]." *Ost-Probleme* 17, no. 16 (1965): 501-505.
While still a communist state, the drafts of Romania's Party statute and that of its constitution indicate that it is committed to distancing itself from the Soviet Union.

596. Colas, Anne. "Une Situation Explosive [An Explosive Situation]." *L'Alternative (Paris)* 14 (January/February 1982): 27-37.
Describes the grave economic, social, and political crisis of the 1980's.

597. Crowther, William E. "The Political Economy of Romanian Socialism." Ph.D. diss., University of California, Los Angeles, 1986. Ann Arbor: UMI, 1986. Order No.:DA862 1050.
Revision published under the same title. New York: Praeger, 1988.
Analyzes the nature of political life in state-socialist political systems.

598. Dawisha, Karen. *Eastern Europe, Gorbachev, and Reform: The Great Challenge.* Cambridge: Cambridge University Press, 1988.
"The Case of Romania" (pp.147-148) discusses the country's energy crisis and foreign debt burden in the 1980's. "Romania: Defiant Ally in Decline" (pp.170-173) narrates Ceaușescu's reluctance to introduce reform.

599. Dima, Nicholas. "Communist Romania: A Model of Social Decay." *Military Intelligence* 13, no. 3 (1987): 22-25.
Profiles developments since World War II and contends that the current socio-political and economic crisis threatens the very core of communist ideology.

600. Durandin, Catherine, and Despina Tomescu. *La Roumanie de Ceaușescu: Essai [Ceaușescu's Romania: Essay].* [Saint-Ouen]: Guy Epaud, 1988.
Essays dealing with aspects of economics, social life, and politics.

601. Dziewanowski, M. K. "The Changing Scene in Rumania." *East Europe* 2 (1917): 15-18.
Changes in higher education, opening of cultural exchanges with the West, efforts to preserve the historical heritage, are some of the ways in which Romania is pursuing the process of "de-satellization." These radical departures from past policies are counter-balanced by cautious ideological maneuvering.

602. Eyal, Jonathan. "Romania: A Hermit Under Pressure." *The World Today* 45, no. 5 (1989): 85-90.
Offers a brief historical overview of the communist regime and its search for legitimacy. Describes the economic and political decline of the last two decades, and mounting opposition from within the Party. Concludes that Romania's best hope is Ceaușescu's demise.

603. Farlow, Robert L. "Romania: Problems of Independence and Development." In *East Central Europe: Yesterday - Today - Tomorrow*, edited by Milorad M. Drachkovitch, 327-348. Hoover Press Publication, 240. Stanford, CA: Hoover Institution Press, 1982.
At the beginning of the 1980's, domestic affairs reflect Ceaușescu's personality cult, nationalism, and emerging dissent. On the economic front, industrialization retains

its dominant role, although growth rates are being scaled down. In foreign relations, Romania continues its independence policy.

604. Farlow, Robert L. "Romania: The Politics of Autonomy." *Current History* 74, no. 436 (1978): 168-171+.
Romania presents a paradox: one of the most restrictive communist states, yet among the most nationalistic. Impressive industrial growth exists alongside dismal living standards. A seemingly autonomous foreign policy is counteracted by adherence to Soviet bloc organizations. Reviews Romania's overtures to the West and notes the growing dissident movement and discontent within the country.

605. Fejtö, François. "Socialisme et Nationalisme dans les Démocraties Populaires (1971-1978) [Socialism and Nationalism in the Peoples' Democracies, 1971-1978]." *Défense Nationale* 34, no. 8 (1978): 21-56.
Contends that the dynamics of social change work against the rigid systems of communist states. Gives examples of social unrest in Romania.

606. Fejtö, François, and Georges Mink. "Roumanie 1965-1980: 15 Ans de 'Ceauşescisme' [Romania 1965-1980: 15 Years of "Ceauşescuism"]." *Notes et Études Documentaires* 4587-4588 (10 October 1980): 55-75.
Discusses the Ceauşescu era in terms of domestic and foreign policy.

607. Fischer, Gabriel. "Romania." In *The Communist States in the Era of Détente: 1971-1977*, edited by Adam Bromke and Derry Novak, 141-159. Oakville, Ontario: Mosaic, [1978].
Discusses Ceauşescu's internal and external political maneuvers.

608. Fischer, Gabriel. "Rumania." In *The Communist States in Disarray, 1965-1971*, edited by Adam Bromke and Teresa Rakowska-Harmstone, 158-179. Minneapolis: University of Minnesota Press, 1972.
Details events from the transition of power of Gheorghiu-Dej to Ceauşescu and analyzes Ceauşescu's leadership style. Despite paradoxical elements in its development course, Romania's unique brand of socialism may survive and succeed.

609. Fischer, Mary Ellen. "Participatory Reforms and Political Development in Romania." In *Political Development in Eastern Europe*, edited by Jan F. Triska and Paul M. Cocks, 217-237. New York: Praeger, 1977.
Describes the political reforms of 1965 and the first multi-candidate elections of March 1975 as examples of Ceauşescu's strategies to consolidate his power over the Romanian Communist Party.

610. Fischer, Mary Ellen. "Political Leadership and Personnel Policy in Romania: Continuity and Change, 1965-1976." In *World Communism at the Crossroads: Military Ascendancy, Political Economy, and Human Welfare*, edited by Steven Rosefielde, 210-233. Boston: Nijhoff, 1980.
Compares members of the Ceauşescu and Gheorghiu-Dej elite circles and probes into patterns of personnel changes that enabled Ceauşescu to grasp and consolidate control.

611. Fischer, Mary Ellen. "Political Leadership in Rumania under Communists." *International Journal of Rumanian Studies* 5, no. 1 (1987): 7-31.
Analyzes features of continuity and contrast in political leadership by using Gheorghiu-Dej, Ceauşescu, and pre-communist rulers as examples.

612. Fischer, Mary Ellen. "Politics, Nationalism, and Development in Romania." In *Diverse Paths to Modernity in Southeastern Europe: Essays in National Development*, edited by Gerasimos Augustinos, 135-168. Contributions to the Study of World History, 20. New York: Greenwood, 1991.
Briefly reviews the economic, social, and political history of Romania with empha-

sis on 1965-1990 and assesses the country's chances to create a democratic political system in the post-Ceaușescu era.

613. Fischer, Mary Ellen. "Romania: The 1990s, Or, After Ceaușescu What?" In *United States-East European Relations in the 1990's*, edited by Richard F. Staar, 173-192. New York: Crane Russak, 1989.
An overview of Romania under Ceaușescu is followed by several scenarios for a post-Ceaușescu succession.

614. Fischer, Mary Ellen. "The Romanian Communist Party and its Central Committee: Patterns of Growth and Change." *Southeastern Europe* 6, part 1 (1979): 1-28.
Presents the nature, size, and makeup of the Party and its Central Committee. The Party faces a dilemma: by encouraging popular participation it allows input into policy making, while a return to centralized control could result in diminished cooperation in ambitious economic plans.

615. Fischer-Galați, Stephen. *The New Rumania: From People's Democracy to Socialist Republic*. Cambridge: M.I.T. Press, 1967.
Reviews the evolution of communist rule and the 1960-1964 road to independence, and discusses Gheorghiu-Dej's legacy of "destalinization" at the beginning of the Ceaușescu regime.

616. Fischer-Galați, Stephen. "Rumänien [Romania]." In *Die Kommunistischen Parteien der Welt*, edited by C. D. Kernig, 432-446. Freiburg: Herder, 1969.
Recaps the history of the Romanian Communist Party from its beginnings through the period of Soviet subordination and its search for independence. Describes Ceaușescu's rise to power, the role and function of mass organizations and of the press, and Romania's position in the international communist movement.

617. Fischer-Galați, Stephen. *The Socialist Republic of Rumania*. Baltimore: Johns Hopkins Press, 1969.
Historical treatment of Romania's integration into the communist party states. The last chapter deals with the Ceaușescu era, Romania's "independent course," and projections for the future.

618. Fisher, William. "Fighting Change: Romania in the Age of Glasnost." *New Leader* 70 (29 June 1987): 11-13.
Romania has become an ideological embarassment for Gorbachev's reform programs.

619. Florescu, Radu R. "Ceaușeschism: Rumania's Road to Communism." *Current History* 64, no. 38 (1973): 212-215+.
Based upon Ceaușescu's speeches. Contends that the unquestioning trust in the Romanian leadership can be attributed to its fair policy towards national minorities, its historical and territorial vision, its attempt to open a dialogue between Party and people. Equality of opportunity, austerity, and a spirit of "socialist puritanism" permeates all levels of Romanian society. Describes Romania's cultural gains, its "miraculous" postwar economic recovery, and its foreign policy. Concludes that Romania's unique approach to communism deserves the coinage of a new expression: Ceaușeschism.

620. Gabanyi, Anneli Ute. "Romanian Pensioners Barred from Moving to Population Centers." *Survey (London)* 29, no. 4 (1987): 114-116.
Commentary on Ceaușescu's 1985 speech to the Third Congress of the People's Council.

621. Gabanyi, Anneli Ute. "Rumänien im Zeichen von Perestrojka und Glasnost: Von der Scheinreform zur Gegenreform [Romania under the Sign of Perestroika and Glasnost: From Illusory Reform to Counter Reform]." *Osteuropa* 39, no. 8 (1989): 746-759.
Differences between Soviet reform policies and Ceaușescu's struggle to maintain

control became evident during Gorbachev's visit to Romania in May 1987. The Soviet Union insisted on international responsibility, while Romania re-emphasized its right to an independent national policy and reiterated its oppostion to any attempt to import reforms.

622. Gabanyi, Anneli Ute. "Rumänien und Gorbatschow [Romania and Gorbachev]." In *Südosteuropa in der Ära Gorbatschow: Auswirkungen der Sowjetischen Reformpolitik auf die Südosteuropäischen Länder,* edited by Walter Althammer, 75-81. Südosteuropa Aktuell, 2. München: Südosteuropa-Gesellschaft, 1987.
Ceauşescu bases his resistance to reform on three arguments: on the ideological argument that privatization runs contrary to the principle of socialist ownership, on the contention that Romania is already engaged in restructuring, and on the political argument that Romania does not allow external involvment in internal affairs.

623. Gabanyi, Anneli Ute. "Der Rumänische Kulturkongress: Permanente Revolution und der Neue Nationalismus [Romania's Congress on Culture: Permanent Revolution and the New Nationalism]." *Osteuropa* 27, no. 2 (1977): 131-137.
Overview of the Bucharest Convention on Political Education and Socialist Culture (1976), known as the Romanian cultural mini-revolution.

624. Gabanyi, Anneli Ute. "Die Verweigerung: Zur Krise in Rumänien [Refusal: The Crisis in Romania]." *Osteuropa* 32, no. 7 (1982): 588-600.
Romania is in a deep economic crisis. Protest movements, passive resistance, and emigration requests intensify. Insisting on independence from the Soviet Union, the government responds with a rapprochement to CMEA and with internal purges of Party cadres.

625. Gabanyi, Anneli Ute. "Der XII. Parteitag der Kommunistischen Partei Rumäniens: Autonomiepolitik im Zeichen der Energiekrise [12th Party Congress of the Communist Party of Romania: Policy of Autonomy in the Energy Crisis]." *Osteuropa* 30, no. 5 (1980): 419-433.
Reports on the rejection of bylaw changes submitted by the Central Committee, on the participation of a Chinese delegation, and on the "Pîrvulescu affaire."

626. Georgescu, Vlad. "Romania in the 1980's: The Legacy of Dynastic Socialism." *Eastern European Politics and Societies* 2, no. 1 (1988): 69-93.
Explores the causes of the existing political and economic decay and assesses the country's short-term outlook.

627. Ghermani, Dionisie. *Rumänien: Marxismus-Leninismus in Theorie und Praxis; Ehrengabe für Dionisie Ghermani zum 65. Geburtstag [Romania: Marxism and Leninism in Theory and Practice; Festschrift for Dionisie Ghermani on his 65th Birthday].* Beiträge zur Kenntnis Südosteuropas und des Nahen Orients, 42. München: Rudolf Trofenik, 1990.
Collection of 34 articles and essays concerning Romania's international relations, economy, and society, published between 1982 and 1988, mostly in *Südosteuropa.*

628. Ghermani, Dionisie. "Rumäniens Reformverdrossenheit - Keine Ansätze von Erneuerung [Romania's Unhappiness with Reforms: No Signs of Change]." In *Wirtschaftsreformen im Ostblock in den 80er Jahren: Länderstudien: Sowjetunion, DDR, Polen, Rumänien, Tschechoslowakei, Bulgarien, Ungarn,* edited by Rolf Schlütter, 107-134. Zeitfragen der Politischen Bildung, 2. Paderborn: Schöningh, 1988.

629. Gilberg, Trond. "Ceauşescus 'Kleine Kulturrevolution' in Rumänien [Ceauşescu's 'Cultural Mini-Revolution' in Romania]." *Osteuropa* 22, no. 10 (1972): 717-728.
Argues that in 1971, the increasing power of industrial planners and managers began threatening the authority of the Communist Party and thus triggered Ceauşescu's swift reaction. Describes similarities and differences between China's cultural revolution and the Romanian mini-version.

630. Gilberg, Trond. "Ceauşescu's Romania." *Problems of Communism* 23, no. 4 (1974): 29-43.
Analyzes the character of Romanian politics and the factors that have shaped it. Describes Ceauşescu's drive to accumulate and consolidate political power and his personality and style as a leader. Discusses the effects of socioeconomic and political modernization, the persistence of mass values inimical to the regime's objectives, and the external political influences, primarily those exercised by the USSR. Concludes that Romania will continue to modernize its economy. However, political problems will become more severe as clashes will develop between political control and modernization and between political cadres and technocrats.

631. Gilberg, Trond. "The Communist Party of Romania." In *The Communist Parties of Eastern Europe*, edited by Stephen Fischer-Galaţi, 281-325. New York: Columbia University Press, 1979.
Examines the structure, policy goals, strategies, successes, and failures of the Party under Ceauşescu.

632. Gilberg, Trond. "Political Leadership at the Regional Level in Romania: The Case of the Judeţ Party, 1968-1978." *East European Quarterly* 9, no. 1 (1975): 97-111.
Studies personnel staffing at the regional party level. First secretary positions are reserved for party line "apparatchiki." As economic experts become increasingly important a "cooptation" process occurs, allowing for limited transfer of political power in exchange for technical expertise.

633. Gilberg, Trond. "Romania: Problems of the Multilaterally Developed Society." In *The Politics of Modernization in Eastern Europe: Testing the Soviet Model*, edited by Charles Gati, 117-159. New York: Praeger, 1974.
Based on a conference held in March 1973, sponsored by the Institute on East Central Europe of Columbia University.
Studies the impact of modernization on communist power.

634. Gilberg, Trond. "Romania: Will History Repeat Itself?" *Current History* 89, no. 551 (1990): 409-412, 431-433.
The legacy of poverty and fear of the Ceauşescu era is clouding hopes for a successful democratization and liberalization.

635. Gilberg, Trond. "Romania's Growing Difficulties." *Current History* 83, no. 496 (1984): 375-379+.
Analyzes the political, economic, social and cultural crises threatening Romania. The crises are the result of failed Party policies. Concludes that, in the regime's view, the crises are still manageable, provided that all disgruntled elements remain isolated from one another. Suggests potential solutions.

636. Graham, Lawrence S. *Romania: A Developing Socialist State*. Boulder: Westview, 1982.
Examines the formation of the Romanian state, its transition to socialism, the rekindling of nationalism in the mid 1960's, socioeconomic transformations under Ceauşescu, the personality-cult, and East-West relations.

637. Hale, Julian. *Ceauşescu's Romania: A Political Documentary*. London: Harrap, 1971.
Profiles political, economic, social and cultural institutions, their policies, and their impact on everyday life under Ceauşescu.

638. Hamelet, Michel P. *La Vraie Roumanie de Ceauşescu [The Real Romania of Ceauşescu]*. Destinus Politiques, 9. Genève: Nagel, 1983.
Flattering description of life in Romania.

639. Hazan, Baruch A. *The East European Political System: Instruments of Power*. Boulder: Westview, 1985.
Presents similarities and differences in Eastern European political regimes (with

numerous references to Romania), by analyzing elections, national assemblies, the parties, the leaders, relations between church and state, the judiciary, and rituals relating to political life.

640. Jelavich, Barbara. *History of the Balkans - Twentieth Century.* Vol.2, 370-378. Cambridge: Cambridge University Press, 1983.
Covers the period 1950-1980 in Romania and reviews domestic developments and reactions to international events.

641. Jowitt, Kenneth. "Background to the 11th Party Congress: Political Innovation in Romania." *Survey (London)* 20, no. 4 (1974): 132-151.
Contends that Ceauşescu's organizational, political and ideological innovations may lead to a dangerous confrontation with the Soviet Union.

642. Jowitt, Kenneth. "An Organizational Approach to the Study of Political Culture in Marxist Leninist Systems." *American Political Science Review* 68, no. 3 (1974): 1171-1191.
Drawing on Ceauşescu's Romania, explains the meaning of political culture and suggests approaches to its study.

643. Jowitt, Kenneth. *Revolutionary Breakthroughs and National Development: The Case of Romania, 1944-1965.* Berkeley: University of California Press, 1971.
Using the history of Romania since the end of World War II as a case study, explains the process of nation-building and modernization, resulting from a violent "breakthrough." Part IV (pp. 231-294) analyzes the Ceauşescu regime and the role of the Party in the world communist movement.

644. Jowitt, Kenneth. "The Romanian Communist Party and the World Socialist System: A Redefinition of Unity." *World Politics* 23, no. 1 (1970): 38-60.
Analyzes Romania's political position within the communist bloc and its ideological interpretation of interparty relations.

645. King, Robert R. "Ansätze zu einer 'Sozialistischen Demokratie' in Rumänien: Mehrfachkandidaturen bei den Wahlen von 1975 [Signs of a 'Socialist Democracy' in Romania: Multiple Candidates in the 1975 Elections]." *Osteuropa* 26, no. 5 (1976): 382-388.
The 1975 elections did not allow for an alternative to Party programs. Nonetheless, options in chosing candidates were available, a deviation from East European norm.

646. King, Robert R. "The Blending of Party and State in Rumania." *East European Quarterly* 12, no. 4 (1978): 489-500.
The Romanian Communist Party considers that each communist party has the right to adapt the principles of Marxism-Leninism to its own situation. Nicolae Ceauşescu advocated combining party and state and introduced two organizational approaches: the "plurality of offices", i.e., individuals who hold simultaneously party and government positions, and the "plurality of attributions" of organizations, i.e., bodies which are subordinated to both party and state organizations. Functions were blended to reduce inefficiency, avoid duplication, and provide greater legitimacy to the Party and its officials. The change could transform the nature of the communist party.

647. King, Robert R. *A History of the Romanian Communist Party.* Hoover Press Publication, 233. Stanford, CA: Hoover Institution Press, 1980.
Traces the development of the RCP from a minor political organization with a disproportionate ethnic minority membership, serving Soviet interests, to its accession to power and transformation into a dominant institution, pursuing an independent and nationalistic policy.

648. King, Robert R. "Reorganisationen in Rumänien: Ceauşescus Umbau der Partei-, Staats-, und Wirtschaftsverwaltung [Reorganization in Romania: Ceauşescu's Restructuring of the Administration of Party, State, and Economy]." *Osteuropa* 24,

no. 1 (1974): 36-46.
Describes reasons for and elements of the reforms affecting Romania's entire administrative structure.

649. King, Robert R. "Romania." In *Communism in Eastern Europe*, edited by Teresa Rakowska-Harmstone and Andrew Gyorgy, 145-167. Bloomington: Indiana University Press, 1979.
Profiles the country's historical development and describes the political structure and Party elite under Ceauşescu, his domestic and foreign policy, and the economic conditions since the 1970's.

650. Kittrie, Nicholas N., and Ivan Volgyes, eds. *The Uncertain Future: Gorbachev's Eastern Bloc*. New York: Paragon House, 1988.
Scholarly papers assessing the economic and political situation in Eastern Europe (with ample references to Romania), at the time of the break up of the monolith.

651. Kristof, Ladis K. D. "The Case of Rumania." *Studies in Comparative Communism* 4, no. 2 (1971): 36-42.
Takes issue with the "Almond-Powell" and "Triska" schemes that discuss Soviet bloc countries in general without acknowledging the unique development of individual East European countries. Argues in favor of continued study of individual societies prior to developing general schemes and highlights problems with Professor Triska's outline when applied to Romania.

652. Lambert, Anthony. "Return of the Vampire." *Geographical Magazine* 61, no. 2 (1989): 16-20.
The West remains oblivious to Ceauşescu's megalomaniacal plans of building the Danube-Black Sea canal, destroying historical sections of the capital as well as 8000 villages, and ruthlessly suppressing any expression of dissent.

653. Lendvai, Paul. "Rumänien [Romania]." In *Die Grenzen des Wandels: Spielarten des Kommunismus im Donauraum*, 255-321. Vienna: Europa, 1977.
Reprints articles and essays, originally published between 1964 and 1974, dealing with natality, economy, domestic and international relations, territorial disputes, minorities, and nationalism.

654. Lhomel, Edith. "Les Ambiguités de l'Autonomie Roumaine [The Ambiguities of Romanian Autonomy]." *Problèmes Politiques et Sociaux* 491 (29 June 1984): 27-28.
A repressive domestic policy has been the prize for an independent foreign policy. In turn, this autonomy confers to the regime some domestic credibility.

655. Lhomel, Edith. "Ceauşescu Dit Non! [Ceauşescu Says No!]." *Problèmes Politiques et Sociaux* 574 (25 December 1987): 23-24.
Ceauşescu opposes reforms.

656. Lhomel, Edith. "Roumanie, l'Année Politique: Un Pouvoir Désavoué, une Population Épuisée [Romania, The Year in Politics: A Discredited Authority, an Exhausted Population]." *Notes & Études Documentaires* 4867-4868 (1988): 191-199.
Reviews events of 1987: demonstrations in Braşov for better salaries and living conditions are brutally repressed. Relations with Hungary deteriorate, while Moscow presses for reforms.

657. Lhomel, Edith, ed. "Roumanie: Pouvoir et Societé [Romania: Power and Society]." *Problèmes Politiques et Sociaux* 536 (16 May 1986).
Collection of articles by well known scholars on Romanian affairs, previously published in leading social science journals.

658. Lhomel, Edith. "La Roumanie sur la Corde Raide [Romania on the Tightrope]." *Notes et Études Documentaires* 4673-4674 (22 June 1982): 31-48.

The economic situation is alarming, the standard of living has plummeted, and open protests are flaring up. Ceauşescu responds locally with repression and internationally with a flurry of diplomatic activities. No positive outcome is foreseen.

659. Lhomel, Edith. "Roumanie: Un Régime aux Abois [Romania: A System at Risk]." *Études* 357, no. 4 (1982): 307-321.
Faced with economic, financial and political difficulties, Romania runs the risk of social instability.

660. Linden, Ronald H. *Communist States and International Change: Romania and Yugoslavia in Comparative Perspective.* Boston: Allen & Unwin, 1987.
Describes causes of international economic and political changes in the 1970's and early 1980's and comparatively analyzes their impact on domestic and foreign policies in two communist states.

661. Lindner, Robert. "Rumänien (Januar 1976 - August 1976) [Romania (January 1976 - August 1977)]." *Osteuropa* 27, no. 5 (1977): 435-440.
The first of a series of reviews of major highlights of internal and external political activities, followed by a detailed chronology. All of the reviews appear in the "Umschau" section of *Osteuropa* as follows: Sept. 1976-Aug. 1977, in v. 28, no. 3 (1978); Sept. 1977-Juni 1978, in v. 28, no. 11 (1978); Juli-Dez. 1978, in v. 29, no. 6 (1979); Jan.-Juni 1979, in v. 29, no. 12 (1979); Juli-Dez. 1979, in v. 30, no. 6 (1980); Jan.-Juni 1980, in v. 31, no. 4 (1981); Juli-Dez. 1980, in v. 32, no. 3 (1982); Jan.-Juni 1980, in v. 32, no. 9 (1982); Juli 1981-Juni 1982, in v. 33, no. 5 (1983); Juli 1982-Juni 1983, in v. 34, no. 1 (1984); Juli 1983-Juni 1984, in v. 34, no. 11 (1984); Juli 1984-Juni 1985, in v. 36, no. 5 (1986).

662. Manea, Ion. "Linkage Between Foreign and Domestic Policy in Contemporary Romania." *Journal of the American Romanian Academy for Arts and Sciences* 5 (1984): 102-127.
Romania's risky foreign policy requires internal stability. Yet the thwarted expectations of the 1965-1971 political thaw have given rise to opposition.

663. McGlynn, Tom R. "Advanced Socialism by the 1990's? Romania's Doubtful Prospects." *World Review* 22, no. 2 (1983): 84-106.
Reviews causes leading to Romania's break with Moscow, Ceauşescu's rise to power, the emergence of the personality cult, and the worsening political and economic prospects.

664. Meier, Viktor. "The Political Dynamics of the Balkans in 1974." In *The World and the Great-Power Triangles*, edited by William E. Griffith, 35-98. Studies in Communism, Revisionism, and Revolution, 21. Cambridge: MIT Press, 1975.
The segment "Rumania" (pp. 38-49) analyzes Ceauşescu's ascent to power and the country's efforts to break out of its satellite status, increase the rhythm of development, and assert its national independence.

665. Meier, Viktor. "Rumänien auf dem Wege der Emanzipation [Romania on the Path of Emancipation]." *Europa-Archiv* 20, no. 1, (1965): 491-498.
Questions if the new Secretary of the Party, Ceauşescu, will continue Gheorghiu-Dej's independent foreign policy course. Domestically, Romania is embarking on a nationalistic policy that has negative implications for minorities.

666. Nelson, Daniel N. "Background Characteristics of Local Communist Elites: Change vs. Continuity in the Romanian Case." *Polity* 10, no. 3 (1978): 398-415.
Reports results of interviews with 42 politicians in four counties (Timiş, Cluj, Braşov, Iaşi). Permanent bureau members at all levels of local government are male, of Romanian heritage, approximately 40 years old, have a university degree in engineering, economics or law, and are Party educated in Bucharest. Women and minorities are underrepresented. Increased emphasis is being placed on competence and specialized skills but not at the expense of committed Party activity.

667. Nelson, Daniel N. *Democratic Centralism in Romania: A Study of Local Communist Politics.* East European Monographs, 69. New York: Columbia University Press, 1980.
    Focuses on sub-national political life and studies socioeconomic and political changes occurring in the process of modernization and development.

668. Nelson, Daniel N. "Development and Participation in Communist Systems: The Case of Romania." In *Political Participation in Communist Systems,* edited by Donald E. Schultz and Jan S. Adams, 234-253. New York: Pergamon, 1981.
    Studies the degree to which socioeconomic development influences citizens' interest and participation in political life.

669. Nelson, Daniel N. "Dilemmas of Local Politics in Communist States." *Journal of Politics* 41, no. 1 (1979): 23-54.
    Argues that in communist systems local level politics determine long-term successes or failures of central communist governments.

670. Nelson, Daniel N. "Issues in Local Communist Politics: The Romanian Case." *Western Political Quarterly* 30, no. 3 (1977): 384-396.
    The meaning of communism for citizens is most directly apparent at the local level. Interviews political participants and analyzes broader theoretical questions regarding the relationship between socioeconomic development or modernization and political change. With socioeconomic "successes," communist political systems will incur increased dissatisfaction and negative consequences.

671. Nelson, Daniel N. "Local Politics in Romania: An Intra-National Comparison." Ph.D. diss., Johns Hopkins University, 1975. Ann Arbor: UMI, 1975. AAD7601546.
    Studies representatives in four counties and concludes that generated socioeconomic changes conflict with the very political system that created them.

672. Nelson, Daniel N. "People's Council Deputies in Romania." In *Communist Legislatures in Comparative Perspective,* edited by Daniel Nelson and Stephen White, 85-110. London: Macmillan, 1982.
    Revised version of a chapter published as "Citizen Participation in Romania: The People's Council Deputy." In *Local Politics in Communist Countries,* edited by Daniel Nelson, 90-120. Lexington: University of Kentucky Press, 1980.
    Based on interviews with deputies and other sub-national elites in Timiş, Cluj, Braşov, and Iaşi, the study investigates the process that allows citizens to become deputies in local people's councils and in the Grand National Assembly.

673. Nelson, Daniel N. *Romanian Politics in the Ceauşescu Era.* New York: Gordon and Breach, 1988.
    Examines the Ceauşescu regime by focusing on three areas: elite-mass relations, local institutions and political dynamics, and military policies.

674. Nelson, Daniel N. "Sub-National Political Elites in a Communist System: Contrasts and Conflicts in Romania." *East European Quarterly* 10, no. 4 (1976): 458-494.
    A "dialectic hypothesis" appears to be supported by findings: socioeconomic change dictated at the national level engenders an evolution of attitudes in local elites that may run contrary to the intentions of central leaders.

675. Nelson, Daniel N. "Vertical Integration and Political Control in Eastern Europe: The Polish and Romanian Cases." *Slavic Review* 40, no. 2 (1981): 210-227.
    The process of horizontal rather than vertical integration creates tensions between central governments and subnational institutions. In an effort to blunt horizontal integration and minimize formation of local loyalties the central government in Romania (1968-1969) resorted to territorial administrative restructuring, created provincial administrators, and periodically rotated subnational personnel.

676. Nelson, Daniel N. "Women in Local Communist Politics in Romania and Poland." In *Women, State, and Party in Eastern Europe,* edited by Sharon L. Wolchik and Alfred

G. Meyer, 152-167. Durham: Duke University Press, 1985.
**Also reprinted in Nelson, Daniel N. *Elite-Mass Relations in Communist Systems.*
London: St. Martin's Press, 1987**.
Examines numbers, characteristics, and roles of women participating in local political activities.

677. Nelson, Daniel N. "Worker-Party Conflict in Romania." *Problems of Communism* 30, no. 5 (1981): 40-49.
In striving to achieve industrialization, urbanization, literacy, and modernization of agriculture the Romanian government may have unleashed forces contradictory to party control. Concludes that the model of "developed socialism" is flawed. The seeds of worker-party conflict are inherent in every communist party state.

678. Nelson, Daniel N. "Workers in a Workers' State: Participation in Romania." *Soviet Studies* 32, no. 4 (1980): 542-560.
Analyzes workers' decision-making authority in a communist party state. Discusses citizenship roles, political participation and socioeconomic equality.

679. Nolting, Orin F. "Local Government Administration in Romania." *Planning and Administration* 2, no. 2 (1975): 33-39.
Describes the organization and administration of local government and national training policies and programs for employee development.

680. Oschlies, Wolf. "Der XI. Parteitag der Rumänischen Kommunistischen Partei: Ceauşescu Ruft zum 'Grossen Sprung' [The 11th Congress of the Romanian Communist Party: Ceauşescu Calls for the 'Great Leap Forward']." *Osteuropa* 25, no. 5 (1975): 319-330.
Detailed account of the deliberations of the 11th Congress of the Communist Party of Romania.

681. Osten, Walter. "Der XI. Parteitag der Rumänischen Kommunistischen Partei: Als Beobachter beim Bukarester Parteitag [The 11th Congress of the Romanian Communist Party: As Observer of the Bucharest Party Congress]." *Osteuropa* 25, no. 5 (1975): 331-337.
Eyewitness account highlighting Ceauşescu's refusal to be Secretary of the Party for life, his opposition to integration into COMECON, and media reports on the event in Moscow, East Berlin, and West European communist party papers.

682. Rady, Martyn. *Romania in Turmoil: A Contemporary History.* London: IB Tauris, 1992.
Looks for clues in Romania's past to explain current events. Depicts the bloody uprising of 1989 and the turmoil characterizing post-revolutionary Romania.

683. Rakowska-Harmstone, Teresa. "Eastern European Communism in the Seventies." In *The Many Faces of Communism,* edited by Morton A. Kaplan, 194-227. New York: Free Press, 1978.
Analyzes development patterns of Eastern European political systems (including Romania) and suggests U.S. policy alternatives for the eighties.

684. *Romania: A Case of Dynastic Communism.* Perspectives on Freedom, 11. New York: Freedom House, 1989.
As part of a symposium organized by the Freedom House, M. H. Botez, A. Brezianu, M. Călinescu, L. Hamos, I. Hosszú, E. Mihaesco, N. Ratesh, G. A. Sencovici, V. Tismăneanu, and D. Tudoran discuss the political and economic crisis in Romania and scenarios for the future. L. Hamos, President of the Hungarian Human Rights Foundation, addresses human rights violations against the Hungarian minority.

685. "Romania 1985: Roundtable Organized by Professor Vlad Georgescu." *Journal of the Romanian Academy of Arts and Sciences* 8-9 (1986): 42-59.
Three panelists discuss the crisis in Romania: K. Jowitt analyzes the political cli-

mate that allows Ceauşescu to maintain power; D. Chirot addresses existing economic conditions; V. Georgescu examines the extreme hardships imposed on the population, dynastic socialism, and the cult of personality.

686. Rothschild, Joseph. *Return to Diversity: A Political History of East Central Europe Since World War II.* New York: Oxford University Press, 1989.
Contains a brief overview of Romania's desatellization under Ceauşescu and the Communist Party's quest for domestic legitimacy.

687. "Rumania: The Cracks Widen." *Soviet Analyst: A Fortnightly Commentary* 16, no. 25 (1987): 1-3.
Commentary on the harsh living conditions, mounting protests, and the Party's propaganda campaign at the end of 1987.

688. Rush, Myron. "Romania's Arranged Succession (1965)." In *How Communist States Change Their Rulers*, 121-129. Ithaca, N.Y.: Cornell University Press, 1974.
The orderly transfer of power from Gheorghiu-Dej to Ceauşescu denied Moscow a perfect opportunity to intervene and modify Romania's policies.

689. Sampson, Steven L. "Regime and Society in Rumania." *International Journal of Rumanian Studies* 5, no. 1 (1987): 41-51.
Focuses on "the nature of mobilization in Ceauşescu's Rumania and the kind of social contract he established with society" (p.42). Speculates on prospects of a post-Ceauşescu era.

690. Sampson, Steven L. "Romania: House of Cards." *Telos* 79 (Spring 1989): 217-224.
Romania, a country with the lowest living standard in Eastern Europe, subjected to the repressive regime of Ceauşescu who feels threatened by *perestroika* from the East and capitalism from the West, is on the verge of collapse. A post-Ceauşescu government may succeed in mobilizing the masses only if such values as education, work ethics, consumerism, or civil liberties are once again included in the public agenda.

691. Schöpflin, George. "Rumania: President Nixon's Visit and the Tenth Party Congress." *The World Today* 25, no. 9 (1969): 369-371.
Highlights three important aspects evident during the Congress: Romania's continued independent foreign policy, the elimination of old Stalinist leaders, and the growth of Ceauşescu's personality cult.

692. Schöpflin, George. "Rumania's Blind Alley." *The World Today* 38, no. 4 (1982): 148-153.
Ceauşescu's strategy for political and economic independence has failed. Romania is showing signs of economic disintegration and political decay. This crisis casts a long shadow on the country's future.

693. Schreiber, Thomas. "Roumanie: L'Année Politique [Romania: The Political Year in Review]." *Notes et Études Documentaires* 4673-4674 (22 June 1982): 207-212.
Angry demonstrations are brutally repressed. Increasingly, the power is concentrated in the hands of Ceauşescu's family. Internationally Ceauşescu steps up his diplomatic offensive.

694. Schultz, Lothar. "Die Zweite Landeskonferenz der Rumänischen KP [The Second National Conference of the Romanian Communist Party]." *Osteuropa* 23, no. 1 (1973): 21-28.
Reviews meeting agenda and argues that increased economic investments, active foreign trade, East-West joint ventures, and a degree of decentralized decision-making are positive and encouraging signs.

695. Schultz, Lothar. "Rumänien auf dem Wege der Reformen [Romania on the Path of Reforms]." *Osteuropa* 19, no. 4 (1969): 245-255.

Following the Soviet invasion of Czechoslovakia, Romania embarked on a program of social, legal, and economic reforms meant to enhance socialist unity and build a homogenous Romanian nation.

696. Schultz, Lothar. "Rumänien im Lichte des X. Parteitages der RKP [Romania in Light of the 10th Congress of the Romanian Communist Party]." *Osteuropa* 20, no. 2 (1970): 97-103.
Reviews the directives of the Party Congress which took place in the aftermath of Nixon's visit (August, 1969), a high point in Romania's successes in foreign policy.

697. Shafir, Michael. "The Future of the Rumanian Leadership." *International Journal of Rumanian Studies* 5, no. 1 (1987): 33-40.
A previous version titled "Coalition and Political Successions in Communist Systems: A Comparative Analysis of the Future of the Rumanian Leadership" was published in *Süd-Ost Europa Forschung* 35, no. 3-4 (1986): 201-222.
Discusses the political succession in post-Ceauşescu Romania.

698. Shafir, Michael. "Romania." In *Leadership and Succession in the Soviet Union, Eastern Europe and China*, edited by Martin McCauley and Stephen Carter, 114-135. Armonk, NY: M. E. Sharpe, 1986.
While leadership and succession in Romania bear similarities to that of other Eastern European countries, Ceauşescu's drive to political primacy, his dynastic government and personality cult are unique. Explores signs of cadre resistance and military threat to Ceauşescu's authority.

699. Shafir, Michael. *Romania, Politics, Economics and Society: Political Stagnation and Simulated Change.* London: Pinter, 1985.
Comprehensive analysis of the Romanian political, economic, and social system under Ceauşescu.

700. Shafir, Michael. "Socialist Republic of Romania." In *Marxist Governments: A World Survey*, edited by Bogdan Szajkowski, 589-639. London: Macmillan, 1981.
Traces the historical roots of Marxism and describes the communist take-over in Romania and the consolidation of power under Gheorghiu-Dej and Ceauşescu. Analyzes the oganizational principles of the Party, the government, and mass organizations. Profiles Romania's educational, religious, and economic life and foreign relations.

701. Smultea, Ilie J. "Ideology and Political Community in Eastern Europe: The Case of Romania." *East European Quarterly* 5, no. 4 (1972): 505-536.
Outlines the impact of such determinants as geographic location, language, culture, history, and foreign relations on current political events. Discusses steps taken by the government to distance the country from Soviet influence.

702. Staar, Richard F. *Communist Regimes in Eastern Europe.* 5th ed. Hoover Press Publication, 381. Stanford, CA: Hoover Institution Press, 1988.
Chapter seven, "Socialist Republic of Romania" (pp. 148-220), discusses governmental and party organization, domestic policy, growing dissent, church-state relations, foreign policy, and Ceauşescu's dynastic and nationalistic socialism.

703. Staar, Richard F. "Nonconformers - The Other Eastern Europe." *The World & I,* 4, no. 7 (1989): 97-101.
Reviews the position of East European communist countries toward the fundamental changes occuring in the Soviet Union. Ceauşescu is rejecting the Soviet reforms and intensifying internal repression.

704. Stuart, Anthony. "Ceauşescu's Land." *Survey (London)* 76 (Summer 1970): 112-121.
Despite a long and costly struggle for progress, a small, militarily indefensible and economically weak country cannot prevail in its quest for independence and prosperity.

705. Szulc, Tad. "Glorifying Mao and the Homeland in Ceauşescu's Romania." *New Republic* 175, no. 17 (1976): 12-16.
Describes Ceauşescu's repressive internal policy as a price paid for his independent policy.

706. Tampke, Jürgen. *The People's Republics of Eastern Europe*. London: Croom Helm, 1983.
Chapter six, "Romania: Mediator Between East and West?" (pp. 83-92), narrates the economic and political situation under Gheorghiu-Dej, which was used by Ceauşescu as the basis for launching his independent foreign policy.

707. Tismăneanu, Vladimir. "Miron Constantinescu or the Impossible Heresy." *Survey (London)* 28, no. 4 (1984): 175-187.
Biographical profile of Miron Constantinescu, Marxist intellectual, historian, sociologist, and member of the party elite under Gheorghiu-Dej and Ceauşescu. However, both dictators rejected him.

708. Tismăneanu, Vladimir. "Personal Power and Political Crisis in Romania." *Government and Opposition* 24, no. 2 (1989): 177-198.
Looks at the Ceauşescu era from the late 1960's period of liberalization to the political decay of the 1980's and offers potential scenarios of succession.

709. Tismăneanu, Vladimir. *Reinventing Politics: Eastern Europe from Stalin to Havel*. New York: Free Press, 1992.
A historical account of Eastern European countries since World War II. Reviews Romanian political development, from its Soviet appointed government, through the de-Stalinization under Gheorghiu-Dej and Ceauşescu's despotic rule, to the revolutionary upheaval of 1989 and the dawn of democracy.

710. Tismăneanu, Vladimir. "The Tragicomedy of Romanian Communism." In *Crisis and Reform in Eastern Europe*, edited by Ferenc Fehér and Andrew Arató, 121-174. New Brunswick: Transaction, 1991.
An initial version appeared in *East European Politics and Societies* 3, no. 2 (1989): 329-376.
While most Soviet-style regimes have embraced *glasnost*, Ceauşescu remains anchored in his grotesque version of orthodox socialism. Reviews the history of the Romanian Communist Party and Ceauşescu's ascent to power.

711. Tontsch, Günther H. "Die Gemischten Partei- und Staatsorgane in Rumänien [The Mixed Party and States Bodies in Romania]." *Osteuropa Recht* 28, no. 2 (1982): 63-93.
Explains the legal organization and importance of bodies that are subordinate to the Central Committee of the RCP and also subordinate to either the National Assembly, the Council of State, or the Council of Ministers.

712. Tontsch, Günther H. *Das Verhältnis von Partei und Staat in Rumänien: Kontinuität und Wandel, 1944-1982 [Relationship between Party and State in Romania: Continuity and Change, 1944-1982]*. Abhandlungen zum Ostrecht, 170. Köln: Wissenschaft und Politik, 1985.
Explores the organization and function of the state-party system by focusing on the development and consolidation of power structures, changes in doctrine, and means to institutionalize modified party-state relations.

713. Triska, Jan F. "Citizen Participation in Community Decisions in Yugoslavia, Romania, Hungary, and Poland." In *Political Development in Eastern Europe*, edited by Jan F. Triska and Paul M. Cocks, 147-177. New York: Praeger, 1977.
Discusses D. Nelson's research on deputies for local people's councils and Nelson's conclusion that in Romania there is diversity in political participation.

714. Verdery, Katherine. "Homage to a Transylvanian Peasant." *Eastern European Politics and Societies* 3, no. 1 (1989): 51-82.

Romania's and Europe's history from the turn of the century to 1987 are seen through the eyes of Petru Bota, a Transylvanian peasant.

715. Wagner, Richard, and Helmuth Frauendörfer. *Der Sturz des Tyrannen: Rumänien und das Ende einer Diktatur [Fall of the Tyrant: Romania and the End of a Dictatorship]*. Reinbek bei Hamburg: Rowohlt, 1990.
Five German-Romanian authors, former members of "Aktionsgruppe Banat," a literary movement suppressed by the Securitate, discuss Ceaușescu's personality, dissident movements and the secret police, Romania's nationalities policy, and Soviet-Romanian relations.

716. Whetten, Lawrence L. *Interaction of Political and Economic Reforms Within the East Bloc*. New York: Taylor & Francis, 1989.
The chapter, "Romania" (pp.85-92), shows how Ceaușescu is continuing to implement his austerity program while resisting reforms. In 1987, labor unrests are indicative of an explosive situation.

717. *Yearbook of International Communist Affairs*. Stanford, CA: Hoover Institution Press, 1961-1991.
Includes annual chapters on Romania, signed by well known scholars.

14. International Business, Finance & Trade

See also the chapter, Most Favored Nation Status

718. Assetto, Valerie J. *The Soviet Bloc in the IMF and the IBRD*. Boulder: Westview, 1988.
In chapter six (pp.139-161) describes the aborted economic reforms of 1967-1972, the recentralization course of 1972-1977, Romania's role as a member of the Bank and Fund, and the economic crisis of 1974-1984. Concludes that the policy of "inducement and punishment" did not make Romania conform to the Fund's conditions of market oriented policy changes.

719. Balussou, Madeleine. "Les Échanges de la Roumanie avec l'O.C.D.E. (1970-1980) [Relations between Romania and OECD (1970-1980)]." *Revue d'Études Comparatives Est-Ouest* 12, no. 4 (1981): 91-114.
Presents Romania's political and economic history as a backdrop for a review of its relations to OECD countries. Discusses exports, trade balance, national debt, and future outlook.

720. Barisitz, Stephan. *Rumäniens Investitionspolitik und ihre Bedeutung für Westliche Anlageexporte [Romania's Investment Policy and its Importance for Western Exports of Installations]*. Forschungsberichte, 160. Vienna: Institut für Internationale Wirtschaftsvergleiche, 1989.
Traces the rise and fall of industrial investments since the 1970's. Concludes that massive imports of technology and equipment are needed so as to avoid an economic collapse.

721. Bethkenhagen, Jochen. "Zur Aussenwirtschaftsreform in Rumänien [On Romania's Foreign Economic Rerform]." *Vierteljahreshefte zur Wirtschaftsforschung* 3 (1971): 221-232.
Discusses the 1971 Foreign Trade Law and questions if the new reform measures will achieve their intended goals.

722. Borstein, Morris. "Comparing Romania and Poland: A Summary." In *East European Integration and East-West Trade*, edited by Paul Marer and John Michael Montias, 390-392. Studies in East European and Soviet Planning, Development, and Trade, 28. Bloomington: Indiana University Press, 1980.
Based on a conference held at Indiana University, Bloomington, October 1976, sponsored by the Joint Committee on Eastern Europe.
Compares foreign trade policies and practices.

723. Botsas, Eleftherios N. "The Big Powers and Interbalkan Economic Relations." *East European Quarterly* 12, no. 3 (1978): 275-282.
Studies the period from the end of World War I to the mid-seventies, and discusses factors influencing anti-trade forces among Balkan countries.

724. Brada, Josef C., and Marvin A. Jackson. "Strategy and Structure in the Organization of Romanian Foreign Trade Activities, 1967-1975." In *East European Economies Post-Helsinki: A Compendium of Papers*, submitted to U.S. Congress, Joint Economic Committee, 1260-1276. Washington, D. C.: U.S. G.P.O., 1977. Committee Print. Y4.Ec7:Eu7/8.
     Studies the Romanian experience with organizational changes within the framework of changes in East European foreign trade activities.

725. Brada, Josef C., and Larry J. Wipf. "Romanian Exports to Western Markets." In *Quantitative and Analytical Studies in East-West Economic Relations*, edited by Josef C. Brada, 37-50. Studies in East European and Soviet Planning, Development, and Trade, 24. Bloomington: Indiana University, International Development Research Center, 1976.
     Compares Romania's export performance in six Western countries with that of other socialist states. Concludes that Romanian exports have faired well, thus setting an example for other CMEA countries.

726. Burakow, Nicholas. "The Dynamic Role of Trade in Development: Romania's Strategy." Ph.D. diss., University of Notre Dame, 1980. Ann Arbor: UMI, 1980. AAD8028452.
     Romania, unlike other Eastern European countries, has moved away from import substitutions toward a strategy of export promotion of manufactured goods. Concludes that Romania's economy presents a dynamic trade model that could be emulated by other developing countries.

727. Burgess, Jay A. "An Analysis of the United States-Romanian Long-Term Agreement on Economic, Industrial, and Technical Cooperation." In *East European Economies Post-Helsinki: A Compendium of Papers*, submitted to U.S. Congress., Joint Economic Committee, 1243-1259. Washington, D. C.: U.S. G.P.O., 1977. Committee Print. Y4.Ec7:Eu7/8.
     Looks at the definition of cooperation within the framework of Romanian foreign trade, discusses motivations for cooperation, and analyzes the text of the Long-Term Agreement.

728. Burgess, Jay A. "Direct Foreign Investment in Eastern Europe: Problems and Prospects of Romania's Joint Venture Legislation." *Law & Policy in International Business* 6, no. 4 (1974): 1059-1104.
     Revised chapter first published as "The Socialist Republic of Romania" In *East-West Business Transactions*, edited by Robert Starr, 272-310. New York: Praeger, 1974.
     Explores Romania's market structure and its efforts to introduce institutional and legal reforms conducive to joint business ventures with Western partners. Focuses on the Control Data and Reşiţa-Renk agreements.

729. Dannenbaum, Anne Henderson. "The International Monetary Fund and Eastern Europe: The Politics of Economic Stabilization and Reform." Ph.D. diss., Yale University, 1989. Ann Arbor: UMI, 1989. AAD9010650.
     To repay national debts, Romania and other Eastern European countries requested IMF standby credits. In return, IMF demanded market-oriented reforms which were met with resistance in Romania.

730. Davey, W. G. "Energy Issues and Policies in Eastern Europe." *Energy Policy* 15 (February 1987): 59-72.
     Reviews energy issues and policies in Eastern Europe, including Romania. Under a new agreement the Soviet Union will continue to supply oil below world market prices in return for increased economic collaboration. Because Romania has not accepted the Soviet conditions for full CMEA/Warsaw Pact integration it faces a political and economic dilemma. Briefly reviews Romania's alternative energy sources and its future prospects.

731. Donaghue, Hugh P. "Control Data's Joint Venture in Romania." *Columbia Journal of World Business* 8, no. 4 (1973): 83-89.
    ROM Control Data SRL became a company 45% owned by Control Data Corporation (U.S.) and 55% owned by a state enterprise of the Romanian government. Describes the history of negotiations leading to the establishment of this first transideological corporation in Romania.

732. *East-West Trade: the Prospects to 1985: Studies Prepared for the Use of the Joint Economic Committee, Congress of the United States.* Washington: U.S. G.P.O., 1982. Committee Print. Y4.Ec7:T67/9.
    Assesses past and future trade patterns for twelve planned economies, including Romania, with the industrialized West. The Romanian study, "Romania: Performance and Prospects for Trade with the U.S. and the West," by Linda Draher and John A. Marten (pp. 237-275), contains a discussion of Romania's hard currency debt, foreign trade, leading imports and exports and projected 1985 trade activity. Includes comprehensive trade and debt statistics.

733. Forrest, Robert. "Romanian-American Economic Relations, 1947-1975." In *Romania Between East and West: Historical Essays in Memory of Constantin C. Giurescu*, edited by Stephen Fischer-Galați, Radu R. Florescu, and George R. Ursul, 385-413. East European Monographs, 103. New York: Columbia University Press, 1982.
    A historical overview, highlighting 1965-1969 trade issues, the Nixon-Ceaușescu visits and the relaxing of trade restrictions, the successful negotiations for MFN status, and the beginning of American-Romanian joint business ventures.

734. Gordon, Lincoln. "The Economic Crisis in Eastern Europe." In *Security Implications of Nationalism in Eastern Europe*, edited by Jeffrey Simon and Trond Gilberg, 29-48. Boulder: Westview, 1986.
    Discusses Romania among other communist states and the causes of the balance-of-payment crisis of 1980-1982.

735. Hall, D. R. "The Iron Gates Scheme and its Significance." *Geography* 57, pt.1, no. 254 (1972): 51-55.
    The Yugoslav-Romanian agreement to harness the waters of the Danube for hydro-electrical power will benefit both countries economically.

736. Hayden, Eric W. "Romania." In *Technology Transfer to East Europe: U.S. Corporate Experience*, 76-104. New York: Praeger, 1976.
    Reports on Romania's cooperation with Control Data and General Tire and Rubber, Co. and on the disputed agreement with Instrument Systems Corp.

737. Henderson, Anne. "The International Monetary Fund and the Dilemmas of Adjustment in Eastern Europe: Lessons from the 1980's and Prospects for the 1990's." *Journal for International Development* 4 (May-June 1992): 245-271.
    Discusses IMF past and current impact on the economic policies and development of Hungary, Romania, and Yugoslavia.

738. Holzman, Franklyn D. *International Trade Under Communism: Politics and Economics*. New York: Basic Books, 1976.
    Refers to Romania's trade and its joint ventures with western firms.

739. Jackson, Marvin R. "Prices and Efficiency in Romanian Foreign Trade." In *Quantitative and Analytical Studies in East-West Economic Relations*, edited by Josef C. Brada, 117-133. Studies in East European and Soviet Planning, Development, and Trade, 24. Bloomington: Indiana University, International Development Research Center, 1976.
    Discusses the difficulties of Romanian attempts to apply price-based efficiency measurements in trade.

740. Jackson, Marvin R., and James D. Woodson, Jr., eds. *New Horizons in East-West Economic and Business Relations*. East European Monographs, 156. New York:

Columbia University Press, 1984.
Papers presented at the third Romanian-American conference on trade and economic cooperation, Bucharest 1978, focusing on East-West trade analysis, legal issues, management and marketing, and East-West trade in the global setting.

741. Kaser, Michael. "Rumania's Economic Relations." *The World Today* 25, no. 9 (1969): 371-375.
    Discusses Romania's position before and during the 10th Congress of the Romanian Communist Party regarding COMECON collaboration.

742. Kretschmar, Robert S., Jr., and Robin Foor. *The Potential for Joint Ventures in Eastern Europe*. New York: Praeger, 1972.
    A special appendix on Romania (pp.109-129) offers a historical, political, and economic overview, discusses trade opportunities, and includes statistical data of use to U.S. business people contemplating joint ventures with Romania.

743. Laux, Jeanne Kirk. "La Roumanie et les Multinationales [Romania and the Multinationals]." *Revue d'Études Comparatives Est-Ouest* 12, no. 4 (1981): 61-89.
    Examines Romania's national development policy in light of its relations to multinational corporations. Discusses the role of international capital in the development of the country. Analyzes strategies to maintain a policy of independence toward East and West.

744. Lavigne, Marie. "Les Pays Socialistes Européens et le Fond Monétaire International [European Socialist Countries and the International Monetary Fund]." *Le Courrier des Pays de l'Est* 291 (January 1985): 29-42.
    Explores Romania's advantages as an IMF member country (1972) and the ways in which IMF conditions influence politics in centrally planned economies.

745. Lawson, Colin W. "National Independence and Reciprocal Advantages: The Political Economy of Romanian-South Relations." *Soviet Studies* 35, no. 3 (1983): 362-375.
    Romania deviated from CMEA joint policies by joining the South's UNCTAD program and the Group of 77 and by claiming developing country status. Romania's actions appear to be motivated by a desire to benefit from West-South concessions, rather than by political considerations.

746. Marer, Paul. "US-Romanian Industrial Cooperation: A Composite Case Study." In *East-West Trade: Theory and Evidence*, edited by Joseph C. Brada and V. S. Somanath, 92-113. Studies in East European and Soviet Planning, Development, and Trade, 27. Bloomington: International Development Institute, 1978.
    Highlights achievements and problems in moving toward an "improved business climate."

747. McElroy, David. "The Control Data Joint Venture in Romania." *International Lawyer* 10, no. 1 (1976): 55-57.
    Negotiations for a joint venture between Control Data Corporation and Romania began in December 1971. The first finished product (computer peripheral equipment) was delivered in December 1974. The negotiations were arduous due to different cultural expectations of Romanian and American workers and the inability of the Romanian economy to adapt quickly to new conditions. The hoped-for production of piece parts and subassemblies in Romania did not materialize.

748. McMillan, Carl H. "East-West Industrial Cooperation." In *East European Economies Post-Helsinki: A Compendium of Papers*, submitted to U.S. Congress, Joint Economic Committee, 1175-1224. Washington: U.S. G.P.O., 1977. Committee Print. Y4.Ec7:Eu7/8.
    Focuses on the 1971 legislation which facilitates Romanian trade with the West.

749. McMillan, Carl H., and D. P. St. Charles. *Joint Ventures in Eastern Europe: A Three Country Comparison*. Montreal: C. D. How Research Institute, 1974.

Discusses laws and regulations governing joint ventures in Romania, Hungary, and Yugoslavia.

750. Montias, John M. "Obstacles to the Economic Integration of Eastern Europe." *Studies in Comparative Communism* 2, no. 3-4 (1969): 38-60.
Discusses inhibiting factors to the economic integration of COMECON states.

751. Montias, John M. "Romania's Foreign Trade: An Overview." In *East European Economies Post-Helsinki: A Compendium of Papers*, submitted to U.S. Congress, Joint Economic Committee, 865-885. Washington, D. C.: U.S. G.P.O., 1977. Committee Print. Y4.Ec7:Eu7/8.
Partial Contents: "Industrialization of Foreign Trade," "Geographical Orientation of Romania's Trade," "Microanalysis of Trade in Machinery," "Romania's Trade by Areas."

752. Montias, John M. "Romania's Foreign Trade Between East and West." In *East European Integration and East-West Trade*, edited by Paul Marer and John Michael Montias, 321-344. Studies in East European and Soviet Planning, Development, and Trade, 28. Bloomington: Indiana University Press, 1980.
Based on a conference held at Indiana University, Bloomington, October 1976, sponsored by the Joint Committee on Eastern Europe.
Uses statistics of trade and development to reveal government trade policies accounting for fluctuations in the share of imports and exports from East and West. The study is followed by "Discussions" by Marvin R. Jackson (pp. 344-349) and Gregory Grossman (pp. 350-354).

753. Moore, Russell, and Eva Nove. "Perspectives of American Importers Dealing with Romanian Exports." In *East-West Trade: Theory and Evidence*, edited by Joseph C. Brada and V. S. Somanath, 28-45. Studies in East European and Soviet Planning, Development, and Trade, 27. Bloomington: International Development Institute, 1978.
Evaluates the Romanian export market through interviews with companies importing from Romania. Makes recommendations for improvement of marketing practices.

754. Morse, David A., and Samuel V. Goekjian. "Joint Investment Opportunities with the Socialist Republic of Romania." *The Business Lawyer* 29, no. 1 (1973): 133-148.
Explores Romanian legislative and administrative reforms enacted to promote foreign trade relations. Discusses the Control Data joint company agreement with Romania.

755. Pascal, Nina S. "The Law of Comparative Advantage and Rumanian Foreign Trade." *International Journal of Rumanian Studies* 5, no. 1 (1987): 63-70.
The ambitious plans for industrialization coupled by a rigid centralized system have been the cause of Romania's present economic collapse.

756. Pissulla, Petra. *Der Internationale Währungsfonds und seine Bedeutung für die Osteuropäischen Länder: Rumänien, Ungarn, Polen [The International Monetary Fund and its Importance for East European Countries: Romania, Hungary, Poland]*. Hamburg: Weltarchiv, 1983.
Reprinted in *Osteuropa Wirtschaft* 29, no. 2 (1984): 97-107; an English version of this article was published in *Intereconomics* 2 (March-April 1984): 64-70.
Discusses membership, claims, agreements, and World Bank credit for Romania (pp.54-75).

757. Portes, Richard. "East Europe's Debt to the West: Interdependence is a Two-Way Street." *Foreign Affairs* 55, no. 4 (1977): 751-782.
At the end of 1976 Romania's estimated debt stands at $2.8 billion, while its net debt ratio to hard currency exports is $1.2 billion. Suggests a response to a potential request for debt relief to Western financial institutions.

758. Reynaud, Pierre Louis. "Le Commerce Extérieur et l'Orientation de la Politique Économique en Roumanie [Foreign Trade and Orientation of Romanian Political Economy]." *Mondes en Dévelopement* 16 (1976): 819-840.
States that efforts to stabilize exchanges and redefine the convertibility of the currency can be relaxed. A liberalization policy in agriculture could lead to increased production.

759. Rohleder, Claus-Dieter. "Rumänien [Romania]." In *Die Aussenwirtschaft Südosteuropas: Entwicklung, Probleme, Perspektiven*, edited by Jens Meier and Johann Hawlowitsch, 46-58. Köln: Wissenschaft und Politik, 1970.
Romania enjoys a special position among Eastern European countries due to its achievements and innovative concepts in international trade and trade policies.

760. Schmiegelow, Michèle. "L'Adhésion de la Roumanie au FMI et la Théorie des Relations Internationales [Romania Becomes a Member of the IMF and the Theory of International Relations]." *Revue Française de Science Politique* 24, no. 1 (1974): 113-123.
Romania is the first Eastern bloc country to join the International Monetary Fund and the World Bank. Explores national and international economic and political implications of this action.

761. Schmutzler, George E. "Gegenwärtiger Stand der Wirtschaftlichen Beziehungen der Bundesrepublik Deutschland zu Rumänien [Current Economic Relations between West Germany and Romania]." In *Osthandel in der Krise*, edited by Stefan Bethlen, 139-149. Berichte und Studien der Hanns-Seidel-Stiftung e.V. München, 10. Vienna: Olzog, 1976.
The German-Romanian trade outlook is not encouraging. Romania is heavily indebted and Germany is reluctant to extend additional credit.

762. Schnitzer, Martin. *U.S. Business Involvement in Eastern Europe: Case Studies of Hungary, Poland, and Romania*. New York: Praeger, 1980.
Looks at characteristics, objectives, and potential of joint equity ventures and industrial cooperative agreements between Romania and the West.

763. Schönfeld, Roland. "Romania's 'Mixed Ownership Companies': A Showcase Example of East-West Industrial Cooperation." *Soviet and Eastern European Foreign Trade* 13, no. 4 (1978): 25-49.
Also appeared in German as "Rumäniens 'Gemischte Gesellschaften': Paradebeispiel Industrieller Ost-West-Kooperation?" in *Osteuropa Wirtschaft*, 22, no. 4 (1977): 301-316..
Romania has embarked upon a policy of inter-enterprise cooperation with more advanced economies in East and West. Mixed production companies have gained acceptance due to mutual existing advantages.

764. Schröder, Klaus. "The IMF and the Countries of the Council for Mutual Economic Assistance." *Intereconomics* 17, no. 2 (1982): 87-90.
Brief discussion on the advantages derived by Romania from its membership in the IMF and the World Bank.

765. Smith, Alan H. "Romanian Economic Relations with the EEC." *Jahrbuch der Wirtschaft Osteuropas* 8 (1979): 323-361.
The EEC, Romania's major trading partner, has been supplying machinery and equipment in exchange for raw material, fuel, and food products. Despite being a GATT member and a "developing country," Romania experiences difficulties with indebtedness and EEC tariff and quota policies. Describes cooperative ventures on Romanian territory and abroad.

766. Tyrka, Stanislaw. "La Pénétration des Sociétés Multinationales dans les Pays d'Europe de l'Est [Penetration of Multinationals in Eastern European Countries]." *Revue d'Études Comparatives Est-Ouest* 7, no. 3 (1976): 89-105.

Reviews legal mechanisms in cooperative ventures between socialist countries (including Romania) and western firms. Analyzes motivations behind the acceptance of foreign capital and the impact of foreign multinationals on the economies of host countries.

767. U.S. Congress. House. Committee on Government Operations. Commerce, Consumer and Monetary Affairs Subcommittee. *The Operations of Federal Agencies in Monitoring, Reporting on, and Analyzing Foreign Investments in the United States: Hearings....* Washington: U.S. G.P.O., 1978. House Hearing. Y4.G74/7:F76/9/pt.3.
"Examination of the Committee on Foreign Investment in the United States, Federal Policy Toward Foreign Investment, and Federal Data Collection Efforts." Vol. 3 (pp. 411-466) contains documentation and correspondence relating to Romania's investment in a Virginia coal mine and its interaction with the International Energy Agency.

768. Vanous, Jan. "Romanian Economic and Foreign Trade Performance in 1988: Mr. Ceauşescu's Dream is Fulfilled - Romania has no Debt and There is not Much Left of its Economy Either." *PlanEcon Report: Development in the Economies of the Soviet Union and Eastern Europe* 5, no. 19-20 (1989): 1-34.
Reports on foreign debt repayment and its disastrous domestic impact. Questions if Ceauşescu would continue this policy or would recognize the needs of the population.

769. Venema, M. P. "Finance and Structure of Major Economic Projects in Eastern Europe: The Romanian Refinery Project." *American Review for East-West Trade* 1, no. 6 (1968): 52-59.
Uses the case of Universal Oil Products Co. refinery project to illustrate U.S. policy of peaceful trade with Eastern Europe.

770. Verzariu, Pompiliu, and Jay A. Burgess. "The Development of Joint Economic and Industrial Cooperation in East-West Trade." In *East European Economies Post-Helsinki: A Compendium of Papers*, submitted to U.S. Congress, Joint Economic Committee, 1225-1242. Washington, D. C.: U.S. G.P.O., 1977. Committee Print. Y4.Ec7:Eu7/8.
Cites the Romanian example in establishing legislation that facilitates joint East-West cooperation. Discusses forms of association, procedures to form a joint venture, financial and operational regulations, and personnel issues.

771. Verzariu, Pompiliu, and Jay A. Burgess. *Joint Venture Agreements in Romania: Background for Implementation.* Washington, D.C.: U.S. Department of Commerce, June 1977. C57.402:R66/2.
Provides an "overview of the principal aspects regarding organization and operation of joint companies in Romania, and introduces interested U.S. firms to main issues encountered by investors..." (p. iii).

772. Zaleski, Eugène. "Transferts de Technologie, Endettement et Perspectives du Commerce Est-Ouest [Technological Transfer, Debt and Outlook of East-West Trade]." *Revue d'Études Comparatives Est-Ouest* 10, no. 4 (1979): 57-68.
Speculates on economic and political reactions of Eastern bloc countries faced with a growing national debt and trade deficit.

773. Zieger, Gottfried, and Josef Fenyves, eds. *Deutsch-Rumänische Wirtschaftskooperation: Internationales Symposium 26.-27. Oktober 1978 in Göttingen [German-Romanian Economic Cooperation: An International Symposium 16-17 October, 1978 in Göttingen].* Studien zum Internationalen Wirtschaftsrecht und Atomenergierecht, 63. Köln: Carl Heymann, 1980.
Listing of papers delivered by Western participants: R. Schönfeld "Deutsch-Rumänische Kooperation in Gemischten Unternehmen;" G. Rohnfelder "Deutsch-Rumänische Kooperation auf dem Finanzmarkt aus der Sicht der Frankfurt Bukarest Bank;" C. J. Gmur "Praxis und Möglichkeiten der Finanzierung von Exporten in

Staatshandelsländer und Entwicklungsländer der Dritten und Vierten Welt;" R. Dittmar "Die Perspektiven der Deutsch-Rumänischen Wirtschaftskooperation;" O. Rudolf "Die Wirtschaftskooperation mit Rumänien aus der Sicht der Deutschen Unternehmen;" K. Schnick "Die Abwicklung von Kompensationsverpflichtungen auf Basis von Rahmenvertragen bzw. Abkommen bei Abschluss von Kaufverträgen Deutscher Maschinen und Anlagen;" K. Reimer "Theorie und Praxis der Gegengeschäfte im Ost-West Handel;" U. Bruns-Wüstefeld "Ausfuhrförderung im Handel mit Rumänien;" K.-H. Fink "Firmenkooperation mit Rumänien;" W. Hendricks "Praktische Probleme der Finanzierung im Warengeschäft zwischen Rumänien und Deutschland;" E. Kissner "Deutsch-Rumänische Wirtschaftskooperation;" H. F. Krull "Die Praxis Deutsch-Rumänischer Firmen-Kooperation."

774. Zloch-Christy, Iliana. *Debt Problems of Eastern Europe.* Cambridge: Cambridge University Press, 1987.
Analyzes the post 1970's indebtedness problems of Eastern European countries, including Romania's debt rescheduling (pp. 113-116). Describes relations with international financial institutions, lending risks to COMECON countries, and trends and prospects for the late 1980's.

775. Zotschew, Theodor D. "Wachstum, Differenzierung und Spezialisierung der Industrieproduktion Ungarn, Rumäniens und Bulgariens in Abhängigkeit vom Aussenhandel [Growth, Differentiation, and Specialization of Export-Dependent Industry Production in Hungary, Romania, and Bulgaria]." *Südosteuropa-Studien* 19 (1972): 17-27.
Exports have shifted from the traditional textile, food, and leader products to machinery, metal, and chemicals. New joint ventures contribute to the development of East-West trade.

15. Law & the Legal System

776. Braun, Aurel. "Socialist Concepts of Sovereignty: The Case for Romania." *Case Western Reserve Journal of International Law* 7, no. 2 (1975): 169-197.
Looks at how Romania interprets the concept of sovereignty in order to defend its autonomy against the Soviet Union.

777. Burgess, Jay A. "Doing Business in Eastern Europe: A Businessman's Look at Romania." *Business Lawyer* 27, no. 2 (1972): 491-528.
Describes legal and legislative restrictions and practical problems related to trade relations with Romania.

778. Burgess, Jay A. "Romania Looks West: An Analysis of Legislative Change in the Foreign Trade Sector during the Sixties." *California Western International Law Journal* 2 (Winter 1971): 16-51.
The reform legislation permitting joint ventures represents a departure from old practices that will define Romania's foreign trade of the 1970's.

779. Buzescu, Petre. *Foreign Investments and the Taxation of Foreign Enterprises and Persons in Romania*. Washington, D.C.: U.S. Library of Congress, Law Library, 1986. LC42.2:R66.
Explains the legal terms and agreements governing Romanian and Western cooperative/coproductive business enterprises.

780. Cismarescu, Michael. *Einführung in das Rumänische Recht: Allgemeine Grundzüge und Tendenzen [Introduction to Romanian Law: General Characteristics and Tendencies]*. Darmstadt: Wissenschaftliche Buchgesellschaft, 1981.
Describes the origins and organization of Romania's state and legal system.

781. Cismarescu, Michael. "Die Gerichtliche Kontrolle von Verwaltungsakten in der Sozialistischen Republik Rumänien [The Judicial Control of Administrative Law in the Socialist Republic of Romania]." *Acta Scientiarum Socialium* 5 (1972): 9-62.
Analysis of the tenet of the August 1965 Constitution and its applications.

782. Cismarescu, Michael. "An Original Legal Experiment in Rumania: The Party and State Bodies." *Review of Socialist Law* 2, no. 1 (1976): 5-13.
Examines the creation of bodies with dual nature subordinated to the organs of both party and state.

783. Cismarescu, Michael. "Reformen im Recht- und Justizwesen Rumäniens, 1965-1970 [Reforms in Romania's Law and Legal System 1965-1970]." *Acta Scientiarum Socialium* 3 (1971): 1-103.
Examines new and revised laws since 1965, with special emphasis on the Penal Code.

784. Cismarescu, Michael. "Rumania's Changing Legal Code." *East Europe* 16, no. 8 (1967): 16-17.
Changes in the 1965 Constitution reflect Romania's pursuit of independence from the Soviet Union and the creation of a specifically Romanian legal system.

785. Cismarescu, Michael. "Die Verfassungsrechtliche Entwicklung der Sozialistischen Republik Rumänien 1965-1975 [The Constitutional Development of the Romanian Socialist Republic, 1965-1975]." *Jahrbuch des Öffentlichen Rechts der Gegenwart* 24 (new series) (1975): 232-285.
Reviews constitutional reforms to date and discusses citizens' rights, socialist democracy, and laws governing citizenship.

786. Frenzke, Dietrich. "Die Entwicklung der Rumänischen Völkerrechtsdoktrin Seit dem Zweiten Weltkrieg [The Development of Romanian International Law since World War II]." *Osteuropa Recht* 19, no. 2-3 (1973): 125-164.
Explores Romanian interpretation of international law during Soviet domination (1948-1955), "peaceful coexistence" (1956-63), and during the time characterized by the doctrine of national sovereignty (since 1964).

787. Frenzke, Dietrich. *Rumänien, der Sowjetblock und die Europäische Sicherheit: Die Völkerrechtlichen Grundlagen der Rumänischen Aussenpolitik [Romania, the Soviet Bloc and European Security: The International Law Foundation of Romanian Foreign Policy].* Berlin: Berlin, 1975.
Examines Romania's doctrine on international law and its application to national sovereignty, European security, and socialist internationalism.

788. Hundt, Florenz. "Doppelbesteuerungsabkommen mit Polen und Rumänien (I-II) [Double Taxation Convention with Poland and Romania (I-II)]." *Betrieb* 28, (1975): 1187-1193, 1239-1244.
A two part article discussing and contrasting the taxation laws of Poland and Romania.

789. Jacobini, H. B. "The Romanian Procuratura." *East European Quarterly* 14, no. 4 (1980): 439-459.
Compares the role and functions of the Procuratura with similar institutions in the West. Traces its development since its inception in 1952 and concludes that it has been successful in discharging its investigation, prosecution, and supervisory responsibilities.

790. Jacobini, H. B. *Romanian Public Law: Some Leading Internal Aspects.* East European Monographs, 223. New York: Columbia University Press, 1987.
Surveys legal institutions, the Procuratura, and administrative law in communist Romania.

791. Kendi, Erich. *Minderheitenschutz in Rumänien: Die Rechtliche Normierung des Schutzes der Ethnischen Minderheiten in Rumänien [Protection of Minority Rights in Romania: Legal Standards of Protection of Ethnic Minorities in Romania].* Untersuchungen zur Gegenwartskunde Südosteuropas, 30. München: Oldenbourg, 1992.
Describes the protection of minority rights in Romania in historical perspective based on international and national law. Places special emphasis on conditions in Ceauşescu's Romania and on post-revolution developments.

792. Leonhardt, Peter. "Der Begriff des Eigentumsrechts in Rumänien [The Concept of Property Right in Romania]." *Jahrbuch für Ostrecht* 12, no. 1 (1971): 127-147.
Examines existing legal interpretation of ownership and types of property under socialist law.

793. Leonhardt, Peter. *Entstehung und Entwicklung des Persönlichen Eigentumsrechts in Rumänien [The Emergence and Development of the Private Property Rights in Ro-*

mania]. Studien des Instituts für Ostrecht - München, 25. Tübingen: Erdmann, 1974. Explores the evolution of the concept of private property in Socialist Romania and the laws and regulations governing its use.

794. Leonhardt, Peter. "Individuelle Bodennützung in Rumäniens Landwirtschaft: Rechtliche Grundlagen und Ihre Jüngsten Änderungen [Individual Land Usage in Romanian Agriculture: Legal Principles and Recent Changes]." *Osteuropa* 40, no. 11 (1990): 1084-1096.
Historical review of laws governing land use and changes introduced after the 1989 revolution.

795. Leonhardt, Peter. "Die Neuere Entwicklung des Individuellen Grundeigentums in Rumänien [Latest Developments in Individual Property Rights in Romania]." *Recht im Ost und West* 22, no. 2 (1978): 110-118.
Discusses policies increasing restrictions on private ownership of land and homes.

796. Leonhardt, Peter. "Die Neuere Verfassungsentwicklung in Rumänien [The Latest Constitutional Developments in Romania]." In *Verfassungs- und Verwaltungsreformen in den Sozialistischen Staaten*, edited by Friedrich Christian Schroeder and Boris Meissner, 179-198. Berlin: Duncker & Humbolt, 1978.
After examining Romania's constitutional history since 1965, concludes that while recent laws have improved in clarity and fairness, no liberalization is visible. The limits of freedom are defined by the Party.

797. Nash, George W. "Rumanian Contracts of Delivery: A Comparative Analysis." *Buffalo Law Review* 17, no. 2 (1968): 375-434.
Discusses mandatory contracting, contracting procedures, form and content of contracts, total and partial invalidity of delivery contracts, modification, performance, and consequences of breach within the context of Romanian economic law.

798. Nelson, Daniel N. "Organs of the State in Romania." *International and Comparative Law Quarterly* 25, no. 3 (1976): 651-664.
Examines Romania's three constitutions, their corresponding laws concerning subnational political organization, and the principles (e.g. democratic-centralism, double-subordination, collective decision making, local autonomy) supposed to govern interactions of political institutions.

799. Pfaff, Dieter. "Wiederbelebung der Kapitalgesellschaften in Rumänien: Rechtsgrundlagen und Rechtsprobleme der 'Gemischten Gesellschaften' [Revival of Investment Companies in Romania: Legal Structure and Legal Concerns of 'Mixed Companies']." *Die Aktiengesellschaft* 19, no. 4 (1974): 106-114.
Summarizes basic characteristics of the new property laws and major issues concerning management, decision-making, and litigation.

800. Pfeifer, Michael George. "Legal Framework for American Direct Investment in Eastern-Europe: Romania, Hungary, and Yugoslavia." *Cornell International Law Journal* 7, no. 2 (1974): 187-203.
Compares strengths and weaknesses of investment laws in the three countries and concludes that, on balance, the Yugoslav law is more favorable to foreign investors. These investment laws represent a positive development for American business and hold great potential for American foreign policy.

801. Roman, George J. "Foreign Trade Law of Romania." *Law and Contemporary Problems* 37, no. 4 (1972): 652-681.
Examines foreign trade since World War II. Discusses foreign trade agreements, joint ventures with free enterprise countries, the national long range plans and their impact on foreign trade, and issues of contracts and arbitration.

802. Tiraspolsky, Anita. "Les Investissements Occidentaux dans les Pays de l'Est [Western Investments in Eastern Countries]." *Le Courrier des Pays de l'Est* 228 (April 1979): 3-19.

Reviews laws and regulations governing joint ventures in Romania, Hungary, and Poland.

803. Veress, Bulcsu. "The Status of Minority Rights in Transylvania: International Legal Expectations and Rumanian Realities." In *Transylvania: The Roots of Ethnic Conflict*, edited by John F. Cadzow, Andrew Ludányi, and Louis J. Eleto, 269-288. Kent, OH: Kent State University, 1983.
A collection of papers, some of which were presented at the Symposium on Transylvania, held on May 18-20, 1979, at Kent State University.
Presents the status of minorities based on international legal definitions regarding recognition, political rights, cultural and linguistic rights, religious rights, economic rights, and legal remedy against abuse.

804. Weiner, Robert. "Romania and International Law at the United Nations." *International and Comparative Law Quarterly* 32 (October 1983): 1026-1034.
Romania's desire to pursue its own foreign policy is reflcted in its concept of international law. The Nation State is Romania's highest governmental organization and Romanian politicians assert that states have a duty not to interfere in the internal affairs of other states.

16. Most Favored Nation Status

See also the following chapters: Ethnic Relations & Human Rights; International Business, Finance & Trade

805. Davidson, Lynne A. "Romania, CSCE and the Most-Favored-Nation Process, 1982-1984." In *The Diplomacy of Human Rights*, edited by David D. Newsom, 187-200. Lanham, MD: University Press of America, 1986.
     Charts the use of the Most Favored Nation lever by Congress to force Romania to improve its human rights record.

806. Heuston, Stephen P. "United States-Romanian Trade Relations: Development and Use of Most-Favored-Nation Trading Status." *George Washington Journal of International Law and Economics* 22, no. 2 (1988): 378-415.
     Reviews the history of Romania's MFN status and US-Romanian trade relations and concludes that linking MFN status to improvement of domestic human rights policies is in the best interest of the United States.

807. Lansing, Paul, and Eric C. Rose. "The Granting and Suspension of Most-Favored-Nation Status for Nonmarket Economy States: Policy and Consequences." *Harvard International Law Journal* 25, no. 2 (1984): 329-354.
     Using Romania as an example, illustrates the need for "more predictable yet flexible arrangements" in trade relations between states with centrally planned economies and the U.S. and offers suggestions for future agreements.

808. Pilon, Juliana Geran. "Why Romania No Longer Deserves to be a Most Favored Nation." *The Heritage Foundation Backgrounder* 441 (26 June 1985): 1-12.
     Although it has benefitted from its MFN status for years, Romania has not lived up to U.S. expectations. Romania remains the most repressive regime in Eastern Europe. Calls for the revocation of MFN status.

809. Pressler, Larry. *Trip Report, A Visit to Eastern Europe in the Wake of the 27th Soviet Party Congress and the Chernobyl Nuclear Accident (Czechoslovakia, Hungary, Yugoslavia, and Romania) on June 28, 1986: A Report to the Committee on Foreign Relations*...Washington: U.S. G.P.O., 1987.Committee Print. Y4.F76/2:S.prt.100-13.
     Contains a capsule summary of Romania's demography, economy, trade, military budget, and historical background. Discusses the Ceaușescu dynasty and personality cult, his foreign policies and relations with the United States, the dismal performance of the economy in 1985 and the austerity policy aimed at repaying Romania's foreign debt. Mentions the plan for urban renewal and the destruction of historical sites and monuments. Discusses human rights abuses, minority and religious persecutions, the decline in services for the elderly, and the regime's oppositon to emigration. Describes conversations with church officials on the utility of MFN status and ecounters with government officials including President Ceaușescu. Presents

and ecounters with government officials including President Ceauşescu. Presents advantages and disadvantages of renewal of MFN status.

810. Ratesh, Nestor. "The Rise and Fall of a Special Relationship." In *The United States and Romania: American-Romanian Relations in the Twentieth Century*, edited by Paul D. Quinlan, 161-175. American-Romanian Academy of Arts and Sciences, 6. Woodland Hills, CA: ARA, 1988.
Discusses the Nixon administration's efforts for a new policy towards Eastern Europe that included recognition of Romania's autonomous policy and granting of MFN status. However, the country's dismal human rights record has negated all premises for a "special relationship."

811. Siljander, Mark D. "An Overview of Post World War II U.S.-Romanian Relations." In *Sources of "Human Rights Violations in Romania,"* edited by Philip S. Cox, 9-21. Washington, D.C.: American Foreign Policy Institute, 1986.
Pleads for revocation of the MFN status in the face of Romania's continued human rights abuses and friendly ties to the Soviet Union.

812. U.S. Congress. House. Committee on Foreign Affairs. Subcommittee on Europe and the Middle East. *Developments in Europe, August 1986: Hearing ... August 7, 1986*. Washington: U.S. G.P.O., 1986. House Hearing. Y4.F76/1:Eu7/25/986-5.
Contains a brief discussion of human rights, details of the destruction of a Bucharest church, harassment of religious believers, and the extension of Most Favored Nation status to Romania.

813. U.S. Congress. House. Commitee on Foreign Affairs. Subcommittee on Europe and the Middle East. *United States-Romanian Relations and Most-Favored-Nation (MFN) Status for Romania: Hearing ... July 30, 1987*. Washington: U.S. G.P.O., 1987. House Hearing. Y4.F76/1:R66/2.
Representative Christopher H. Smith (New Jersey) presents a written statement, which includes a *Wall Street Journal* editorial of July 16, 1987 entitled "The Romanian Problem" and a compendium of quotations from human rights leaders and other knowledgeable individuals regarding opinions about renewal of MFN status and the Ceauşescu regime. A second prepared statement is submitted by Rozanne L. Ridgway, Assistant Secretary of State for European and Canadian Afairs, in which a recommendation for continuation of MFN status is supported, contending that MFN status is a weapon in the struggle for human rights. Also included are questions and answers dealing with the Jackson-Vanik Amendment, Hungarian minorities in Romania, Ceauşescu's policy of "Horizon," Romanian-U.S. dialogue on MFN status, statistics on emigration, and Romanian-PLO and Romanian-Libyan relations.

814. U.S. Congress. House. Committee on Ways and Means. *Disapproval of Extension of Presidential Authority to Waive Freedom of Emigration Requirements under Section 402 of the Trade Act of 1974 with Respect to Romania: Adverse Report ...* Washington: U.S. G.P.O., 1982. Committee Report. Y1.1/8:8:97-743.
The Committee members warn Romanian authorities that, in the future, strong emphasis will be placed on Romania's human rights record and emigration policies.

815. U.S. Congress. House. Committee on Ways and Means. Subcommittee on Trade. *Emigration Waiver to the Socialist Republic of Romania and the Hungarian People's Republic and Nondiscriminatory Treatment of the Products of Romania: Hearing ... June 15, 1978*. Washington: U.S. G.P.O., 1978. House Hearing. Y4.W36:95-85.
Monitors Romania's emigration trends to the U.S., West Germany, and Israel and its performance in meeting reciprocity commitments under the U.S.-Romanian Trade Agreement.

816. U.S. Congress. House. Committee on Ways and Means. Subcommittee on Trade. *Extension of MFN Status to Rumania, Hungary, and the People's Republic of China:*

Hearings ... July 12 and 13, 1982. Washington: U.S. G.P.O., 1982. House Hearing. Y4.W36:97-78.

Shows ten years of Romanian emigration statistics and testimony of over 60 witnesses including representatives from East Watch International, American-Romanian National Committee for Human Rights, and B'nai B'rith International. Includes several submissions from private individuals, companies and human rights organizations.

817. U.S. Congress. House. Committee on Ways and Means. Subcommittee on Trade. *Most-Favored-Nation Trading Status for the Socialist Republic of Romania, the Hungarian People's Republic, and the People's Republic of China: Hearing ... June 10, 1986.* Washington: U.S. G.P.O., 1987. House Hearing. Y4.W36:99-102.

Includes statements filed by the Committee on Human Rights in Romania (Hungarian Human Rights Foundation), the testimony of Jeri Laber, Executive Director of the U.S. Helsinki Watch Committee, and the testimony of Nina Shea, Program Director, International League of Human Rights. Supplemental materials include letters from business leaders supporting MFN status, and correspondence and reports by various associations, organizations, and individuals.

818. U.S. Congress. House. Committee on Ways and Means. Subcommittee on Trade. *Most-Favored-Nation Treatment with Respect to the Products of the Socialist Republic of Romania: Hearing ... July 18, 1977.* Washington: U.S. G.P.O., 1977. House Hearing. Y4.W36:95-33.

Administration and public witnesses discuss human rights, emigration, and trade issues in hearings on possible continuation of MFN status for Romania.

819. U.S. Congress. House. Committee on Ways and Means. Subcommittee on Trade. *Presidential Recommendation to Continue Waivers Applicable to Romania, Hungary, and the People's Republic of China, and to Extend the Trade Act Waiver Authority: Hearing ... July 14, 1983.* Washington: U.S. G.P.O., 1983. House Hearing. Y4.W36:98-22.

Witnesses express reservations due to Romania's continued human rights abuses. Appended materials include a paper by Catherine Fitzpatrick (Helsinki Watch Committee) entitled "Romania: Human Rights in a Most Favored Nation" (pp. 107-123), Kentucky Senate Resolution No. 31, requesting non-renewal of MFN status for Romania, documents on repression of ethnic Hungarians, and a tabular summary of Romanian emigration denials or delays. Expressions of support of and opposition to continuation of MFN status by witnesses are also recorded.

820. U.S. Congress. House. Committee on Ways and Means. Subcommittee on Trade. *Report of the Subcommittee on Trade to the U.S. House of Representatives on Continuation of Nondiscriminatory (Most-Favored Nation) Treatment to Products Imported from the Socialist Republic of Romania, September 26, 1978.* Washington: U.S. G.P.O., 1978. Committee Print. Y4.W36:WMCP95-106.

Report to inform House members on the current status of the freedom of emigration requirements as they apply to Romania. Concludes by recommending an extension of the Most Favored Nation Status to Romania.

821. U.S. Congress. House. Committee on Ways and Means. Subcommittee on Trade. *Report on Trade Mission to Central and Eastern Europe ....* Washington: U.S. G.P.O., 1984. Committee Print. Y4.W36:WMCP98-29.

An overview of Romania's geography and economy is followed by highlights of trade relations since MFN status was extended to Romania in 1975. Human rights, emigration, and minority issues are commented upon and meetings with Romanian officials, including President Ceauşescu, and a visit to the Grand National Assembly are described. The members of the delegation express their concerns that opportunities for U.S. business are diminishing. They recommend that growth of bilateral commercial relations be facilitated despite periods of low potential.

822. U.S. Congress. House. Committee on Ways and Means. Subcommittee on Trade. *Trade Waiver Authority Extension. Hearing ... June 10, 1980.* Washington: U.S.

G.P.O., 1981. House Hearing. Y4.W36:96-123.
Reviews emigration performance. Civic and political leaders testify for and against extension of Jackson-Vanik waiver authority.

823. U.S. Congress. House. Committee on Ways and Means. Subcommittee on Trade. *Trade Waiver Authority Extension: Hearing ... June 22, 1981.* Washington: U.S. G.P.O., 1981. House Hearing. Y4.W36:97-18.
Recommends a 12 month trade waiver extension for freedom of emigration for several countries including Romania. Emigration from Romania has risen since the Trade Agreement has been in effect. Includes an analysis of emigration performance, practices, and procedures, with monthly and yearly emigration statistics of Romanians to the United States from FY 1975 through FY 1980 as well as Jewish Romanian emigration to Israel from FY 1976 through FY 1981. Also included are letters from Romanian/ American citizens and residents requesting reunification of their families and testimony by the American-Romanian Cultural Foundation recommending extension of the MFN status for Romania.

824. U.S. Congress. House. Committee on Ways and Means. Subcommittee on Trade. *Waiver of Freedom of Emigration Requirement to the Socialist Republic of Romania and the Hungarian People's Republic: Hearing ... June 22 and July 9, 1979.* Washington: U.S. G.P.O., 1979. House Hearing. Y4.W36:96-30.
Administration and public witnesses express their views on extension of MFN status to Romania. Central to the discussion is emigration and the extent to which Romania is providing reciprocity for U.S. trade concessions.

825. U.S. Congress. Senate. Committee on Finance. *Background Materials Relating to the United States-Romanian Trade Agreement.* Washington: U.S. G.P.O., 1975. Committee Print. Y4.F49:T67/33.
Discusses the effects of MFN status on Romanian imports and exports.

826. U.S. Congress. Senate. Committee on Finance. *Background Materials Relating to United States-Romanian Trade and the Extension of the President's Authority to Waive Section 402 of the Trade Act of 1974.* Washington: U.S. G.P.O., 1976. Committee Print. Y4.F49:T67/38.
Reports on emigration from Romania and on U.S. trade with Romania.

827. U.S. Congress. Senate. Committee on Finance. Subcommittee on International Trade. *Continuation of the President's Authority to Waive the Trade Act Freedom of Emigration Provisions: Hearing ... July 29, 1983.* Washington: U.S. G.P.O., 1983. Senate Hearing. Y4.F49:S.hrg.98-399.
A hearing on the President's recommendation that a twelve month waiver of the freedom of emigration provision be extended to Romania. Includes witness statements, documents, correspondence, and statistics which support opinion for and against the waiver. Includes a U.S. Helsinki Watch Report, articles from leading U.S. and foreign newspapers and journals on Romanian human rights abuses, a bibliography of periodical articles published in the West on minority oppression in Romania (July 1982-May 1983), a statement by the Committee for Human Rights in Romania prepared by Laszló Hamos on behalf of the Committee for Human Rights in Romania, and a prepared statement by Nina Shea, Program Director of the International League of Human Rights, on the League's Family Reunification Project.

828. U.S. Congress. Senate. Committee on Finance. Subcommittee on International Trade. *Continuing Presidential Authority to Waive Freedom of Emigration Provisions: Hearing ... August 8, 1984.* Washington: U.S. G.P.O., 1985. Senate Hearing. Y4.F49:S.hrg.98-1219.
Examines continuing Most Favored Nation status for Romania, Hungary, and the People's Republic of China. Includes a review of human rights policies, emigration, religious persecution, and mistreatment of ethnic minorities, especially Hungarians. Reprints include correspondence, articles and reports from the underground Hungarian Press of Transylvania.

829. U. S. Congress. Senate. Committee on Finance. Subcommittee on International Trade. *Continuing the President's Authority to Waive the Trade Act Freedom of Emigration Provisions: Hearing ... July 12, 1978.* Washington: U.S. G.P.O., 1978. Senate Hearing. Y4.F49:P92/3.
Witnesses testify on Romania's emigration and human rights record. Business leaders and administration representatives discuss U.S.-Romanian trade in view of possible extension of the Trade Agreement providing for MFN status.

830. U. S. Congress. Senate. Committee on Finance. Subcommittee on International Trade. *Continuing the President's Authority to Waive the Trade Act Freedom of Emigration Provisions: Hearing ... July 19, 1979.* Washington: U.S. G.P.O., 1979. Senate Hearing. Y4.F49:T67/44.
Oral and written testimony for and against MFN treatment for Romania.

831. U.S. Congress. Senate. Committee on Finance. Subcommittee on International Trade. *Extension of the President's Authority to Waive Section 402 (Freedom of Emigration Requirements) of the Trade Act of 1974: Hearing ... July 21, 1980.* Washington: U.S. G.P.O., 1980. Senate Hearing. Y4.F49:T67/46.
A hearing on the right to emigrate and its status in Romania and other countries. Includes correspondence with the Romanian Embassy in Washington, lists and addresses of Romanian Jews seeking to emigrate, a letter of an American Romanian Committee for Assistance to Refugees official on emigration violations, and discussions on deteriorating social conditions of minorities. Arguments for and against extension of waiver are provided.

832. U.S. Congress. Senate. Committee on Finance. Subcommittee on International Trade. *MFN Status for Hungary, Romania, China, and Afghanistan: Hearing ... July 23, 1985.* Washington: U.S. G.P.O., 1986. Senate Hearing. Y4.F49:S.hrg.99-341.
Review of human rights performance, oppression of minorities, and freedom of emigration. Witnesses express opposing views. Appendix includes a paper by Joseph Ţon of the Romanian Missionary Society, entitled "Religious Persecution in Romania" (pp. 410-440), documenting discrimination of pastors and the desperate need for new church buildings.

833. U.S. Congress. Senate. Committee on Finance. Subcommittee on International Trade. *MFN Status for Romania: Hearing ... August 1, 1986.* Washington: U.S. G.P.O., 1987. Senate Hearing. Y4.F49:S.hrg.99-1008.
Includes several prepared statements on violations of human rights in Romania. Human rights abuses are highlighted in testimony given by representatives of the U.S. Helsinki Watch Committee, and the International Human Rights Law Group, Washington, D.C. The Hungarian Human Rights Foundation's Committee on Human Rights in Romania filed a statement dealing with anti-minority measures. Several other organizations testified to the persecution of the Hungarian minority in Transylvania. Business leaders testify in favor of MFN status as a foundation of trade opportunities for U.S. firms and their workers and as a tool for U.S. policy in general.

834. U.S. Congress. Senate. Committee on Finance. Subcommittee on International Trade. *Most Favored Nation Status for Romania, Hungary and China: Hearing ... July 27, 1981.* Washington: U.S. G.P.O., 1981. Senate Hearing. Y4.F49:F27.
A public hearing discussing whether to continue to wave the Trade Act Freedom of Emigration provisions for Romania. Appendixes include reprints of articles on ethnic problems, religious and emigration issues in the *London Times* and other newspapers, and personal letters as well as statements from Amnesty International.

835. U.S. Congress. Senate. Committee on Finance. Subcommittee on International Trade. *Review of the President's Decision to Renew Most-Favored-Nation Status for Romania, Hungary, and China: Hearing ... August 10, 1982.* Washington: U.S. G.P.O., 1982. Senate Hearing. Y4.F49:P92/4.
Romanian emigration to the U.S. and Romania-U.S. trade are the focal points.

Includes statistics on both aspects, along with correspondence relating to the issue of human rights violations within Romania and testimonies for and against continuing Most Favored Nation Status.

836. U.S. Congress. Senate. Committee on Foreign Relations. Subcommittee on European Affairs. *Romania, Most Favored Nation Status: Hearing ... February 26, 1986.* Washington: U.S. G.P.O., 1986. Senate Hearing. Y4.F76/2:S.hrg.99-674.
Presents statements and testimony on the possible extention of MFN status to Romania. The major theme is the human rights issue and its violation in Romania. Also included is the persecution of Hungarian minorities. Appended are supporting articles reproduced from the *Wall Street Journal, New York Times, Christian Science Monitor*, and several journals.

17. Philosophy, Ideology & Historiography

837. Anrod, Wener. "Zum Ideologischen Wandel in der Politik Rumäniens [Ideological Change in Romanian Politics]." *Zeitschrift für Politik* 20, no. 4 (1973): 361-374.
Analysis of Romania's international political and economic initiatives and Ceaușescu's ideological arguments in support of his deviant position.

838. Bacon, Walter M., Jr. "Romania: Neo-Stalinism in Search of Legitimacy." *Current History* 80, no. 465 (1981): 168-172+.
Theoretically, communist regimes enjoy broad popular support. In practice, they must resort to methods of coercion, consumerism, and nationalism to legitimize their existence. Examines Romania's apparent assertive foreign policy and its Stalinist domestic strategies.

839. Bacon, Walter M., Jr. "Romania." In *Communism in Eastern Europe*, edited by Teresa Rakowska-Harmstone, 162-185. 2nd ed. Manchester: Manchester University Press, 1984.
Romania, an anomaly combining domestic Stalinism with "partial alliance" to COMECON and the Warsaw Pact, is reinterpeting Marxism-Leninism to legitimize its nationalistic policy.

840. Botez, Mihai. "East-European Intellectuals and the National-Communist State: A View from Bucharest." *Praxis International* 8, no. 3 (1988): 350-359.
Discusses the relationship between intellectuals under communism and the totalitarian state.

841. Brown, J. F. "Conservatism and Nationalism in the Balkans: Albania, Bulgaria, and Romania." In *Central and Eastern Europe: The Opening Curtain?*, edited by William E. Griffith, 283-313. Boulder: Westview, 1989.
States that the three Balkan countries face political and economic uncertainty at home, as well as a precarious future. In Romania, Ceaușescu's successor will have to deal not only with domestic chaos, but also with the increasing pressures of *perestroika*.

842. Cioranescu, George. "Zum 100. Jahrestag der Unabhängigkeit Rumäniens: Historiographie mit Aktuellem Bezug [100th Anniversary of Romanian Independence: Historiography with Reference to the Present]." *Osteuropa* 27, no. 12 (1977): 1048-1056.
The fight for territorial integrity and independence is a dominant theme throughout Romanian history. Reviews contributions of Romanian historians to the centennial celebration of independence and Ceaușescu's own interpretation of historical events that support the country's current policy of independence.

843. Cismarescu, Michael. "Das Neue Programm der Rumänischen Kommunistischen Partei: Historische Legitimität und Nationaler Kommunismus [The New Program

of the Romanian Communist Party: Historical Legitimation and National Communism]." *Österreichische Osthefte* 18, no. 2 (1976): 160-168.

844. Deletant, Dennis. "Literature and Society in Romania since 1948." In *Perspectives on Literature and Society in Eastern and Western Europe*, edited by Geoffrey A. Hosking and George F. Cushing, 121-161. New York: St. Martin's Press, 1989.
Fatalism and opportunism induced a number of writers to adopt an attitude of acquiescence with party cultural policies. Nonetheless, there existed voices of defiance and opposition to the regime. Reviews major writers and trends since 1945, with special emphasis on the period after Ceauşescu's election to First Secretary.

845. Deletant, Dennis. "The Past in Contemporary Romania: Some Reflections on Current Romanian Historiography." In *Historians and the History of Transylvania*, edited by Laszló Peter, 133-158. East European Monographs, 332. New York: Columbia University Press, 1992.
An earlier version of this chapter appeared in *Slovo* 1, no. 2 (1988): 77-91.
Ceauşescu's distortion of national identity is achieved by denying and villifying Romania's association with Rome. Considers the role of language and history in shaping Romanian historical consciousness.

846. Deletant, Dennis. "Rewriting the Past: Trends in Contemporary Romanian Historiography." *Ethnic and Racial Studies* 14, no. 1 (1991): 64-86.
Analyzes the reasons for Ceauşescu's reappraisal of the Roman period of Romania's history.

847. Dion, Michel. "L'Identité Ethnique en Roumanie [Romanian Ethnic Identity]." *Cahiers Internationaux de Sociologie* 93 (July-December 1992): 251-268.
Analyzes some of the elements connected to the theory of national identity and focuses on the adoption in the 1970's of protochronism as state ideology.

848. Fischer, Gabriel. "Nationalism and Internationalism in Hungary and Rumania." *Canadian Slavonic Papers* 10, no. 1 (1968): 26-41.
Socialist societies and intra-bloc attitude is influenced and constantly redefined by nationalism.

849. Fischer-Galaţi, Stephen. "'Autocracy, Orthodoxy, Nationality' in the Twentieth Century: The Romanian Case." *East European Quarterly* 18, no. 1 (1984): 25-34.
In the 1960's, Ceauşescu's nationalistic policy sought legitimization from the Orthodox Church. The diaspora denounced Ceauşescu's Romanian Orthodox Church as a communist collaborator and viewed communist nationalism as incompatible with Orthodox traditions. Explores the relationship between the Romanian Orthodox Church and the ruling elite, as reflected in the case of Valerian Trifa, the Archbishop of the Romanian Orthodox Episcopate of America, who was deported from the United States for failing to declare his former affiliation to the Iron Guard.

850. Fischer-Galaţi, Stephen. "France and Rumania: A Changing Image." *East European Quarterly* 1, no. 2 (1967): 107-114.
Resurrection of traditional Franco-Romanian ties by the government is only one of the many political strategies to achieve independence from Moscow. For the younger generation, however, France has lost its relevance as an economic and political benefactor.

851. Fischer-Galaţi, Stephen. "Marxist Thought and the Rise of Nationalism." In *Security Implications of Nationalism in Eastern Europe*, edited by Jeffrey Simon and Trond Gilberg, 69-79. Boulder: Westview, 1986.
Ceauşescu's socialist patriotism is compatible with the nationalism of the Romanian right.

852. Fischer-Galaţi, Stephen. "Myths in Romanian History." *East European Quarterly* 15, no. 3 (1981): 327-334.

The accepted historical mythology, culminating with the exaltation of Nicolae Ceauşescu, is rooted in the search for legitimacy of the Romanian Communist Party. Analyzes the attempt to justify territorial rights and communist policies by using national and revolutionary traditions.

853. Fischer-Galaţi, Stephen. "Romanian Nationalism." In *Nationalism in Eastern Europe*, edited by Peter F. Sugar and Ivo J. Lederer, 373-395. Seattle: University of Washington Press, 1969.
Investigates to what extent Ceauşescu's claim to the national historic legacy of Romania is justified and necessary in the face of post-Stalinist Soviet pressure.

854. Gabanyi, Anneli Ute. "Ceauşescus Nationaldogmatische Kulturpolitik - Ein 'Dritter Weg'? [Ceauşescu's Dogmatic National Cultural Policy - A 'Third Path'?]." *Osteuropa* 26, no. 3 (1976): 194-201.
Presents highlights of the 1974 cultural policy, a continuation of Ceauşescu's 1971 theses on culture and ideology. Discusses literary works reinterpreting events from the recent past in a nationalistic light and the political motivations that allowed these to be published.

855. Gabanyi, Anneli Ute. *Partei und Literatur in Rumänien seit 1945 [Party and Literature in Romania Since 1945]*. Untersuchungen zur Gegenwartskunde Südosteuropas, 6. München: Oldenbourg, 1975.
Reviews Romania's policy on culture and creative expression from its Soviet dominated beginnings, through its short lived thaw in 1953-1957, to the Ceauşescu liberalization (1965-1968) and cultural revolution (1971-1974).

856. Ghermani, Dionisie. "Theorie und Praxis der Rumänischen Historiographie der Nachkriegszeit (1948-1978) [Theory and Practice of the Post-War Romanian Historiography (1948-1978)]." *Südostdeutsches Archiv* 21 (1978): 105-117.
Ceauşescu led a campaign for the rehabilitation of historical figures and in 1976 mandated that historical writings depict Romania's heroic past. Historians used this challenge to publish works that, under a thin ideological veneer, offer a high standard of scientific research.

857. Gilberg, Trond. "Eurocommunism and Romania." In *Eurocommunism Between East and West*, edited by Vernon V. Aspaturian, Jiri Valenta, and David P. Burke, 181-201. Bloomington: Indiana University Press, 1980.
Explores the impact of the Italian, French, and Spanish Communist Parties on policies and on the ideology of the Romanian Communist Party and its leader.

858. Gilberg, Trond. *Nationalism and Communism in Romania: The Rise and Fall of Ceauşescu's Personal Dictatorship*. Boulder: Westview, 1990.
Contents highlights: "Radicalism and Marxism," "Romania as a Modernizing Society," "Implementing Ceauşescuism: The Vehicle of the Party," "Modernization, Ceauşescu Style," "The Transformation of the Social Structure," "The Mass Culture of Ethnicity and Nationalism," "Societal Change and Instability," "Romania, Perestroika, and Glasnost," "Romania - Abberant or Typical?"

859. Gilberg, Trond. "Religion and Nationalism in Romania." In *Religion and Nationalism in Soviet and East European Politics*, edited by Pedro Ramet, 328-351. Rev. ed. Durham: Duke University Press, 1989.
Religion has experienced a revival despite efforts to eradicate it. Nationalism and orthodoxy are inextricably intertwined and are characteristic of Ceauşescu's dysfunctional policies.

860. Gilberg, Trond. "State Policy, Ethnic Persistence and Nationality Formation in Eastern Europe." In *Ethnic Diversity and Conflict in Eastern Europe*, edited by Peter Sugar, 185-235. Santa Barbara, CA: ABC-Clio, 1980.
Based on a conference of ethnicity in Eastern Europe, Seattle, June 11-13, 1976.

In the 1960's Romania embarked upon "national communism." Discusses this state policy and its impact on minority populations.

861. Giurchescu, Anca. "The National Festival 'Song to Romania:' Manipulation of Symbols in the Political Discourse." In *Symbols of Power: The Esthetics of Political Legitimation in the Soviet Union and Eastern Europe*, edited by Claes Arvidsson and Lars Erik Blomqvist, 163-171. Stockholm: Almqvist & Wiksell, 1987.
Shows how folkloric traditions and rituals are used by the Ceauşescu government to misrepresent reality, articulate ideological propaganda, and ultimately legitimize power.

862. Hartl, Hans. *Nationalismus in Rot: Die Patriotischen Wandlungen des Kommunismus in Südosteuropa [Red Nationalism: Communist Patriotic Transformations in Southeast Europe]*. Schriftreihe der Studiengesellschaft für Zeitprobleme, Zeitpolitik, 1. Stuttgart: Seewald, 1968.
The chapter "Rumänien: Nationaler Sozialismus" (pp. 26-52) discusses Ceauşescu's 1965 theses, the concept of national specific as determinant factor in judging history, literature, and art, and the role of the nation in socialism in light of Marxist-Leninist ideals.

863. Hartl, Hans. "Zuerst Sind Sie National [First They Are National]." *Der Europäische Osten* 13, no. 145 (1976): 212-219.
In contrast to the classics of communism and to other East bloc country ideology, the Romanian Communist Party proclaims that in socialism the national takes precedence over the international.

864. Hitchins, Keith. "Historiography of the Countries of Eastern Europe: Romania." *American Historical Review* 97, no. 4 (1992): 1064-1083.
Reviews the processes of nation-building from the 19th century, discusses Ceauşescu's July theses which marked the beginning of nationalism and the cult of personality.

865. Jackson, Bill Frank. "A Study in the Ideology of a National Communism: Romanian Elite Concepts Comprising Romanian Communist Ideology as Manifested on the Domestic and International Scenes." Ph.D. diss., University of Southern Mississippi, 1972. Ann Arbor: UMI, 1972. AAD7226555.
Compares and contrasts Soviet and Romanian ideology and practice as applied to domestic and international policy issues.

866. Karnoouh, Claude. *L'Invention du Peuple: Chronique de Roumanie [People's Creation: Romanian Chronicle]*. Paris: Arcantére, 1990.
Essays, some previously published, illustrating manifestations of national identity as reflected in ethnology, social organization, culture, philosophy, or history.

867. Kellogg, Frederick. "The Structure of Romanian Nationalism." *Canadian Review of Studies in Nationalism* 11, no. 1 (1984): 21-50.
Analyzes the "pillars" of Romanian nationalism: language, religion, educational traditions, fear of external threats, and the economy.

868. King, Robert R. "Ideological Mobilization in Romania." In *Eastern Europe's Uncertain Future: A Selection of Radio Free Europe Research Reports*, edited by Robert R. King and James F. Brown, 266-282. New York: Praeger, 1977.
Investigates the impact of ideological indoctrination emphasizing nationalism and patriotism on economic efficiency, on education and youth, and on controlling the cultural elite and mobilizing the masses.

869. Kuhns, Woodrow J. "Political Nationalism in Contemporary Eastern Europe." In *Security Implications of Nationalism in Eastern Europe*, edited by Jeffrey Simon and Trond Gilberg, 81-108. Boulder: Westview, 1986.
Analyzes Ceauşescu's ideology of nationalism.

870. Lendvai, Paul. *Eagles in Cobwebs: Nationalism and Communism in the Balkans.* Garden City, NY: Doubleday, 1969.
Study of nationalism and its impact on political developments in Yugoslavia, Albania, Bulgaria, and Romania. Chapter six, "Romania: A Quiet Revolution" (pp.262-349), reviews historical relations between the Soviet Union and Romania, the post-World War II communist takeover, and Romania's drive for national independence. Focuses on domestic and foreign relations under Ceauşescu.

871. Meier, Viktor E. *Neuer Nationalismus in Südosteuropa [New Nationalism in South-East Europe].* Opladen: Leske, 1968.
The chapter "Rumänien: Nationale Souveranität als Ordnungsprinzip" (pp.9-26) contends that an independent posture and ideology are no substitute for a sound domestic policy and economy. Since the internal structure is weak, future difficulties appear unavoidable.

872. Nasta, Mihail. "Un Départagement des Termes dans l'Ontologie de Constantin Noica [Classification of Terms in Constantin Noica's Ontology]." *International Journal of Rumanian Studies* 4, no. 2 (1984): 23-52.
Explores Noica's work since the 1960's and his special attention to language.

873. Nemoianu, Virgil. "Mihai Şora and the Traditions of Romanian Philosophy." *Review of Metaphysics* 43, no. 3 (1990): 591-605.
A review of Romanian contributions to the history of philosophy followed by a discussion of the significance of Şora's writings.

874. Pilon, Juliana Geran. "Anti-Individualist Chords in the Romanian-Marxist Rhapsody." *Studies in Soviet Thought* 19, no. 3 (1979): 233-238.
Examines *The History of Romanian Philosophy*, a 1972 collection of essays written by contemporary Romanian Marxists. Commends the precursors of contemporary Romanian Marxists for correctly opposing anarchism. By rejecting anarchism, Romanian philosophers reject the autonomy of individual choice and the primacy of self, and embrace the ideals of controlled scientific socialism.

875. Pilon, Juliana Geran. *The Bloody Flag: Post-Communist Nationalism in Eastern Europe: Spotlight on Romania.* Studies in Social Philosophy & Policy, 16. New Brunswick: Transaction, 1992.
After tracing the process of awakening of ethnic consciousness, focuses on Ceauşescu's megalomaniacal nationalism.

876. Pilon, Juliana Geran. "Objectivity in Romanian-Marxist Ethics: Dissonant and Equivocal Variations on a Kantian Theme." *Studies in Soviet Thought* 20, no. 2 (1979): 177-190.
Analysis of the "objectivity" concept and its anti-individualist meaning, based on Ioan Grigoraş' text *Principles of Socialist Ethics.*

877. Pilon, Juliana Geran. "The Romanian Distinction Between Negative and Positive Liberty." *Studies in Soviet Thought* 23, no. 2 (1982): 131-140.
Analyzes political freedom as explained by Nistor Prisca in *The Fundamental Rights and Obligations of the Citizens in RSR.* Concludes that negative liberty (the non-interference duty of the state) is practically and theoretically impossible in a state that abolishes private property.

878. Price, George W. "Nationalism in the Romanian Military: Ceauşescu's Double-Edged Sword." In *Security Implications of Nationalism in Eastern Europe*, edited by Jeffrey Simon and Trond Gilbert, 277-294. Boulder: Westview, 1986.
Discusses the role of nationalism as a means to gain legitimacy for the regime, buttress foreign policy positions, and gain control of the military.

879. Schöpflin, George. "Rumanian Nationalism." *Survey (London)* 20, no. 2-3 (1974): 77-104.

Explores nationalistic tendencies as reflected in economic policies, pronatalist legislation, international relations, etymology and vocabulary, historiography, and terrritorial claims.

880. Shafir, Michael. "L'Involution Idéologique du Parti Communiste Roumain [Ideological Regression of the Romanian Communist Party]." *Temps Modernes* 45, no. 522 (1990): 4-24.
Faced with *glasnost* and *perestroika*, Ceauşescu reverts to Stalinist positions and rejects reform as a deviation from true communist doctrine.

881. Shafir, Michael. "The Men of the Archangel Revisited: Anti-Semitic Formations among Communist Romania's Intellectuals." *Studies in Comparative Communism* 16, no. 3 (1983): 223-243.
Reviews cultural politics under Gheorghiu-Dej and Ceauşescu and concludes that anti-Semitic writers have once again become active and enjoy the protection of Ceauşescu's elites.

882. Shafir, Michael. "Political Culture, Intellectual Dissent, and Intellectual Consent: The Case of Romania." *Orbis* 27, no. 2 (1983): 393-420.
Originally published as Research Paper, No. 38. Jerusalem: Hebrew University of Jerusalem, Soviet and East European Research Center, 1978.
Examines the historic relationship between the communist regime and the Romanian creative intelligentsia and suggests that a series of factors have produced acquiescence or have kept intellectual dissent from being openly expressed.

883. Shafir, Michael. "Xenophobic Communism - The Case of Bulgaria and Romania." *The World Today* 45, no. 12 (1989): 208-212.
Both countries are trying to stem reforms by rekindling traditional national and ethnic animosities. This manipulation of the social consensus is termed "xenophobic communism."

884. Verdery, Katherine. *National Ideology under Socialism: Identity and Cultural Politics in Ceauşescu's Romania*. Berkeley: University of California Press, 1991.
Study of nationalism during the last decades of communist rule, focusing on the debate between Ceauşescu's ethnocentric minstrels and those advocating reason.

885. Verdery, Katherine. *Romanian Identity and Cultural Politics under Ceauşescu: An Example from Philosophy*. Occasional Papers of East European Studies, 17. Washington: Wilson Center, 1990.
Studies Noicans' and ethnophilosophers' definition of culture, values, and national identity and its relation to the organization of power.

886. Zwick, Peter. *National Communism*. Boulder: Westview, 1983.
Discusses Ceauşescu's Stalinist leadership style and his domestic and foreign policies. Concludes that Romanian national communism is not an abberation within international communism, but "an acceptable, normal pattern of behavior."

18. Protest, Dissent & Revolution

See also the chapter Ethnic Relations & Human Rights

887. Brown, J. F. *Surge to Freedom: The End of Communist Rule in Eastern Europe.* Durham, NC: Duke University Press, 1991.
In "Romania: The Uprising" (pp.199-220) the author revisits the last dark decades of Romania's history, from the "systematization," personality cult, and staunch opposition to reform to the "spirit of Timișoara" and the violent overthrow of Ceaușescu.

888. Bugajski, Janusz, and Maxine Pollack. *East European Fault Lines: Dissent, Opposition, and Social Activism.* Boulder: Westview, 1989.
Traces the evolution and manifestations of dissent, e.g. social activism, political and human rights movements, religious and economic activities, campaigns for minority rights, and the rock-and-roll subculture.

889. Călinescu, Matei, and Vladimir Tismăneanu. "The 1989 Revolution and Romania's Future." *Problems of Communism* 40, no. 1-2 (1991): 42-59.
Describes Ceaușescu's last days in power, the revolution, the dictator's trial and execution, and the legacy cast by the old regime on the country's democratic future.

890. Connor, Walter D. "Dissent in Eastern Europe: A New Coalition?" *Problems of Communism* 29, no. 1 (1980): 1-17.
Focuses on the Jiu Valley miners' strike and Paul Goma's letter of protest in 1977. Asserts that Eastern European intellectuals and workers, while actively protesting against communist regimes, have acted independently without forming a coalition across social classes.

891. Deletant, Dennis. "Crimes Against the Spirit." *Index on Censorship* 18, no. 8 (1989): 25-28.
Describes the growing opposition to Ceaușescu's policies.

892. Dempsey, Judy. "Romania Since Solidarity." *Workers under Communism* 3 (Winter 1983): 19-22.
The lessons of Solidarity were lost on Romania's communist elite, who so far has been successful in suppressing any isolated expression of dissent. A cohesive opposition movement has yet to emerge.

893. Durandin, Catherine. "Sortir de l'Hiver? [The End of Winter?]." *Esprit* 147 (February 1989): 8-14.
In France, the image of an independent Romania has been replaced with that of a brutally repressive regime. Encouraged by *perestroika*, Paul Goma, Mihai Botez, and Bujor Nedelcovici are part of a growing dissident movement.

894. Durandin, Catherine. "Une Voix de l'Opposition Roumaine [One Voice from Romania's Opposition]." *L'Autre Europe* 15/16 (1988): 58-70.
Discusses the political agenda of the dissident movement, "Romanian Democratic Action."

895. Eyal, Jonathan. "Why Romania Could Not Avoid Bloodshed." In *Spring in Winter: The 1989 Revolutions*, edited by Gwyn Prins, 139-160. Manchester: Manchester University Press, 1990.
Four cardinal mistakes led to the uprising and Ceauşescu's execution: his abuse of people; his misreading of shifting geopolitical interests; his nationalistic policies; and his lack of understanding of social dynamics.

896. Freund, Emil. "Nascent Dissent in Romania." In *Dissent in Eastern Europe*, edited by Jane Leftwich Curry, 60-68. New York: Praeger, 1983.
Papers from a conference sponsored by the American Council of Learned Societ-ies' Joint Committee on Eastern Europe.
Overview of voices of dissent since the 1970's presented by occupational, reli-gious, and demographic groups.

897. Gabanyi, Anneli Ute. "Das 'Bukarester Tauwetter:' Rumänische Literaturpolitik im Zeichen der Dissidentenbewegung [The 'Bucharest Thaw:' Romanian Literary Policy in the Context of the Dissident Movement]." *Osteuropa* 27, no. 12 (1977): 1038-1047.
A chronology of the literary dissident movement initiated by writer Paul Goma. The official government reaction is a mix of tolerance and terror, instituting a new model of censorship.

898. Gabanyi, Anneli Ute. *Die Unvollendete Revolution: Rumänien Zwischen Diktatur und Demokratie [The Incomplete Revolution: Romania Between Dictatorship and Democracy]*. Series Piper, 1271. München: Piper, 1990.
Analytical account of the revolution. Gives credence to the theory that the revolu-tion was instigated by Moscow in an effort to topple Ceauşescu and install a pro-Soviet government.

899. Georgescu, Vlad. "Romanian Dissent: Its Ideas." In *Dissent in Eastern Europe*, edited by Jane Leftwich Curry, 182-194. New York: Praeger, 1983.
Papers from a conference sponsored by the American Council of Learned Societ-ies' Joint Committee on Eastern Europe.
Deals with the philosophical contents of open letters of dissent.

900. Ghermani, Dionisie. "Rumänien: Der Rumänische Widerstand [Romania: Romanian Resistance]." In *Selbstbestimmung für Mittel- und Osteuropa*, 117-119. Knjiznica Sloboda, 9. Brugg: Adria, 1988.
Resistance is manifest in the writings of survivors of communist persecution or in active and passive workers' protests. Tragically such actions find no echo in the pages of the Western press, whose readers are over-exposed to dramatic events.

901. Goma, Paul. "'État Ouvrier' et Classe Ouvrière ['Worker's State' and Working Class]." *L'Alternative (Paris)* 1 (November-December 1979): 17-19.
Outlines the emergence (1977) and manifestations of the dissent movement and the regime's repressive response.

902. Harsanyi, Doina, and Nicolae Harsanyi. "Romania: Democracy and the Intellectu-als." *East European Quarterly* 27, no. 2 (1993): 243-260.
Discusses cases of intellectual dissent and forms of protest ranging from artistic candor to cultural self-isolation.

903. Karatnycky, Adrian, Alexander J. Motyl, and Adolph Sturmthal. *Workers' Rights, East and West: A Comparative Study of Trade Unions and Workers' Rights in West-ern Democracies and Eastern Europe*. N.p.: League for Industrial Democracy, 1980.

Profiles the organization of the first independent trade union in Romania (SLOMR, 1979) and the repressive reaction of the Ceauşescu government (pp.78-86). Reproduces SLOMR documents (pp.134-143).

904. King, Arthur. "Religion and Rights: A Dissenting Minority as a Social Movement in Romania." *Social Compass* 28, no. 1 (1981): 113-119.
Describes the origins, achievements, and collapse of the Christian Committeee for the Defense of Freedom of Religion and Conscience (ALRC). Consisting primarily of Romanian Baptists, this organization served as a vehicle for ideological dissent. The government successfully weakened the movement by exploiting internal differences and facilitating emigration of its leaders to the West.

905. Loupan, Victor. *La Révolution n'a pas eu Lieu: Roumanie, l'Histoire d'un Coup d'État [The Revolution Did Not Take Place: Romania, the History of a Coup]*. Paris: Robert Laffont, 1990.
Describes the events of December 1989 as a political coup, involving a spontaneous mass rebellion. Sketches portraits of Ceauşescu and of the principal characters who manipulated the December political events.

906. Portocală, Radu. *Autopsie du Coup d'État Roumain: Au Pays du Mensonge Triomphant [Post-Mortem of the Romanian Coup: In the Country of the Triumphant Lie]*. Paris: Calmann-Levy, 1990.
Contends that the 1989 revolution was scripted in Moscow.

907. Ratesh, Nestor. *Romania: The Entangled Revolution*. The Washington Papers, 152. New York: Praeger, 1991.
Describes Romania in the last decade of communist dictatorship, the unrest in Timişoara that ignited the revolution, and the "recycled communism" that rules Romania today.

908. Sampson, Steven L. "Is Romania the Next Poland?" *Critique (Glasgow)* 16 (1983): 139-144.
Explores differences between socioeconomic and political attitudes of workers and intellectuals in Romania and Poland, and concludes that a Solidarity type movement is unlikely to appear in Romania.

909. Sampson, Steven L. "Muddling Through in Rumania: (or Why the Mămăliga Doesn't Explode)." *International Journal of Rumanian Studies* 3, no. 1-2 (1981): 165-176.
Questions why there is silence and apathy in face of increasing suffering. Contends that Romania has not reached the state of genuine crisis and citizens continue to seek solutions to apparently insolvable problems.

910. Sampson, Steven L. "Reply to My Critics: Issues for Discussion." *International Journal of Rumanian Studies* 3, no. 1-2 (1981): 180-185.
Follow-up to his article "Muddling Through in Rumania."

911. Shafir, Michael. "Who is Paul Goma?" *Index on Censorship* 7, no. 1 (1978): 29-39.
Profiles the dissident movement and its leader, the writer Paul Goma. The movement is supported by intellectuals and workers alike.

912. Simpson, John. *Dispatches from the Barricades: An Eye-Witness Account of the Revolutions that Shook the World, 1989-90*. London: Hutchinson, 1990.
Part five, "Bucharest - A Darker Revolution" (pp.186-253), describes the violent overthrow of Ceauşescu.

913. Tănase, Virgil. *Le Dossier Paul Goma: L'Écrivain Face au Socialisme du Silence [The Paul Goma File: The Writer Facing the Socialism of Silence]*. Cahiers de l'Est, 2. Paris: Albatros, 1977.
Supported by texts, letters, and diary entries of Paul Goma, narrates the fight of this Romanian writer for basic human rights.

914. *Tearing Down the Curtain: The People's Revolution in Eastern Europe*. London: Hodder & Stoughton, 1990.
"Romania: The Half-Finished Revolution" (pp. 124-146) narrates the events lead-ing to the revolutionary explosion of December 1989, the capture and trial of the Ceauşescus, and the post-revolutionary tentatives for reform, as seen by a team from *The Observer*.

915. Thon, F. "La Violence Politique dans les Pays de l'Est: Roumanie [Political Vio-lence in Eastern Countries: Romania]." *Études Polémologiques* 42, no. 2 (1987): 127-131.
Lists groups of people at risk and government methods of intimidation and repres-sion. Contends that organized opposition is on the rise.

916. Tismăneanu, Vladimir. "The Rebellion of the Old Guard." *East European Reporter* 3, no. 4 (1989): 23.
Discusses the open letter challenging Ceauşescu's dictatorship (March 1989) signed by six veterans of the Romanian Communist Party and gives background informa-tion on the signatories. Reproduces the full text of the letter.

917. Tismăneanu, Vladimir. "The Revival of Politics in Romania." In *The New Europe: Revolution in East-West Relations*, edited by Nils H. Wessell, 85-99. Proceedings of the Academy of Political Sciences, vol. 38, no.1. Montpelier, VT: Academy of Po-litical Sciences, 1991.
Charts the end of the Ceauşescu regime and argues that the spontaneous revolution was usurped by "apparatchiks." Romania's future will be defined by resolving the conflict between democracy and neo-communism.

918. U.S. Commisssion on Security and Cooperation in Europe. *Revolt Against Silence: The State of Human Rights in Romania (An Update)*. Washington: U.S. G.P.O., 1989. Committee Print. Y4.Se 2:101-1-10.
The destruction of villages continues and human rights abuses are on the increase. In spite of repressive measures a dialogue between dissidents and the regime is emerging.

19. Religion

See also the following chapters: Ethnic Relations & Human Rights; Most Favored Nation Status; Protest, Dissent & Revolution

919. Beeson, Trevor. *Discretion & Valour: Religious Conditions in Russia and Eastern Europe.* Rev. ed. London: Collins, 1982.
    Chapter 11 (pp.350-379) describes Romanian church organizations, theological education, religious publications, denominations, church attendance, and religious freedom.

920. Berindei, Mihnea. "Religion et Politique en Roumanie [Religion and Politics in Romania]." *International Journal of Rumanian Studies* 5, no. 1 (1987): 107-128.
    The marked increase in the number of believers in most denominations, especially among Catholics and neo-Protestants, demonstrates the failure of the regime's religious policy.

921. Broun, Janice A. "Catholics in Rumania: A History of Survival." *America* 150, no. 18 (1984): 357-361.
    Overview of persecutions suffered by Catholics and Eastern- and Latin-Rite Church members. Despite mistreatments, church attendance is up and the ratio of priests to people has increased. The future of the church remains in danger.

922. Broun, Janice A. "The Latin-Rite Roman Catholic Church in Romania." *Religion in Communist Lands* 12, no. 2 (1987): 168-184.
    Traces the history of this resilient church and its persecution under communism.

923. Broun, Janice A. "Religion in Romania: The Truth Behind the Image." *Freedom at Issue* 77 (March 1984): 10-13.
    The government proclaims full religious freedom while arresting believers and banning two major churches.

924. Broun, Janice A. "Rumania's Churches Behind the Facade of Liberalism." *America* 150, no. 9 (1984): 165-169.
    The proclaimed church-state harmony masks considerable tensions. Those protesting state policies are harassed or imprisoned.

925. Calciu-Dumitreasa, Gheorghe. "The Persecution of the Orthodox Church in Romania." In *Sources of "Human Rights Violations in Romania,"* edited by Philip S. Cox, 22-36. Washington, D.C.: American Foreign Policy Institute, 1986.
    Discusses atheism in communist Romania, persecution of the clergy, political assassinations, and the so-called "independent policy," a ploy to fool the West.

926. Delvoy, P. "The Church in Romania." *Pro Mundi Vita Dossiers. Dossier Europe/ North America* 4 (November-December 1978): 2-30.
Outlines church-state relations regarding abortion and divorce. Describes the Orthodox Church as the guardian of Romanian identity and explains its organization, clerical education, monastic life, and its relation to non-Orthodox churches. Concludes that coexistence between church and state is possible.

927. Doens, I. "L'Église Orthodoxe Roumaine [Romanian Orthodox Church]." *Irénikon* 41 (1968): 414-443.
Summary of discussions between Patriarchs Justinian and Athenagoras (1967) on inter-Orthodox concerns and relations to other Christian churches.

928. Eileen Mary, Sister. "Orthodox Monasticism in Romania." *Religion in Communist Lands* 8, no. 1 (1980): 22-27.
Monasteries are supported by the state and are visited by thousands of vacationers and pilgrims. Monastic life is an integral part of the national identity.

929. Finklestone, Joseph. *Dangers, Tests and Miracles: The Remarkable Life Story of Chief Rabbi Rosen of Romania as Told to Joseph Finklestone*. London: Weidenfeld and Nicolson, 1990.
Chronicles the controversial diplomatic balancing act of Romania's Chief Rabbi to safeguard the faith, traditions, and culture of the Jewish community during the Ceauşescu regime.

930. Ghermani, Dionisie. "Iuliu, Kardinal Hossu, Märtyrer der Rumänischen Griechisch-Katholischen Kirche [Iuliu, Cardinal Hossu, Martyr of the Romanian Greek-Catholic Church]." In *Die Führung der Kirche in den Sozialistishen Staaten Europas*, edited by Gabriel Adrianyi, 131-138. München: Berchman, 1978.
Profiles Iuliu Hossu, Bishop of Cluj, arrested in 1948, who fought to his death for the reinstatement of the Greek-Catholic Church.

931. Ghermani, Dionisie. "Kirche und Menschenrechte in Rumänien [Church and Human Rights in Romania]." *Kirche in Not* 34 (1986): 159-167.
Examines the discrepancy between constitutional religious rights and their implementation.

932. Ghermani, Dionisie. "Die Lage der Kirche in Rumänien: Bilanz und Aussicht [The State of the Church in Romania: Status and Future]." In *Religionsfreiheit und Menschenrechte*, edited by Paul Lendvai, 203-214. Graz: Styria, 1983.
While religious rights are guaranteed by the Constitution, churches and believers continue to be persecuted. Explores the situation of the Catholic, Uniate, and Greek-Orthodox Churches at the beginning of the 1980's.

933. Ghermani, Dionisie. "Rumänien [Romania]." In *Religions- und Glaubensfreiheit als Menschenrechte*, edited by Rudolf Grülich, 90-102. Ackermann-Gemeinde, 30. München: Ackermann-Gemeinde, 1980.
Warns that after Helsinki, religious rights remain elusive and believers are persecuted and imprisoned.

934. Ghermani, Dionisie. "Rumäniens Griechisch-Katholische Kirche [Romania's Greek-Catholic Church]." *Kirche in Not* 30 (1982): 146-150.
Despite papal intervention the Uniate Catholic Church remains outlawed.

935. Ghermani, Dionisie. "Rumäniens Kirchenpolitik und Moskaus 'Perestrojka' [Romania's Policy on Religion and Moscow's 'Perestroika']." *Kirche in Not* 36 (1988): 107-115.
Gorbachev's rehabilitation of the Russian Orthodox Church is seen as a provocation by Ceauşescu. Notwithstanding worldwide protests, Ceauşescu intensifies the destruction of churches and historical monuments.

Uniate Church has Survived]." In *Burgen-Regionen-Völker: Festschrift für Franz Hieronimus Riedl zur Vollendung des 80. Lebensjahr*, edited by Theodor Veiter, 265-272. Ethnos, 27. Vienna: Braumüller, 1986.
Asserts that the Greek-Catholic Church, abolished by the communists in 1948 and forcefully integrated into the Orthodox Church, is still active underground.

937. Ghermani, Dionisie. "Zur Lage der Kirchen in Rumänien [On the Situation of Churches in Romania]." *Kirche in Not* 35 (1987): 181-189.
Notes the growing dependency of the church on the state and warns that Ceauşescu is systematically destroying religion and churches. Calls on Western governments to intensify pressure for religious rights.

938. Ghermani, Dionisie. "Zur Situation der Christen in Rumänien [On the Situation of Christians in Romania]." *Kirche in Not* 29 (1981): 176-181.
Repressive measures taken against believers and the atheistic campaign led by the media have not achieved their goal.

939. Ghermani, Dionisie. "Zwangsatheisierung in Rumänien [Atheism by Force in Romania]." *Kirche in Not* 28 (1980): 73-76.
Far from succeeding in obliterating religion, atheistic campaigns have succeeded in increasing the number of believers.

940. Grossu, Sergiu. *Le Calvaire de la Roumanie Chrétienne [The Calvary of Christian Romania]*. Paris: France-Empire, 1987.
Describes religious persecution, suffering, and underground resistance of believers.

941. Havadtoy, Alexander. "The Oppression of the Hungarian Reformed Church in Romania." In *Sources of "Human Rights Violations in Romania,"* edited by Philip S. Cox, 46-53. Washington, D.C.: American Foreign Policy Institute, 1986.
Discusses state control of the church, the incident of the recycling of Bibles into toilet paper, and the continuous harassment of ministers by the Securitate.

942. Hitchins, Keith. "The Romanian Orthodox Church and the State." In *Religion and Atheism in the U.S.S.R. and Eastern Europe*, edited by Bohdan R. Bociurkiw, John W. Strong, and Jean K. Laux, 314-327. Carleton Series in Soviet and East European Studies, [6]. London: Macmillan, 1975.
Ceauşescu recognizes the Church as a useful social force and allows it to function under conditions more favorable than those existing in other socialist states.

943. Niculescu, Pavel. "Problems and Persecution of the Neoprotestants in Romania." In *Sources of "Human Rights Violations in Romania,"* edited by Philip S. Cox, 54-59. Washington, D.C.: American Foreign Policy Institute, 1986.
Outlines the rise of neo-Protestantism and the persecution suffered by believers.

944. Pope, Earl A. "Church-State Relations in Romania." *Kyrkohistorisk Arsskrift* 77 (1977): 291-297.
The relationship between church and state in the 1970's appears to have stabilized.

945. Pope, Earl A. "Ecumenism in Eastern Europe: Romanian Style." *East European Quarterly* 13, no. 2 (1979): 185-212.
Since the beginning of the twentieth century, the Romanian Orthodox Church has shown an active participation in the ecumenical movement. Traces its history and examines the role of the Church in the development of Eastern European ecumenism.

946. Pope, Earl A. "The Orthodox Church in Romania." *Ostkirchliche Studien* 31 (December 1982): 297-310.
Despite efforts of atheistic socialization, religion continues to play an important role in the life of young and old. Considers the possibility of a dialogue between Marxists and theologians.

947. Pope, Earl A. "Protestantism in Romania." In *Protestantism and Politics in Eastern Europe and Russia: The Communist and Postcommunist Eras,* edited by Sabrina Petra Ramet, 157-208. Christianity under Stress, 3. Durham: Duke University Press, 1992.
Highlights relevant features of the history of Protestantism in Romania and discusses the relationship between the socialist state and neo-Protestant communities during and after the Ceauşescu dictatorship.

948. Pope, Earl A. "The Significance of the Evangelical Alliance in Contemporary Romanian Society." *East European Quarterly* 25, no. 4 (1991): 493-518.
Profiles neo-Protestant churches and their fight against religious persecution, culminating in the 1989 revolutionary confrontation. Currently, new opportunities emerge that may lead to better relations between church and state.

949. Scarfe, Alan. "The Evangelical Wing of the Orthodox Church in Romania." *Religion in Communist Lands* 3, no. 6 (1975): 15-19.
Historical account of the emergence of the Brethren Movement and the Lord's Army.

950. Scarfe, Alan. "Romanian Baptists and the State." *Religion in Communist Lands* 4, no. 2 (1976): 14-20.
Discusses Pastor Ţon's papers of 1973/1974, in which he accuses Romanian authorities of legal rights infringements against Baptists and of threatening the "doctrinal assertion of Christ's Lordship over His Church." The state reacted with harassment and persecution.

951. Stolojan, Sanda. "Persécution et Résistance Religieuse en Roumanie [Persecution and Religious Resistance in Romania]." *L'Alternative (Paris)* 9 (1981): 17-19.
A history of state-church relations since the communist takeover, followed by a report on Ceauşescu's repressive measures against human rights activism and neo-Protestant militancy.

952. Transylvanicus [pseud.]. "The Catholic Church in Romania." In *Sources of "Human Rights Violations in Romania,"* edited by Philip S. Cox, 37-45. Washington, D.C.: American Foreign Policy Institute, 1986.
An American-Hungarian priest from Transylvania discusses the persecution of the Catholic Church in communist Romania.

953. U.S. Congress. Senate. Committee on Foreign Relations. *Protecting and Promoting Religious Rights in Eastern Europe and the Soviet Union: Hearing ... June 12, 1984.* Washington: U.S. G.P.O., 1984. Senate Hearing. Y4.F76/2:S.hrg.98-912.
Statements by scholars, pastors, and others with religious affiliations on the treatment of religious groups and activists within Romania. Supporting articles published in newspapers and religious journals are included. Individual stories of human rights abuses against Christians comprise the major portion of the testimony.

954. U.S. Congress. Senate. Committee on Foreign Relations. Subcommittee on European Affairs. *Religious Persecution Behind the Iron Curtain: Hearing ... November 14, 1985.* Washington: U.S. G.P.O., 1986. Senate Hearing. Y4.F76/2:S.hrg.99-835.
Includes information on the persecution of Christians and ethnic and other religious minorities in Eastern Europe including Romania.

955. Villiers, Miranda. "The Romanian Orthodox Church Today." *Religion in Communist Lands* 1, no. 3 (1973): 4-7.
The Church is tolerated due to its deep national roots. A spiritual revival can be observed in monastic life, theological education, and interconfessional relations.

956. Webster, Alexander F. C. "Prophecy and Propaganda in the Romanian Orthodox Patriarchate." *East European Quarterly* 25, no. 4 (1992): 519-524.
Portrays three church leaders: a communist collaborator, a prophet-like dissident, and a "progressive realist." Discusses their interaction with political life during and after Ceauşescu.

20. Sociology

957. Batistella, Roger M. "Health Services in the Socialist Republic of Romania: Structural Features and Cost-Containment Policies." *Journal of Public Health Policy* 4, no. 1 (1983): 89-106.
Highlights differences between the Soviet Union and Romania in medical manpower policies, requirements for continuing education, and attitudes towards biomedical research.

958. Beck, Sam. "Changing Styles of Drinking: Alcohol Use in the Balkans." *East European Quarterly* 18, no. 4 (1985): 395-413.
Addresses the overindulgence in alcohol consumption which is linked to socioeconomic changes (e.g. urbanization and shift from farm to industrial labor) in Balkan societies in general, and in Romania in particular.

959. Cernea, Michael. "Cooperative Farming and Family Change in Romania." In *The Social Structure of Eastern Europe: Transition and Process in Czechoslovakia, Hungary, Poland, Romania, and Yugoslavia*, edited by Bernard Lewis Faber, 259-279. New York: Praeger, 1976.
Studies the impact of collectivization on economic roles and task assignments within families and remarks on their relevance in a cross-cultural perspective.

960. Cernea, Michael. "Macrosocial Change, Feminization of Agriculture and Peasant Women's Threefold Economic Role." *Sociologia Ruralis* 18, no. 2-3 (1978): 107-124.
The rapid industrialization of post-war Romania led to a massive migration of male peasants to urban factories and created a disequilibrium of the villages' sex-ratio. Agriculture has become a female dominated sector. Lingering customs and traditions still affect tendencies of emancipation in Romanian peasant women.

961. Cheetham, Tom, II. "Cooperativization as a Strategy for Modernization: The Romanian Case." Ph.D. diss., Brown University, 1981. Ann Arbor: UMI, 1981. AAD8209039.
Reviews agricultural development. Describes the creation of cooperatives, peasant response to the process, and the role of farm managers as mediators between state directives and local community needs.

962. Chirot, Daniel. "The Corporatist Model and Socialism." *Theory and Society* 9, no. 2 (1980): 363-381.
Describes communist Romania's political and economic organization in terms of the corporatist model developed by Mihail Manoilescu.

963. Chirot, Daniel. "Sociology in Romania: A Review of Recent Works." *Social Forces* 51, no. 1 (1972): 99-102.

Within the broad framework of reemerging sociological inquiry in Romania, discusses five Romanian works published in 1970 on sociological impacts of rapid industrialization and collectivization.

964. Cole, John W. "Familial Dynamics in a Romanian Worker Village." *Dialectical Anthropology* 1, no. 3 (1976): 251-265.
Focuses on the village of Mîndra in southern Transylvania and discusses the developmental cycle of the family, the processes which establish, maintain, or alter relations among families, and their relationship to the transformation of the Romanian economy at large.

965. Cole, John W. "Field Work in Romania: An Introduction." *Dialectical Anthropology* 1, no. 3 (1976): 239-249.
Studies socialist transformation in villages in Braşov county (Transylvania) and how it affects the formation and operation of cooperative farms, development of opportunities for and access to industrial employment, interethnic relations, social organization of communes and interrelationships of all these factors.

966. Cristea, Pietro. "L'Industrialisation, le Mouvement Migratoire et les Changements Social-Professionnels en Roumanie [Industrialization, the Migrant Movement and Social and Professional Changes in Romania]." *Revue Internationale de Sociologie* 7, no. 2, part 1 (1971): 239-244.
Increased social and professional mobility and higher educational achievements contribute to the disappearance of class and social differences.

967. Denitch, Bogdan. "Sociology in Eastern Europe: Trends and Prospects." *Slavic Review* 30, no. 2 (1971): 317-339.
Surveys general trends in Eastern European sociology, mentioning Romania's 1965 revival of sociology as an academic discipline and describing the organization of lines of activity.

968. Elliott, Joyce E., and William Moskoff. "Decision-Making Power in Romanian Families." *Journal of Comparative Family Studies* 14, no. 1 (1983): 39-50.
Examines marital decision-making in Romania, a country with a strong patriarchal tradition, yet with one of the world's highest levels of women in the labor force. Shows considerable equality in major household decisions. These results do not correlate well with findings of "double-burden" studies. Concludes that the collected data may reflect women's opinions as to the expected answer, rather than reality. Equality in decision-making may not be indicative of marital equality.

969. Filiti, Gregoire. "La Classe Ouvrière en Roumanie [The Working Class in Romania]." *Notes et Études Documentaires* 4511-4512 (10 May 1979): 139-158.
Following a historical overview, discusses current organization of labor, earnings, standard of living, productivity, and organized and spontaneous opposition.

970. Fischer, Mary Ellen. "Women in Romania: Public Policy and Political Participation." In *Papers for the V. Congress of Southeast European Studies, Belgrade, September 1984*, edited by Kot K. Shangriladze and Erica W. Townsend, 145-157. Columbus, OH: Slavica, 1984.
Examines the steadily increasing participation of women in political life. Nonetheless, women tend to occupy lower positions and cluster in economic sectors traditionally associated with their gender. No substantive alleviation of the triple burden of job, home, and childen, is visible.

971. Gilberg, Trond. "Modernization in Romania." *Balkanistica* 5 (1979): 100-139.
While similar to that of other communist states, Romania's modernization process has an accelerated pace and is more comprehensive. Looks at the organizational and administrative infrastructure of development, the impact of its socioeconomic programs, and its quest to create the "new socialist man."

972. Gilberg, Trond. "Modernization, Human Rights, Nationalism: The Case of Romania."
In *The Politics of Ethnicity in Eastern Europe*, edited by George Klein and Milan J.
Reban, 185-211. East European Monographs, 93. ASN Series in Issue Studies (USSR
and East Europe), 2. New York: Columbia University Press, 1981.
Studies the conflicting relationships in communist political systems among modernization, human rights, and nationalism. Concludes that a change in communist
policy concerning either human rights or nationalism is unlikely.

973. Gilberg, Trond. *Modernization in Romania since World War II.* New York: Praeger,
1975.
Studies the socioeconomic and political concepts, agents, and processes of modernization as well as the relationship between post World War II Romanian society and
its political system.

974. Gilberg, Trond. "Rural Transformation in Romania." In *The Peasantry of Eastern
Europe*, edited by Ivan Volgyes, vol.2, 77-122. New York: Pergamon, 1979.
Although some political and socioeconomic successes have been registered,
Ceauşescu's ambitious program of ideological indoctrination has failed to eliminate
the old value system and create the "new socialist individual."

975. Gilberg, Trond. "Social Deviance in Romania." In *Social Deviance in Eastern Europe*, edited by Ivan Volgyes, 113-158. Boulder: Westview, 1978.
The communist regime attempts to impose a unified code of behavior on its citizens. Offers examples of infractions and concludes that the party has failed to impose its socialist behavioral norm.

976. Hoivik, Tord. "The Development of Romania: a Cohort Study." *Journal of Peace
Research* 11, no. 4 (1974): 281-296.
A survey of Romania's development gleaned from official and other statistics dealing with people born in 1900, 1930, and 1960. Describes childhood and youth,
consumption patterns, living conditions, and historical events. Concludes that, despite war and its aftermath, Romania's achievements are impressive, and its development may be considered a success. However, Romania failed in the realization of
active values, such as political activities, social creativity, and intellectual freedom.
The fear of letting Marxist theory evolve hinders Romania.

977. Joan, Aluas. "Migration Paysanne en Roumanie [Peasant Migration in Romania]."
Revue Internationale de Sociologie 7, no. 2, part 1 (1971): 283-285.
Surveys peasants' opinion on their profession and concludes that, due to mobility,
industrialization, and changes in lifestyle, farming ranks very low socially and pro-
fessionally. Only 4.2% of 247 respondents declared farm work as profession of
choice.

978. Kideckel, David A. "Agricultural Cooperativism and Social Process in a Romanian
Commune." Ph.D. diss., University of Massachusetts, 1979. Ann Arbor: UMI, 1979.
AAD79-20855.
Applies a theoretical analysis of cooperative agricultural organizations to the spe-
cific conditions of formation and functioning of the Hîrseni Cooperative Farm (Re-
gion Braşov).

979. Kideckel, David A. "The Dialectic of Rural Development: Cooperative Farm Goals
and Family Strategies in a Romanian Commune." *Journal of Rural Cooperation* 5,
no. 1 (1977): 43-61.
Studies the aims of the Hîrseni Cooperative Farm and the means used to achieve
these aims (1963-1975), in light of a shrinking and aging cooperative farm labor
force.

980. Kideckel, David A. "Drinking Up: Alcohol, Class, and Social Change in Rural Romania." *East European Quarterly* 18, no. 4 (1985): 431-446.
Traces the historical and cultural significance of alcohol production and consump-

tion in Țara Oltului. Drinking was viewed as a positive force that maintained community interaction. In socialist Romania heavy alcohol consumption has become a venue for social mobility and social status.

981. Kideckel, David A. "Secular Ritual and Social Change: A Romanian Case." *Anthropological Quarterly* 56, no. 2 (1983): 69-75.
Based on fieldwork in Comuna Hîrseni (Transylvania), describes the role of collective farm delegate assemblies (*adunări generale*) in generating and influencing social change. The meetings reveal differences in outlook on work and social life between workers and political leaders and thus achieves a separation rather than a convergence of opinions.

982. Kideckel, David A. "The Social Organization of Production on a Romanian Cooperative Farm." *Dialectical Anthropology* 1, no. 3 (1976): 267-276.
Examines the organization of a Romanian agricultural production cooperative (CAP) in relationship to national policy and to imperatives of the local community. Concludes that CAP administrations function with some degree of success through responsiveness to village social organizational demands. CAPs still encounter difficulties, such as worker alienation, poor communication, and poor overall management, all playing a major role in impeding production and the introduction of socialism in Romanian villages.

983. Kideckel, David A. *The Solitude of Collectivism: Romanian Villagers to the Revolution and Beyond.* Ithaca: Cornell University Press, 1993.
Describes the daily life of villagers in Oltenia and how their personal struggle influenced and was influenced by the socialist state in the Ceaușescu years, during the revolution, and its aftermath.

984. Kolaja, Jiri. "Notes on Romanian Sociology." *Acta Sociologica* 17, no. 1 (1974): 78-82.
After World War II, communist Eastern Europe banned sociology as an academic discipline. In Romania, sociology is gradually returning to academic life. Offers a brief survey of Romanian sociological publications published between 1970 and 1971.

985. Masson, Daniele. "Roumanie: La 'Societé Socialiste Multilateralement Développée' et sa Paysannerie [Romania: The 'Multilaterally Developed Socialist Society' and its Peasants]." In *Paysans et Nations d'Europe Centrale & Balkanique*, 257-267. Paris: Maisonneuve et Larose, 1985.
Industrialization and collectivization have turned peasants into wage earners. The communist state is dismantling the very class that supposedly confers its historical legitimacy.

986. Moskoff, William. "Child Care in Romania: A Comparative Analysis." *East European Quarterly* 15, no. 3 (1981): 391-397.
Compares child care in the United States and in Romania. Although Romanian parents distrust state run nurseries for children under the age of one, Romanian nurseries compare favorably to facilities in the U.S. For after-school care, Romania's children appear to have less structured support than American children.

987. Moskoff, William. "The Problem of 'Double Burden' in Romania." *International Journal of Comparative Sociology* 23, no. 1-2 (1982): 79-88.
Examines whether socialism has helped Romanian women in reducing the magnitude of the double burden. The percentage of Romanian women in the economically active population is highest among countries of Eastern Europe and the Soviet Union and among the highest in the world. Romanian women, however, shoulder a disproportionate share of the household labor. This is due in part to the persistent patriarchal values. Concludes that socialism has failed in helping women alleviate "double-burden." Suggests investments in social services and labor-saving consumer durables and a departure from longstanding patriarchal traditions.

988. Moskoff, William. "Pronatalist Policies in Romania." *Economic Development and Cultural Change* 28, no. 3 (1980): 597-614.
Since 1966 the Romanian government has implemented a series of measures to reverse declining birth rates. In evaluating Romania's demographic policies, concludes that the lack of kindergarten facilities, the small size of living quarters, the educational attainment of women, and the "double-burden," all contribute to the failure of the state to achieve higher birth rates. Incentives offered by the Romanian socialist government fall short of advantages offered to women in other Eastern European countries.

989. Moskoff, William. "Sex Discrimination, Commuting, and the Role of Women in Rumanian Development." *Slavic Review* 37, no. 3 (1978): 440-456.
Women have increasingly become the dominant workforce in the agricultural sector. The double burden of full-time work outside the home and responsibility for child care have kept women in lower paying jobs. Men commute to cities offering skilled, higher salaried positions.

990. Nelson, Daniel N. "Romania." In *Survey Research and Public Attitudes in Eastern Europe and the Soviet Union*, edited by William A. Welsh, 436-481. New York: Pergamon, 1981.
Reports on results of a public attitude and behavior survey concerning media habits, family and women, work, leisure time, moral and ethical preferences, life aspirations, social problems, politics, and ideology.

991. Nelson, Daniel N. "Romania: Participatory Dynamics in 'Developed Socialism'." In *Blue-Collar Workers in Eastern Europe*, edited by Jan F. Triska and Charles Gati, 236-252. London: Allen & Unwin, 1981.
Examines the quality and quantity of workers' participation in the organization and management of production and political decision-making and its impact on the communist government.

992. Oschlies, Wolf. "Junge Nachbarn im Osten: Rumäniens Jugend: Selbstbewusst, Leistungsmotiviert, Patriotisch [Young Neighbors in the East: Romania's Youth: Confident, Motivated, Patriotic]." *Deutsche Jugend* 2 (1981): 62-64.
Sociological research, anchored in traditional methods, is making a comeback. Data on young adults is better developed than elsewhere in Eastern Europe and reveals positive character traits.

993. Oschlies, Wolf. *Rumäniens Jugend - Rumäniens Hoffnung [Romania's Youth - Romania's Hope]*. Jugend in Osteuropa, 3. Sozialwissenschaftliches Forum, 9. Köln: Böhlau, 1983.
Discusses results of studies (conducted from the 1960's to the 1980's) concerning social integration, vocational guidance, professional satisfaction, culture, and expectations of youth.

994. Oschlies, Wolf. *Soziale Mobilisierung in Rumänien [Social Mobilization in Romania]*. Berichte, 47. Köln: Bundesinstitut für Ostwissenschaftliche und Internationale Studien, 1973.
Looks at processes of change from a traditional to a modern way of life and how these changes affect settlements, work habits, aspirations, and needs.

995. Petyt, K. M. "Romania: A Multilingual Nation." *International Journal of the Sociology of Language* 4 (1975): 75-101.
Provides descriptive data on language use in Romania, a country with numerous language minorities. Compares findings with existing sociolinguistic models and typologies.

996. Ronnås, Per. "Agrarian Change and Economic Development in Rural Romania: A Case Study of the Oaş Region." *Geografiska Annaler Series B - Human Geography* 69, no. B1 (1987): 41-53.

Studies uneven economic growth and its impact on the community of a region poorly suited for collectivization of agriculture or for the creation of a manufacturing environment.

997. Sampson, Steven L. "Elites and Mobilization in Romanian Villages." *Sociologia Ruralis* 24, no. 1 (1984): 30-51.
Rural elite cadres include individuals with formal leadership positions, village professionals, or people who command a local following. To mobilize village people, elite cadres must know what form of authority to espouse — either "bureaucratic-administrative" or "egalitarian." The way elite cadres succeed in balancing demands from above and moral claims from below determines if the leadership is efficient or poor. The constraints rural elite cadres face stem from the structure of their social, economic, and political environment.

998. Sampson, Steven L. "Feldioara: The City Comes to the Peasant." *Dialectical Anthropology* 1, no. 4 (1976): 321-347.
Development of the village of Feldioara, located in southern Transylvania, is occurring according to planned growth under governmental control. Gives a description of the spatial, demographic, economic, social, and political components of the town in addition to a detailed account of the planned urban transformation of this village. Feldioara, once grown to a town, will serve as a social, economic, and political center for the surrounding villages in a process called "systematization."

999. Sampson, Steven L. "Ideology and Rationality in Romanian Development Strategies." In *Economy, Society, and Culture in Contemporary Romania*, edited by John W. Cole, 43-74. Research Report, 24. Amherst: University of Massachusetts, Department of Anthropology, 1984.
The village of Feldioara is used to depict the dysfunctions existing between supralocal "systematization" planning and execution at the village level.

1000. Sampson, Steven L. "The Informal Sector in Eastern Europe." *Telos* 66 (Winter 1985/86): 44-66.
Based on anthropological research work conducted in Romania, states that Eastern European societies revolve around two poles: formal state organizations and informal unauthorized structures. The latter fulfill tasks left unmet by state institutions and are used by political elites to maintain their political power and achieve economic objectives.

1001. Verdery, Katherine. "Ethnic Stratification in the European Periphery: The Historical Sociology of a Transylvanian Village." Ph.D. diss., Stanford University, 1977. Ann Arbor: UMI, 1977. AAD77-12712.
Follows a bi-ethnic Transylvanian village from the turn of the century to the communist transformation of agriculture and analyzes changes in village life brought about by changing elite policies.

1002. Vianu, Ion. "Le Mythe de l'Occident en Roumanie [The Myth of the West in Romania]." *Cahiers Vilfredo Pareto* 18, no. 53 (1980): 67-74.
The migration of the best Romanian minds to the West has less to do with a search for economic opportunities and more with an act of liberation and of total disregard of consequences.

21. Urban & Rural Planning & Development

1003. Beck, Sam. "The Impact of Social Engineering on Rural Life in Rumania." *Human Ecology Forum* 18 (Fall 1989): 23-26.
The plan for territorial "systematization," scheduled for completion by the year 2000, will result in the destruction of thousands of villages. The mounting international outcry may pressure the government to reconsider its designs for social restructuring.

1004. Boutrais, Jean, and Jean Paul Charvet. "Bucarest: Étude de Géographie Urbaine [Bucharest: Study in Urban Geography]." *Revue Géographique de l'Est* 7, no. 3 (1967): 265-363.
Studies the restructuring of Bucharest according to socialist economic principles. Urban planners attempt to erase existing differences between center city and outskirts.

1005. Church, Gordon. "Bucharest: Revolution in the Townscape." In *The Socialist City: Spatial Structure and Urban Policy*, edited by R. A. French and F. E. Ian Hamilton, 493-506. Chichester: Wiley, 1979.
Discusses the Bucharest townscape as an example of "socialist urban gestalt."

1006. Daniel, Odile. "Les Politiques du Logement en Hongrie et en Roumanie [Housing Policies in Hungary and Romania]." *Le Courrier des Pays de l'Est* 274 (June 1983): 35-49.
Compares issues and solutions based on a ten year assessment of housing policies in the two countries.

1007. Danta, Darrick. "Ceauşescu's Bucharest." *Geographical Review* 83, no. 2 (1993): 170-182.
Focuses on Ceauşescu's two phases of transformation of the capital: 1965-1980, planning and restructuring the outskirts and 1980-1989, destruction of large sections of the historical city center.

1008. Giurescu, Dinu C. *The Razing of Romania's Past: International Preservation Report*. Washington, D.C.: United States Committee of the International Council on Monuments and Sites, 1989.
Surveys the architectural heritage and Ceauşescu's demolition of traditional urban and rural areas and their replacement with tenement apartment buildings.

1009. Heller, Wilfried. "Zum Studium der Urbanisierung in der Sozialistischen Republik Rumänien: Ein Literaturbericht [On the Study of Urban Development in the Socialist Republic of Romania: A Review of Literature]." *Die Erde* 105, no. 2 (1974): 179-199.
Overview and discussion of Romanian works on geography, sociology, and eco-

nomics as an introduction to the interdisciplinary nature of urban development in Romania.

1010. Oschlies, Wolf. "Tausenden Rumänischer Dörfer Droht die Vernichtung [Thousands of Romanian Villages are Threatened with Destruction]." *Osteuropa* 38, no. 11 (1988): 1002-1007.
Discusses Ceauşescu's program of rural "systematization," and its devastating internal and international policy consequences.

1011. Parent, Michel. "Les Villages Après la Systématisation [Villages after Systematization]." *Monuments Historiques* 169 (June/July 1992): 25-30.
Overview of Ceauşescu's plan for "systematization" of urban and rural areas and observations for post-revolutionary options.

1012. Reed, John. "'Territorial Systematization' or Systematic Terror?" *Uncaptive Minds* 2, no. 6 (1989): 31-33.
Monitors domestic and international protests as Ceauşescu implements his plan to liquidate thousands of Romanian and Hungarian villages.

1013. Rey, Violette. *Braşov: Une Vocation Urbaine [Braşov: A Urban Calling]*. Paris: Bibliothèque Nationale, 1975.
Focuses on urban development and its social consequences in the 1960's and 1970's.

1014. Ronnås, Per. "Centrally Planned Urbanization: The Case of Romania." *Geografiska Annaler Series B - Human Geography* 64, no. B2 (1982): 143-151.
Examines two stages of administrative reforms and the rapid urban development: from the late forties to 1966 and from 1966 to 1977.

1015. Ronnås, Per. "Stadtewächstum und Raumentwicklung in Rumänien [Urban Growth and Regional Development in Romania]." *Osteuropa* 38, no. 11 (1988): 1008-1021.
Study of Romania's demographics and its relationship to urban planning from the post World War II period to the Ceauşescu program of rural "systematization."

1016. Ronnås, Per. "Turning the Romanian Peasant into a New Socialist Man: An Assessment of Rural Development Policy in Romania." *Soviet Studies* 41, no. 4 (October 1989): 543-559.
Analyzes Ceauşescu's program of phasing out large number of villages. Discusses its ideological, economical, and political aims, its feasibility, and probable effects.

1017. Ronnås, Per. "Urbanization in Romania: A Geography of Social and Economic Change Since Independence." Ph.D. diss., Economic Research Institute, Stockholm School of Economics, 1984.
Follows Romania's evolution from a semi-feudal agrarian society to a socialist industrialized economy. Analyzes population development, ethnic structure, economic and industrial transformations, and patterns of urban growth from 1877 to 1980.

1018. Rosière, Stephane. "Le Programme de Systématisation du Territoire Roumain [The Restructuring of Rural Settlement in Romania]." *Temps Modernes* 45, no. 522 (1990): 46-82.
Discusses origins and goals of the program, its strategies for implementation, and the international outcry and condemnation it elicited.

1019. Sampson, Steven L. "Urbanization - Planned and Unplanned: A Case Study of Braşov, Romania." In *The Socialist City: Spatial Structure and Urban Policy*, edited by R. A. French and F. E. Ian Hamilton, 507-524. Chichester: Wiley, 1979.
Study of the importance of national urban development planning when implemented or ignored, as applied to the Transylvanian city of Braşov.

1020. Sandelin, Ejvind. "Urbanisme Selon Ceauşescu: Bucarest a Perdu Son Coeur, la Roumanie a Failli Perdre son Âme [Town Planning According to Ceauşescu:

Bucharest has Lost its Heart, Romania Nearly Lost its Soul]." *Cahiers de l'Institut d'Aménagement et d'Urbanisme de la Région d'Ile-de-France* 93 (June 1990): 9-24.
Describes the disastrous results of the urbanization plans.

1021. Simonitsch, Pierre. "Wohnungsbau in Rumänien: Eine Frage der Prioritäten [Housing Construction in Romania: A Question of Priorities]." *Neue Heimat* 1 (1972): 34-42.
Discusses construction and availability of housing based on statistical data and projected goals for the five-year plan.

1022. Sporea, C., and K.-E. Wädekin. "Land-Stadt-Wanderung und Pläne zur Dorferneuerung in Rumänien [Urban Migration from Rural Areas and Plans for Municipal Reorganization in Romania]." *Osteuropa* 27, no. 2 (1977): 125-130.
Since the mid-1960's, thousands of agricultural workers migrated to industrialized centers. Settlements appeared around larger cities. The 1971-1975 central plan stipulated the elimination of small villages and the resettlement of the population in newly created urban communities. In the next 20 years differences between city and village life were supposed to disappear.

1023. Tomescu, Marian. "A Note on Urban Growth in Romania." *Ekistics* 39, no. 233 (1975): 258.
A very brief article on the development of cities and towns in Romania between 1948 and 1968. Also includes a graph for growth in Bucharest and a hypothesis for 1980.

1024. Turnock, David. "Bucharest: The Selection and Development of the Romanian Capital." *Scottish Geographical Magazine* 86 (1970): 53-68.
Describes the development of the city from its first historical confirmation (1457) to a modern, industrialized city of 1.5 million in 1966.

1025. Turnock, David. "The Changing Romanian Countryside: The Ceauşescu Epoch and Prospects for Change Following the Revolution." *Environment and Planning C: Government and Policy* 9, no. 3 (1991): 319-340.
Reviews rural economic planning under Ceauşescu and the resulting radical redistribution of population between town and country. Outlines prospects for development.

1026. Turnock, David. "City Profile: Bucharest." *Cities* 7, no. 2 (1990): 107-118.
Offers a historical review of the city's development to the end of the Ceauşescu regime.

1027. Turnock, David. "Housing Policy in Romania." In *Housing Policies in Eastern Europe and the Soviet Union*, edited by J. A. A. Sillince, 135-169. London: Routledge, 1990.
After two decades of growth, economic difficulties have brought housing construction to a virtual standstill. The crisis in housing availablility is exacerbated by a constant flux of urban in-migration, crime, and counter-productive policies.

1028. Turnock, David. "The Planning of Rural Settlement in Romania." *Geographical Journal* 157, Part 3 (1991): 251-264.
Analyzes the strategy of "systematization," a coercive program aimed at stemming the flight from rural to urban settlements by providing local access to employment and services. Examines prospects of change after Ceauşescu's fall.

1029. Turnock, David. "Restructuring of Rural Settlement in Romania." *Slavonic and East European Review* 54, no. 1 (1976): 83-102.
Presents a history of rural planning in Romania in light of the official call of the Romanian Communist Party in 1965 for rural development. Over a twenty year period, two-thirds of the country's villages are scheduled to disappear as this policy

intends to achieve a more efficient use of village land and water and a better organization of services.

1030. Turnock, David. "Romania." In *Planning in Eastern Europe*, edited by Andrew H. Dawson, 229-273. London: Croom Helm, 1987.
Studies the role and implementation of economic planning since 1948, including Ceauşescu's policy of "systematization" and its impact on urban and rural settlement patterns.

1031. Turnock, David. "Romania: Ceauşescu's Legacy." *Geography* 75, Pt.3, no. 328 (1990): 260-263.
Bulldozed villages, pollution, and destroyed historical landmarks are some of the scars inflicted by Ceauşescu on Romania's landscape.

1032. Turnock, David. "Romanian Villages: Rural Planning under Communism." *Rural History* 2, no. 1 (1991): 81-112.
Reviews the "systematization" program from its beginning to the "Bulldozer Politik" of the late 1980's. After the revolution, the program was abandoned. However, an alternate urbanization strategy ought to be considered.

1033. Turnock, David. "Spatial Aspects of Modernization in Eastern Europe: The Romanian Case." *Contact: Journal of Urban and Environmental Affairs* 11, no. 2 (1979): 113-142.
Thirty years of socialism have brought about a degree of progress. Nonetheless, there are still sharp contrasts between industrialized areas and backward regions. Regional inequality cannot be attributed solely to capitalist conditions.

1034. Turnock, David. "Urban Development and Urban Geography in Romania: The Contribution of Vintilă Mihăilescu." *GeoJournal* 14, no. 2 (1987): 181-202.
Examines the relationship between urban development and urban geography since the turn of the century in light of the work of Vintilă Mihăilescu (1890-1978).

1035. Turnock, David. "Urban Development in a Socialist City: Bucharest." *Geography* 59, pt. 4, no. 265 (1974): 344-348.
Looks at existing trends of high density development as a means to prevent loss of agricultural land. Various schemes to link urban settlements with industrial estates are explored.

Author Index

Numbers used in the index refer to entry numbers, not page numbers.

Subject Index

Numbers used in the index refer to entry numbers, not page numbers.

About the Compilers

OPRITSA D. POPA, a Humanities and Social Sciences Librarian at Shields Library, University of California, Davis, defected from Romania in 1969. After the fall of communism, she initiated the successful book drive *Books for Romania, USA*, that brought a quarter of a million scholarly publications to Romanian libraries. She lectured in Romania and is the author of numerous articles and book chapters on international librarianship. In 1992 she received the American Library Association's prestigious Humphry Award in "recognition of significant contributions to international librarianship."

MARGUERITE E. HORN is Principal Serial Cataloger at Shields Library, University of California, Davis. She is currently on the editorial committee of the *NASIG Newsletter* and was the editor of *Bibliofile*, the Brown University Library Newsletter.

ISBN 0-313-28939-5

EAN

9 780313 289392

HARDCOVER BAR CODE

DATE DUE

GAYLORD			PRINTED IN U.S.A.